YOUR FIRST PAGE

First pages and what

Your

they tell us about

First

the pages that follow them

Page

REVISED WORKSHOP
AND CLASSROOM EDITION

PETER SELGIN

broadview press

BROADVIEW PRESS – www.broadviewpress.com
Peterborough, Ontario, Canada

Founded in 1985, Broadview Press remains a wholly independent publishing house.
Broadview's focus is on academic publishing; our titles are accessible to university and college
students as well as scholars and general readers. With over 600 titles in print, Broadview has
become a leading international publisher in the humanities, with world-wide distribution.
Broadview is committed to environmentally responsible publishing and fair business practices.

Library and Archives Canada Cataloguing in Publication

Title: Your first page : first pages and what they tell us about the pages that follow them /
    Peter Selgin.
Names: Selgin, Peter, author.
Description: Revised workshop and classroom edition. | Includes index.
Identifiers: Canadiana 20190110473 | ISBN 9781554814732 (softcover)
Subjects: LCSH: Authorship—Study and teaching. | LCSH: Rhetoric—Study and teaching.
Classification: LCC PN181 .S45 2019 | DDC 808.0071—dc23

Broadview Press handles its own distribution in North America:
PO Box 1243, Peterborough, Ontario K9J 7H5, Canada
555 Riverwalk Parkway, Tonawanda, NY 14150, USA
Tel: (705) 743-8990; Fax: (705) 743-8353
email: customerservice@broadviewpress.com

Distribution is handled by Eurospan Group in the UK, Europe, Central Asia,
Middle East, Africa, India, Southeast Asia, Central America, South America, and the
Caribbean. Distribution is handled by Footprint Books in Australia and New Zealand.

Canada

Broadview Press acknowledges the financial support of the
Government of Canada for our publishing activities.

Edited by Juliet Sutcliffe
Book design by Michel Vrana

PRINTED IN CANADA

CONTENTS

CONTENTS

CONTENTS

CONTENTS

G. Style 251

CONTENTS

Introduction

THIS BOOK GREW OUT OF AN EXPERIMENT UNDERTAKEN AT several workshops and conferences to discover how much useful critical commentary and helpful feedback could be extracted from a single page, the first, of works in progress. The experiment was first performed at the New York Round Table Writers' Conference at the General Society of Mechanics and Tradesmen Library in Manhattan, whose main reading room soars to three stories topped by a magnificent skylight. I asked participants there to submit— in advance, anonymously—the first pages of their works in progress to form a pool from which they'd be drawn at random and discussed.

More than thirty authors participated, joining me in the large room packed with people. Since the submissions were anonymous, none of us knew which faces in the crowd belonged to which pages under scrutiny. One by one I selected them from the pool, with copies made available to audience members. Together we listened as the first pages were read out loud. Then I gave my comments and opened the floor to discussion.

The experiment could not have been more successful. As expected, nearly all of the first pages raised concerns that opened up broader areas of discussion. I got the sense—as did everyone in that room—that most, if not all, the challenges pertaining to many of the works in progress were there in those first pages, that much of what those authors needed to hear they heard that afternoon, enough to guide them toward a next draft of the entire work.

Since that first experiment I've conducted other "first page workshops," mostly at Antioch University's Graduate Creative Writing Program in Culver City, Los Angeles. I also started a blog called *Your First Page*, to which authors were invited to submit first pages of works in progress for analysis. More than a hundred authors contributed pages.

My purpose with this book is to offer you the chance to take part in an extended first-page workshop from which you may draw inspiration, ideas, wisdom, and perhaps a few warnings and suggestions with respect to your own works in progress.

1

* * *

So many things happen on the first page of a book. There, within a paragraph or two, and sometimes even within the first sentence, a bond is formed between reader and writer, one that will endure—hopefully—for as many pages as the work is long.

That bond is established in a number of ways. At the simplest level, it is the same—or very similar to—the bond formed between two people when one speaks to the other for the first time. If you are walking down a city street and someone walking the other direction stops you and says, "Excuse me, can you please tell me the time?" in that instant, however briefly and tentatively, a bond is formed between you and this total stranger who demands your attention; it is up to you to decide whether and how much attention you're willing to provide him or her. If you happen to know the time, you'll probably extend the bond (and your courtesy) accordingly; if not, you'll excuse yourself and continue on your way. On the other hand, had the same stranger said to you, "Hey, you! Gimme a thousand bucks!" odds are you'd have kept walking.

In a similar way, authors make demands upon their readers. When a reader picks up a book or opens a magazine to an essay or short story, she opens herself to this interaction with a perfect stranger. Rather than meet on a street, author and reader agree to meet on a page. Once that initial invitation has been accepted, from that point on *it's entirely up to the author to establish that bond and make it endure throughout the length of the work.*

Though authors may make all kinds of demands on readers ("Do you have the time?" "Gimme a thousand bucks!"), readers owe authors nothing. Unless the reader is being paid to write a review, or the book is an assignment for a literature or creative writing class, the only thing compelling readers to keep reading is what's there on the page. And what's there on the first page is all that compels them to read the next page, and so on.

How is this bond established between writer and reader? First, by engaging the reader's empathy by means of *a human voice speaking a shared language.* When people speak to us, we tend to listen. This is no less true with strangers than it is with those we know and love. Often strangers command as much or more attention than loved ones. *Excuse me, can you tell me the time?* Our shared human nature compels us to pay attention to each other, at least to the point where we can be fairly sure we want nothing to do with this person whose voice has reached out to us (*Gimme a thousand bucks!*). Up to that moment, and as long as the voice that reaches out to us is human, since we're human too, we are likely to pay attention.

So, the first rule for engaging and establishing a bond with your reader: speak in their language and with a human voice. That sounds easy and obvious. It's neither. Of hundreds of stories I read every year from my students, for every one whose first sentence appeals to me with a human voice, others assail me with mannerisms, pretensions, verbal gamesmanship, and shock tactics— i.e., with the voice of an overeager writer *writing*. And as hard as it is to ignore a human voice (*Can you please tell me the time?*), nothing is easier to resist than the sound of a writer writing.

But many other things can go wrong on that first page, errors resulting in confusion, frustration, or a blurry, imprecise experience for the reader. Those countless manuscripts that editors reject daily? They are all being rejected for the same reason: for having failed—somehow, at some level—to successfully bond with their readers.

Another reason for that failed bond: the lack of a mediating or filtering agency or authority arbitrating between the author (who only *knows about* the story and its characters) and the story (fiction or nonfiction) itself. In works of fiction especially—but also in nonfiction narratives—there needs to be such an entity or agent. In other words, a narrator.

I hear you say to yourself, *Of course a story has a narrator: how can it not have a narrator?* Yet as you'll see in many of the pages that follow, stories often lack this vital agency or filter. What we get instead is an author taking over or intruding or trying to intrude into the world of his or her story, presenting us with unfiltered information about the characters and their situations and the settings they inhabit, rather than *injecting us directly* into their world through the agency of a narrator, so as to give us not *information about an experience,* but the *experience itself.* Whether they realize it or not, readers of stories don't want information; they want experiences.

Creating and engaging a proper narrator: that is the second big thing that goes right or wrong within the first page.

Establishing viewpoint, controlling diction, grounding readers in setting, action, and scene, pinpointing the inciting incident of a story, engaging and perpetuating plot, setting-up and paying-off moments, knowing when to obey and when to flout conventions, differentiating between events and routine, descriptions and opinions, conclusions and the evidence from which they are drawn, between authenticity and clichés, between style and mannerisms—all these things matter. And they matter starting from the first page of a book or a story.

One problem with so many writing books: they fail to provide authentic examples of less-than-successful writing; some present made-up examples so obviously contrived as to be ludicrous. Here you'll find genuine first pages of works in progress by actual authors.

There's this advantage too of analyzing and working from real first pages of works in progress: instead of offering up generalizations about how things *should* be written, or asking writers to mirror and learn from examples of published works, readers of this book become part of the creative process, one that asks, "What are the particular issues raised by this piece of writing; what does it contract to do; what promises does it hold out; how are those promises met or broken? According to the terms it establishes, how is this first page working, or isn't it? If not, why not?"

Consequently, generalizations are avoided, and the non-specific "how to write" becomes "how to extrapolate general principles and specific remedies from concerns raised by particular pieces of writing." It's up to you to extrapolate as you see fit.

Before we proceed, a few last words about guide books like this one, and the business of giving and getting critical feedback. Criticism of creative work, work into which an artist has potentially invested not only her heart and spirit, but years of labor, is risky business. Emotions run high; feelings get hurt. Telling an author, "Check your ego at the door," is easy. Doing so—for the author—is not.

It's also true that any artist who submits to criticism too easily, taking every word of praise or censure to heart and amending her work accordingly, will most likely end up with something that tries to please everyone and pleases no one. At some point we have to hold tight to our visions.

On the other hand, those who pay no attention to their critics are as likely to lose out in the end. Assuming they have any desire to reach an audience with their words, and assuming that audience consists of people outside of family and friends, sooner or later their work will be subjected to the judgments of strangers. If sooner (before they submit to publishers), they'll have recourse in revision; if later, they'll have a pile of rejection slips.

Each author must find the right balance between receptivity and mulishness. It helps too to know which opinions are worth listening to. But before you dismiss every opinion offered by me in this book, I ask only that you consider what I have to say, that it be food for thought.

Whatever choices you end up making for your work, if you make them thoughtfully, you will have every chance of succeeding.

May this book help you make the right choices for your first pages, and all the pages that come after.

I.

Opening Strategies

I ONCE SPOKE WITH A NEW YORK CITY FIREMAN WHOSE JOB included talking suicidal "jumpers" down from building edges and bridges. He told me something that has stayed with me ever since. He said that in every case, without exception, when the person jumped, the look on his or her face was always the same. It said, in essence, "Wrong decision."

Forgive me for opening on such a grisly note. But every opening of a book or a story is a fateful plunge. The choices we make in those first few sentences, paragraphs, and pages determine not only how what we've written gets read, but whether it will be read at all.

Readers have no obligation to read what we've written. If we want them to spend their precious time with our words, we owe them every courtesy. They owe us nothing.

"Grab the reader by the throat," so we've been told, suggesting that nothing short of bodily assault will gain a reader's attention. I disagree.

Still, there's something to be said for a throat-grabbing opening:

> *Hale knew, before he'd been in Brighton three hours, that they meant to murder him.*[1]
>
> *They threw me off the hay truck about noon.*[2]
>
> *A screaming comes across the sky.*[3]
>
> *One morning, Gregor Samsa awoke from uneasy dreams to find himself transformed into a gigantic beetle.*[4]

---

1   Graham Greene, *Brighton Rock* (1938).
2   James M. Cain, *The Postman Always Rings Twice* (1942).
3   Thomas Pynchon, *Gravity's Rainbow* (1973).
4   Franz Kafka, "The Metamorphosis" (1915). Translation by the author.

Those opening sentences do more than grab our throats. They pull us to the brink of a story and push us in.

To gain a reader's interest you needn't resort to assault or sensationalism. Imagine yourself a guest at a dinner party. To make an impression you can pull the tablecloth out from under the place settings; that will do the trick. Or you can tinkle your wine glass, lean into the ensuing silence, and—with commanding composure—say something like, "It is a truth universally acknowledged, that a single man in possession of a good fortune, must be in want of a wife."[5] No china broken, no necks bruised.

There are countless ways to, as Kafka might have put it, "crack open the frozen sea" of a novel, memoir, or short story. In her essay, "Beginnings at their Best," Julie Pratt identifies seven types of "winning" opening strategies:

1. Ominous
2. Mysterious
3. Peculiar
4. Familiar
5. Sensory
6. Provocative
7. Humorous

These seven strategies may be combined, as in the opening to António Lobo Antunes's *The Land at the End of the World*:

> The thing I liked best about the zoo was the roller-skating rink under the trees and the very upright black instructor describing slow ellipses as he glided effortlessly backward over the concrete surface, surrounded by girls in short skirts and white boots, who, if they spoke, doubtless did so in the same gauzy tones as those voices you hear at airports announcing the departure of planes, cotton syllables that dissolve in the ear just as the remnants of a piece of candy do on the curled shell of the tongue.

This opening is sensory ("cotton syllables that dissolve in the ear," "candy ... on the curled shell of a tongue") as well as familiar ("the same ... tones as those voices you hear at airports announcing the departure of planes"). And isn't there something faintly ominous about those "slow ellipses"? As you read on, you'll see that these strategies can be combined.

---

5   Jane Austen, *Pride and Prejudice* (1813).

1. Who Speaks? *Choosing Narrators*

One question that our openings must answer: Who speaks to us? From where, when, and with what attitude and perspective, through what set of sensibilities?

Every piece of writing has a narrator, a persona distinct from the author especially chosen to serve the material, to select and filter its ingredients and make a particular impression, and who functions, largely by way of constraints, as an organizing principle.[6]

In writing this essay, do I want my narrating persona to be coy, clever, cranky, cute? Breezy or hardboiled? I have many personas in my authorial kit bag. Should I deploy the self-deprecating buffoon, or the professorial pedant? Do I plunge directly into my topic or scene, or wade in slowly, as my father used to wade into the swim-hole where he took me and my brother, inch by inch, making wincing sounds as though he were stepping into a vat of boiling oil?

Here is how Marilyn Robinson wades into *Housekeeping*, her first novel:

> My name is Ruth. I grew up with my younger sister, Lucille, under the
> care of my grandmother, Mrs. Sylvia Foster, and when she died, of her
> sisters-in-law, Misses Lily and Nona Foster, and when they fled, of
> her daughter, Mrs. Sylvia Fisher. Through all these generations of elders we
> lived in one house, my grandmother's house, built for her by her husband,
> Edmund Foster, an employee of the railroad, who escaped this world years
> before I entered it. It was he who put us down in this unlikely place.

A few sentences later:

> Sometimes in the spring the old lake will return. One will open a cellar
> door to wading boots floating tallowy soles up and planks and buckets
> bumping at the threshold, the stairway gone from sight after the second
> step. The earth will brim, the soil will become mud and then silty water,
> and the grass will stand in chill water to its tips. Our house was at the
> edge of town on a little hill, so we rarely had more than a black pool in
> our cellar, with a few skeletal insects skidding around on it. A narrow
> pond would form in the orchard, water clear as air covering grass and
> black leaves and fallen branches, all around it black leaves and drenched

---

6   Except in the case of some metafictional, postmodern, or otherwise experimental works in which author and narrator are supposedly one and the same, and even in those cases I would argue that a narrator has been created.

grass and fallen branches, and on it, slight as an image in an eye, sky, clouds, trees, our hovering faces and our cold hands.

Here, setting is character. The character of the grandfather is subsumed by that of the house in which he grew up, and in which most of the action of the novel will occur.

Like most great openings, the opening of *Housekeeping* melds all seven "winning" strategies: ominous, mysterious, peculiar, familiar, sensory, provocative, and humorous. Forthright but gentle, with her narrator's voice barely raised above a whisper, Robinson seduces without force, effortlessly, by means of sensual summary exposition. Were this a painting, it would be all background: the foreground figures have yet to emerge.

2. Dramatic Openings

In her memoir, *The Glass Castle*, Jeanette Walls takes a more headlong, Burt-Lancaster-plunging-into-the-surf approach:

> I was sitting in a taxi, wondering if I had overdressed for the evening, when I looked out the window and saw Mom rooting through a Dumpster. It was just after dark. A blustery March wind whipped the steam coming out of the manholes, and people hurried along the sidewalks with their collars turned up. I was stuck in traffic two blocks from the party where I was heading.
>
> Mom stood fifteen feet away. She had tied rags around her shoulders to keep out the spring chill and was picking through the trash while her dog, a black-and-white terrier mix, played at her feet. Mom's gestures were all familiar—the way she tilted her head and thrust out her lower lip when studying items of potential value that she'd hoisted out of the Dumpster, the way her eyes widened with childish glee when she found something she liked. Her long hair was streaked with gray, tangled and matted, and her eyes had sunk deep into their sockets, but still she reminded me of the mom she'd been when I was a kid, swan-diving off cliffs and painting in the desert and reading Shakespeare aloud. Her cheekbones were still high and strong, but the skin was parched and ruddy from all those winters and summers exposed to the elements. To the people walking by, she probably looked like any of the thousands of homeless people in New York City.

In starting her memoir with scene rather than summary, Walls commits herself to a narrative strategy that puts the emphasis on drama and suggests more than it tells or states. Background is subordinated, if not entirely suppressed; description and action dominate.

As do most successful openings, this one answers as many questions as it raises; it gives us everything we need to inhabit the moment at hand while inviting us to wonder how such a moment came to be. How does a well-off New Yorker have homeless, dumpster-rutting parents? Ominous, peculiar, sensory, familiar ("the mom she'd been when I was a kid"). Setting aside that the glib irony of this coincidental encounter makes it read more as fiction than nonfiction, still, we feel that we know this woman, despite never having really known anyone in her situation. We get to know her through a specific event (Mom rooting through dumpster) and through her reaction to that event (how she describes it to us).

3. Colluding with Readers / Second Person

In opening his novel, *The Crimson Petal and the White*, Michael Faber eschews drama as well as vivid or sensual scene painting. Instead, with his first words he breaks the so-called "fourth wall," buttonholing us, daring us to enter his fictional world:

> Watch your step. Keep your wits about you; you will need them. This city I am bringing you to is vast and intricate, and you have not been here before. You may imagine, from other stories you've read, that you know it well, but those stories flattered you, welcoming you as a friend, treating you as if you belonged. The truth is that you are an alien from another time and place altogether.

Defying readers in the first paragraph takes guts; it may not be a winning strategy, but it is certainly provocative and peculiar, and it settles, decidedly and immediately, the question of who is telling the story, establishing beyond any doubt the disposition of the narrator, namely "in your face."

In rare cases, collusion takes the extreme form of pressing the reader into service as the protagonist, as Jay McInerney does in his novel, *Bright Lights, Big City*:

You are not the kind of guy who would be at a place like this at this time in the morning. But here you are, and you cannot say that the terrain is entirely unfamiliar, although the details are fuzzy.

Depending on the reader's disposition, this approach may or may not work. With second person address especially there's the risk of the reader folding her arms and refusing to play along, saying to herself, "You're right: I am not that kind of guy."

4. Character Narrator

In the right hands, the matter of who speaks to us can be settled in as few as three words: "Call me Ishmael."

With first-person narrators, the answer to the question "who is speaking to us?" tends to be straightforward, but with an unnamed, third-person narrator things get complicated, with the line between narrator and author often so thin and porous it seems nonexistent, to where even authors can't be sure where they stand in relation to their material. Often, with fictional works in progress especially, but with memoir, too, occasionally, it comes to pass that there is no narrator at all, really, no mitigating persona, no point-of-view, no unique set of sensibilities—apart from the author's—through which events are filtered for the reader. In that case, I call the result *default omniscience*, something I discuss at the start of Chapter II and throughout the first-page analyses in this book.

5. Where to Start?
Biblical Openers

Even once we've settled the question of who is telling our stories, we face another big question. Namely: *where* to start. At what point should we enter our stories? Even as I write these words, I face the dilemma. Speaking of beginnings, where to begin?

Why not with the most famous beginning of all?

In the beginning God created the heavens and the earth.

And the earth was without form, and void; and darkness was upon the face of the deep. And the Spirit of God moved upon the face of the waters.

And God said, Let there be light: and there was light.[7]

Unlike most mere mortals, God has no trouble getting His story off the ground. Then again, He has a distinct advantage, since unlike our stories His truly begins at the beginning, so there's no question of going back any further—say, to the day *before* God created the heavens.

"All sensation," philosopher Henri Bergson declared in *Matter and Memory*, "is already memory." What we call "consciousness" is mainly a product of the past. In telling human stories, we can hardly overlook the thing that most shapes our humanity, our histories, what we remember, and even things we may not remember but that have shaped us nevertheless. Every human story has its "back story," one that goes back and back and back, presumably, to the very beginning of time: *In the beginning, God created the heavens and the earth.*

Fortunately, theory and practice differ, otherwise all stories would have the Bible, or an equivalent, as prologue, as does James A. Michener's *Hawaii*. It opens:

Millions upon millions of years ago, when the continents were already formed and the principal features of the earth had been decided, there existed, then as now, one aspect of the world that dwarfed all others. It was a mighty ocean, resting uneasily to the east of the largest continent, a restless ever-changing, gigantic body of water that would later be described as pacific.

Unlike God, who in his prolificacy he resembled, Michener didn't feel compelled to create the earth first before flooding it. Still, in reaching so far back for this opening, he suggests the epic scope of what follows.

---

7   Genesis 1:1–3. In *Restaurant at the End of the Universe*, Book II of Douglas Adams's five-book Hitchhiker's "Trilogy," he gives us this version of that beginning: "In the beginning, the universe was created. This made a lot of people very angry, and has been widely regarded as a bad idea."

6. Setting the Scene:
The Wide-Angle Establishing Shot

Charles Dickens opens *A Tale of Two Cities* with the rhetorical equivalent of what, in a movie, would be a wide-angle establishing shot:

> It was the best of times, it was the worst of times, it was the age of wisdom, it was the age of foolishness, it was the epoch of belief, it was the epoch of incredulity, it was the season of Light, it was the season of Darkness, it was the spring of hope, it was the winter of despair, we had everything before us, we had nothing before us, we were all going direct to Heaven, we were all going direct the other way—in short, the period was so far like the present period, that some of its noisiest authorities insisted on its being received, for good or for evil, in the superlative degree of comparison only.

Rather than plunge us into the heart of the story, such an opening serves as a sort of *framing device*, an imposing ornate gate through which we pass to get to the story. Call it the red-carpet treatment. But gate and carpeting are there not merely to flatter but to orient us. Along with all the pomp and paradox, Dickens lays out the period in which his story is set, a time when plain-faced queens and large-jawed kings (and vice versa) occupied the thrones of England and France.

7. Beginning at the End

Some stories begin at the beginning, while others end where they start. Madison Smartt Bell's *Ten Indians* starts: "Don't know I can say how it all started, but I tell you how it almost finished up." When Orhan Pamuk's novel *My Name Is Red* begins, his protagonist is already dead. His corpse speaks to us from the bottom of the well where his murderer has deposited it/him.

Trading beginnings for endings is an old trick, but not a bad one. As unsure as we are as to where to begin our stories, we tend to know how they'll end.

Martin Amis knew:

> This is the story of a murder. It hasn't happened yet. But it will. (It had better.) I know the murderer, I know the murderee. I know the

time, I know the place. I know the motive (*her* motive) and I know the means. I know who will be the foil, the fool, the poor foal, also utterly destroyed. And I couldn't stop them, I don't think, even if I wanted to. The girl will die. It's what she always wanted. You can't stop people, once they *start creating*.[8]

In cases like this, who can say that the beginning isn't the end, and vice versa? We're reminded of a Möbius strip, or the Ouroboros, the serpent swallowing its own tail to form a circle, though the fictional "tale" isn't being ingested so much as being born ass-first.

Such is the case with *Finnegans Wake*, Joyce's last, most ambitious, and least-read (also least readable) novel. Joyce's novel begins (and ends):

riverrun, past Eve and Adam's, from swerve of shore to bend of bay, brings us by a commodius vicus of recirculation back to Howth Castle and Environs.

The same novel ends (and begins):

Whish! A gull. Gulls. Far calls. Coming, far! End here. Us then. Finn, again! Take. Bussoftlhee, mememormee! Till thous-endsthee. Lps. The keys to. Given! A way a lone a last a loved a long the

Joyce solves the problem of beginnings and endings by having neither and both. Like the universe that it tries to encompass, *Finnegans Wake* has no center or edges. It never starts and it never ends.

8. Literary Births

Though most writers prefer to plunge straight into the middle of their stories, beginning at the beginning has advantages. For one thing, it lets readers experience events "in real time," as they unfold, without having to make temporal adjustments as they go. Superficially, real life happens this way. Why not life on the page? In fact, many stories (usually longer ones or novels) begin at the beginning of their protagonist's life, with their birth.

---

8   *London Fields* (1989).

I was born in the year 1632, in the city of York, of a good family, though not of that country, my father being a foreigner of Bremen, who settled first at Hull. He got a good estate by merchandise, and leaving off his trade, lived afterwards at York, from whence he had married my mother, whose relations were named Robinson, a good family in that country, and after whom I was called Robinson Kreutznear; but by the usual corruption of words in England we are now called, nay, we call ourselves, and write our name, Crusoe; and so my companions always called me.

Since 1719, when Defoe used the technique in *Robinson Crusoe*, countless authors have given birth to their protagonists on page 1, including Dickens, who titles Chapter 1 of *David Copperfield* "I am born," then opens with his narrator wondering whether he'll turn out to be the hero of the book we hold—a doubt not shared by canny readers who've seen the words "David Copperfield" stamped across the book's spine and title page. As opening gambits go, it's not all that sincere, so we can't entirely blame Holden Caulfield when, a hundred and one years later, he calls it crap:

If you really want to hear about it, the first thing you'll probably want to know is where I was born, and what my lousy childhood was like, and how my parents were occupied and all before they had me, and all that David Copperfield kind of crap, but I don't feel like going into it, if you want to know the truth.[9]

One obvious disadvantage of starting our stories with the birth of our hero is that the event isn't likely to form part of the hero's experience, since he can't possibly remember it.

Well, most of us don't remember being born. As with all things fictional, here too we find exceptions:

I was slapped and hurried along in the private applause of birth—I think I remember this. Well, I imagine it anyway—the blind boy's rose-and-milk-and-gray-walled (and salty) aquarium, the aquarium overthrown, the uproar in the woman-barn ...

So Harold Brodkey's *The Runaway Soul* (which itself runs away to 833 pages) squares up to us, with a narrator who dares to tell us what colors he saw in the

---

9   J.D. Salinger, *The Catcher in the Rye* (1951).

womb. Thus we are prepared for—or forewarned about—the coming performance. "Performance" is the word: Brodkey's protagonist has yet to breathe his first and already the world applauds. Or at least his creator imagines that it will.

The trouble with starting stories at the beginning—not just with a character's history, with their birth, but even with, say, a hypothetical heroine packing her hypothetical bags for a hypothetical trip to Italy—is that the story, if it has begun at all, has only just barely begun; there's little drama greasing the wheels, only the vague anticipations of a voyage whose repercussions remain to be seen. Like a car engine started on a frozen day, you have to wait for it to warm up before bringing it up to speed.

9. *In Medias Res: The Inciting Incident*

This is why most stories start *in medias res* or "in the middle of things." The term comes from the ancient Roman poet Horace, who advised aspiring epic poets to go straight to the heart instead of starting at the beginning. That "heart" may be near the end or close to the beginning of the string of events that form a narrative. In any event, the action of the story is well underway.

Katherine Shonk's 2001 short story, "My Mother's Garden," about a woman trying to convince her mother to abandon her home in a Chernobyl suburb, begins *in medias res*:

> Spring had come to my hometown. When I got off the bus at the entrance to the contamination zone, Oles was standing at the guard station in a lightweight uniform instead of his padded military jacket, his gun swung loosely over his back. The thaw seemed to have improved his unusually sullen mood; he nodded his appreciation of the flowered fabric I'd brought for his wife and let me pass through the gate without even looking at my documents.

Stories that start *in medias res* don't actually start in the middle of the story being told. Rather they start with or close to an *inciting incident*: the event that propels the protagonist out of her status quo existence and into a novel circumstance or circumstances that put that status quo into relief or perspective. Most modern narratives are written this way, with the inciting incident occurring, or alluded to, within the first page or pages.

Often the inciting incident is conveyed by the first sentence:

They threw me off the hay truck about noon.

None of them knew the color of the sky.

One August afternoon, when Ajay was ten years old, his elder brother, Aman, dove into a pool and struck his head on the cement bottom.

The first quoted sentence, from James M. Cain's, *The Postman Always Rings Twice*, explains how Frank, a drifter, winds up at the diner where he falls for Cora, wife of Nick "the Greek" Papadakis, the owner, whom Frank and Cora ultimately plot to murder. Had Frank not been thrown off that hay truck, the most famous crime novel ever would lack an inciting incident.

In the second quote the reason none of the characters in Stephen Crane's short story know the color of the sky is because they're the exhausted survivors aboard "The Open Boat" (a lifeboat) that has delivered them from a shipwreck: the inciting incident.

The last quote is from Akhil Sharma's short story "Surrounded by Sleep," about a young Indian boy who believes himself marked by his brother's accident, and who—to comfort himself—conjures up a cardigan-wearing God that is half Clark Kent, half Mr. Rogers. The demarcation between Ajay's previous, status quo existence as happy child and that of the story's present circumstances (which have him appealing to God to fulfill his special fate so Aman's death won't be in vain) is clearly marked. Given the circumstances, to begin with the pool accident seems not only reasonable, but compulsory.

The precise location of an inciting incident isn't always obvious. In a story about an alcoholic man's downward spiral, is the inciting incident the alcoholic's first drink, or his hundred and first—the one that he swears will be his last? When does a drunk begin to be a drunk? When he thinks he's become one, or when his friends tell him he is? Or when he wakes up in a puddle of his own vomit, or in jail, or in the psychiatric ward of a hospital? Or when he gets fired from his job? Or when his wife and children leave him? Or when he finds himself begging coins and cigarettes on Skid Row?

Inciting incidents can be slippery things. So we're left with the same question: *where to begin?* In the end, where to start may have to be determined by the extent to which an event catapults a character out of his or her routine.

10. The Covenant: *Taking the Leap*

There are, of course, an infinite number of possible opening strategies, possibly as many as there are stories, and each of those strategies comes in countless variations. These are just some examples.

The point is that in telling our stories we have to start somewhere, and where we start matters enough to shape everything that follows. No sooner do we set down the first words of a story than we create, or begin creating, a world—one with its own laws, its own language, its own possibilities and limitations. The covenants of that world are established word by word, line by line, paragraph by paragraph, for reader and writer—but especially for the writer, who'll be bound by them throughout the rest of the work.

Just as in the Bible God makes His covenant with Abraham, we make ours with our readers: we lay down the laws of the worlds they'll inhabit for as long as they keep reading. Or they'll reject that world and its laws and pick up someone else's book, or go about some other business, defrosting the fridge or doing laundry.

In beginning our stories we stand on the edge of a precipice or bridge, but with no fireman there to talk us down. We have to do it ourselves, word by word, but only after we've taken the plunge, hoping our readers will follow us.

Seven Deadly Sins:
Common Errors

I READ THEM ALL THE TIME. STORIES WHERE SCENES DISAPPEAR before my eyes, where the point-of-view is as slippery as a greased tadpole, where authors play hard to get with vital statistics: fictional stories that beg to be memoirs, and memoirs that yearn to be fiction, not to mention stories built on the quicksand of cliché ... errors so glaring I can practically see them through the envelopes in which they've been submitted to the literary journals I edit.

Seven: a curious number, the lowest natural number that cannot be represented as the sum of the squares of three integers. It's the number of sides to a heptagon, of days in the week, of colors in a rainbow. There are seven seas, seven continents, seven Wonders of the Ancient World. Number of notes in the traditional diatonic scale: seven. Rome had seven kings and as many emperors. Noah brought seven pairs of every clean animal onto the ark. The House of Wisdom has seven pillars (Proverbs 9:1); seven things are detestable to the Lord (Proverbs 6:16–19). There are seven virtues and seven deadly sins, not to mention (in bifurcation theory as applied to the mathematical study of dynamical systems) seven types of elementary catastrophes.[1]

Seven also happens to be the number of common errors—errors of style, substance, and structure—routinely encountered by me in the works of beginning and even advanced fiction writers, fundamental errors that present themselves with alarming frequency. Think of them, if you like, as the fiction writer's Seven Deadly Sins.

Here they are—in order of deadliness.

---

1   1. Fold, 2. Cusp, 3. Swallowtail, 4. Butterfly, 5. Hyperbolic Umbilic, 6. Elliptic Umbilic, 7. Parabolic Umbilic.

1. Default Omniscience:
Failure to Properly Engage a Narrator and Inhabit That Narrator's Perspective

A story or a novel is as much about how it's told—by means of what structure, through what voice or voices, from which viewpoint(s)—as about what happens. In fiction, means and ends are inseparable: method is substance. You may have all the ingredients—a plot, characters, dialogue, description, setting, conflict— but if they aren't bound by a specific, consistent, and rigorously controlled view- point, you have nothing.

In workshops I've been known to write across the black (or white) board:

NO POINT-OF-VIEW = NO STORY

I'm not talking minor gaffs and glitches ("As she looked out her bedroom window, Sally heard the door click open behind her and there stood Dawson ..."). I mean errors so deep rooted no line-editing can set them right, blunders that call into question not only the author's grasp of a particular moment or scene in a story, but fiction's primary purpose: to render experiences.

Fiction's stock in trade is human experience, and experience is subjective: things don't just happen; they happen insofar as characters feel and react to them. Subjectivity requires a nervous system. That no two nervous systems respond identically to stimuli gives fiction its raison d'être.

To be authentic, fictional experiences should pass through a subjectivity filter. They must be sorted and sifted either through the sensibility of a char- acter or characters or that of a so-called omniscient narrator—one who, to a variable extent, shares their nervous systems and perspectives on events. Unless this subjective filter or narrator has been created and is firmly in place, what's conveyed to the reader isn't experience, but *information*.

An example:

Hank could have passed for Lila's grandfather. His white mustache added to his years, yet he kept himself trim and thought himself as fit as the younger fathers. He was nuts about Lila, who still loved him, though lately she'd grown distant. She was no longer his little girl; in fact, she secretly wished that he would act his age. She especially hated it when he pretended to pull coins and other things out of her ears. Why was he so goofy? But all adolescent girls pass through a phase where they hold their fathers in mild contempt.

At first glance, nothing seems wrong with this paragraph. But on closer inspection problems arise. While the first sentence ("Hank could have passed for Lila's grandfather") is neutral-objective, the second sentence ("thought himself ... fit") shifts us into Hank's personal, subjective viewpoint. Though the third sentence seems to dip into Lila's feelings about him, the thought expressed by it could still be from Hank's viewpoint. However—unless we assume that Lila's secret is not a secret—the fourth, fifth, and sixth sentences plunge us fully into Lila's consciousness. With the final sentence we get yet another shift in perspective, to an omniscient, generalized view of all adolescent girls' relationships with their fathers.

The cumulative result of all these subtle and not-so-subtle shifts is that as a reader I am never clear whose experience I am getting. The point-of-view isn't solid; the filter is loose or distorted, hence my ability to share the experiences offered in this passage is inhibited. I get all the information necessary to construct an experience, but constructing an experience isn't the same as having or *inhabiting* one. It's the difference between groceries and a meal.

For readers to inhabit our stories we must first somehow inhabit them ourselves. And yet we authors don't really live in our stories, nor can we be expected to, since we're obliged to sit at our desks in front of our computers. This is why we create narrators. The narrator lives inside the story; he (or she or it) is our emissary to the world of that story.

Notice I said we have to *create* narrators. Narrators don't create themselves, nor should they ever be confused with their authors, from whom they exist separately. Nor should authors second guess or in any way intrude upon their narration. When they do, they violate point-of-view; the narrative filter is detached, displaced, distorted, or destroyed. Experience degenerates into information. We call the result *author intrusion*, and it blurs and finally dissolves the fictional dream.

Point-of-view can never be incidental or accidental. It's as fundamental as the choice between present and past tense, formal and informal diction, dramatization versus summary or exposition.

Of all problems plaguing amateur works, none is more common—or more fatal—than mishandling of point-of-view. Typically, the problem results not from a chosen viewpoint being violated (though this, too, happens frequently), but because no viewpoint has been properly established to begin with, so there's nothing to violate.

Example: In a story about a waitress named Linda, we read, "People didn't think Linda was as pretty as she used to be." Arguably, this could be Linda's own view of things. If so, it's a harsh view, presented with the blunt objectivity of a Gallup poll. Earlier in the same story we're told, "Linda was a waitress and an alcoholic; everyone knew that." Here, too, the perspective could *arguably* be Linda's. But it's a weak argument, since alcoholics—those in the throes of their addiction, anyway—are generally the last people to label themselves as such. Since this pronouncement is made early in the story (first paragraph, third line), readers can't be blamed for taking it not as Linda's subjective opinion, but as an omniscient narrator's objective verdict.

Ultimately, though, this turns out to be Linda's story, presented to us, by and large, from her perspective. So I'm thrown by those moments when the viewpoint turns objective with statements like "Lately, people had been all too concerned about [Linda]" (presumably these are the same generalized people who think Linda's looks aren't what they used to be). Or is this Linda's subjective viewpoint wearing an omniscient, objective mask? At the very least it's confusing. At worst it's inauthentic and unconvincing.

Again, the problem here goes deeper than a minor lapse or two. The problem is that the author hasn't embedded herself sufficiently *by way of her chosen narrator* into her character's psyche, or into any particular mindset. Had she done so, none of these lapses would have occurred. They would have been impossible.[2]

Another example: In a story where eight-year-old Aidan takes his first plane trip to France, the author sabotages his point-of-view strategy (and his story with it) in several ways: first, by straying into passive constructions ("It was the longest plane trip that Aidan had ever been on") that locate the viewpoint beyond the character's personal, subjective experience (as opposed to "Aidan yawned and shifted in his seat; he'd never been on such a long plane ride before"), then by drifting into an equally inadvertent omniscience ("They [Aidan and his kid sister] knew they had better behave themselves"), and finally by sliding into diction that yanks us abruptly out of Aidan's eight-year-old psyche ("The only *dietary adjustment* [italics mine] was having to eat goat's milk for breakfast," as opposed to "Aidan spat out his breakfast: his mother had served it to him with goat's milk. The taste reminded him

---

2   The italicized phrase is important, since there has to be that mediating presence between author and story. The author's job is to convey the experience of the narrator; hence, it is the narrator's experience that matters, not the author's experience.

of his armpits."). In each instance the author has failed to inhabit Aidan, to plant himself and the reader along with him *by way of a realized and engaged third-person narrator* firmly in Aidan's psyche, to see, feel, think, act, and react with him.

By resisting such immersion and commitment, by insisting on mixing our own ideas and sensibilities with those of our narrators and the characters whose experiences they convey, we keep readers at a vague, inconsistent distance from the worlds we want them to inhabit. The resulting experience in this case is neither Aidan's nor Linda's—nor that of a true omniscient narrator, but a case of *default omniscience*: omniscience without plan, passion, or purpose, that fails to offer us a consistent, clear, reliable filter. It does the opposite. It muddies things up.

Does this mean we shouldn't create omniscient narratives or narrators? Of course not. It means only that we should do so knowingly.

Does this mean we must restrict ourselves to a single perspective or point-of-view? Not at all. Almost anything we do in our fiction, no matter how outrageous or experimental, can work if done consistently and with authority.

But too often writers simply neglect to make this most crucial of choices. They assume that point-of-view isn't that important, or that it's something that can be fixed later on—which is like getting a flu shot after you've caught the flu.

Let either your characters' or your omniscient narrator's perspectives serve as the organizing principle of your stories, the source of every idea expressed in your narratives. Nothing should reach the reader that hasn't passed through this point-of-view filter.

Point-of-view is the rock on which fiction is built. It can't be added or subtracted any more than a canvas can be added to a finished painting.

Remember:

NO POINT-OF-VIEW = NO STORY

2. False Suspense:
Capricious Withholding of Information

A fiction writer's job is to tell stories, not to hide them. This should be obvious but isn't always. Look at this first paragraph from a first page examined later in this book:

She got off the bus, grateful to be away from all the thoughts that had intruded upon her mind throughout the journey. Across the park the remnant of an ancient society loomed at the end of the path, its stones bright under the hot sun. Inside, students trained for the upcoming campaign. She headed toward the inevitable, the blood-filled battlefield of her future reclaiming the forefront of her thoughts. No one wandered the streets, they were busy working, as she should have been. While she normally skipped her first class, today she had a good excuse. She had a vision to report.

As a workshop leader, but also as the editor of a literary journal, I often read stories like this, where, within the first page or paragraph, I find myself confused, wondering: Who is this woman? Where is she coming from? Where is she going? What "campaign"? "First class" in *what*? What am I reading and why am I reading it?

When authors trade in *false suspense*, they are essentially saying to their readers: keep reading and you'll figure out what in blazes is going on.

The problem with such a strategy is that it assumes saintly forbearance on the part of readers, who don't read to learn information already known to the characters (who may be presumed to know, for instance, their own identities), but to share in their experiences and to learn, with them, the answers to questions far more relevant and urgent, such as: *What will happen next? How will X respond if Y happens? What effect will X's response have on Z?* Plot questions. While writers may hope to raise philosophical and moral questions in their readers, plot questions are what keep them reading.

And whatever else we do, we have to keep our readers reading, bearing in mind that readers are rude. The slightest twinge of hunger or bladder urge may prompt them to put your story or memoir down and never pick it up again. Readers hold all the cards. They can be rude; you can't afford to be.

One way to be rude is to tease people. Writers who capriciously withhold information are doing just that. They do so for other reasons, too, chief among these being that they don't trust their stories, or worse, they have no stories to tell. No wonder they try to hide them.

The classic example of a strategy based on withheld information is the "and then she woke up" story, in which the reader discovers, at the last possible moment, that what she's been reading was only a dream, that all this time Pamela has been sound asleep and safe in her bed, with no purple giraffes chasing her after all. That may be good for Pamela, but it's a terrible way to tell a story and a worse way to treat your reader, who invested in a fictional reality only to have it yanked out from under her. The perpetrator of such a bait-and-switch story might defend himself by saying, "Well, Pamela didn't know she was dreaming, therefore I'm not withholding any information to which my character is privy." Pamela may not know she's dreaming, but her author knows perfectly well, and if he's being honest with himself and his material, instead of leading us down the garden path to "Gotcha!," he'll provide such clues as will make it fairly obvious that we are reading not reality, but a dream. Then, of course, he'll have to go fish for a more substantial plot.

Though false suspense may carry some readers along for a few pages, for most readers it will eventually result in frustration. The solution is straightforward enough: Have a story to tell and tell it. Never withhold information. That's a bold imperative, yet in stating it I'm not alone. Eudora Welty (who knew a thing or two about storytelling) said as much in response to a persistent question unintentionally raised in her readers by one of her short stories: "I had not meant to mystify readers by withholding any fact," she wrote apologetically, "*it is not a writer's business to tease*" (italics mine).[3]

When you ask readers to read a story, novel, or memoir, you're asking them to take a journey with you, one that will lead them up a steep climb of rising action to the summit where a climax typically occurs, leaving the reader with an unprecedented view of the world they have inhabited, as well as (ideally) a broadened, deepened, or enhanced awareness of human nature, the world, and life in general.

As author, you're charged with equipping the reader with the tools necessary not only to arrive at the summit, but to appreciate the view from there. That means withholding nothing crucial or basic (hardtack, maps, rope, food and water), while providing nothing sooner than necessary (champagne, binoculars), since the journey is arduous. Every unneeded bit of information makes it more so.

False suspense weighs your reader down with useless, nagging questions. Burden them with it, and you not only make the climb harder, you spoil the view from the top when they get there, since the answers to such questions are rarely worth the effort.

When writing fiction, it's better to be generous than to withhold. Proof:

---

3   Eudora Welty, "Is Phoenix Jackson's Grandson Really Dead" in *The Eye of a Story: Selected Essays and Reviews.*

My father wanted to show me something, but he wouldn't say what. He only said I should go get my gun, my thirty-six-aught-six, and follow him. This happened just outside Bend, Oregon, where we lived in a ranch house surrounded by ten acres of woods. I was twelve at the time: old enough to shoot a gun, young enough to fear the dark.

This opening to Benjamin Percy's story "The Woods," about an obdurate father teaching his "pantywaist" son to hunt deer, is nothing if not generous. Look at the amount of information provided by this opening paragraph. The protagonist is a twelve-year-old boy who is afraid of the dark and who presumably hunts with his father. The setting: Bend, Oregon. I think of that Robert Frost poem, "Provide, Provide." That's what author Percy does here: he provides his readers with information. He communicates; he shares, he gives. He is bountiful; he holds nothing back. So different from the author hiding behind a veil of mystery or coyness.

All of which is to say it pays to be generous.

3. Dramatized Routine or Status-Quo Syndrome:
Failure to Distinguish between Events and Routine

No matter how intrinsically exotic or sensational a routine may be, readers aren't interested in routine.

Say you've written a story set in the future. In that future your hero, Matt Starhopper, travels on the first day of each month to a space station located on one of the moons of B1620-26, the farthest known planet at the core of the globular M4 cluster. Along the way he encounters the usual ominous space aliens, treacherous asteroid fields, and gravitational follies. His journey is rendered with a Flemish master's eye for detail, an astronomer's embrace of planetary lore, and a speculative imagination that would make Jules Verne blush. Yet as she turns pages, though she admires and respects the author's work, though she finds it stylish and authentic, our reader feels her attention flagging, her eyelids drooping. Why? What's gone wrong?

In a word: routine. Consciously or not, the reader is aware that, however sensational from a twenty-first-century earthling's perspective, Matt

Starhopper has taken this voyage many times before, and will take it many times more. Nothing on the page suggests otherwise, just as nothing on the page suggests that this voyage departs in any significant way from the others. On the contrary, the reader senses that he is being told about a general, not a specific, voyage. So he pushes on, faithfully, in the hope of soon encountering those two blessed words that signal the start of a true fictional voyage: "One day ..."

It's that "one day" (or its equivalent) that pricks the reader's ears, that says, "Listen up: something extraordinary is about to happen." The key word is "extraordinary," an antonym of "routine" and the antidote for it. Whether your characters journey daily to a distant moon or just down the hallway to the bathroom, what matters to readers is the singular event that distinguishes one such voyage from all others and makes for a story.

Another example of dramatized routine:

> Mornings, the rhythmic tapping would wake me: *thunk, thunk, thunk*— the sound of my brother's hammer pounding wood. I'd roll over and squint at the clock. 7:30 am. I'd get out of bed and find him sitting against the floor, cross-legged, his back to the closet door. Above his ears that protruded too prominently, his short hairs would stick up in several places. Not a gray hair in sight. Sometimes, seeing his innocent joy, it would be easy for me to forget that he was forty-eight years old.

Here, instead of a specific, concrete, singular event or moment, this opening confronts us with a conditional, generalized routine. However, except to see it departed from, readers aren't interested in routine or status quo. With good storytelling, the exception implies the routine. We extract the general from the particular, not vice versa.

Compare with:

> A rhythmic tapping wakes me. *Thunk, thunk, thunk.* I roll over and squint at the clock. 7:30 am. I get out of bed and find my brother in his room, leaning against the closet door, pounding his toy hammer against the floorboards, smiling. Above his ears that protrude too prominently, his short hairs stick up in several places. Not a gray hair in sight. Seeing his innocent joy, it's easy to forget he's forty-eight years old.

Note how this version of the same opening expunges the conditional tense. Generally, the conditional tense has a deadening effect. It tells readers not what characters are doing or do, but what they "would" (i.e., generally) do. "Hal would sit on the steps of the town hall with both middle fingers erect for whoever happened to pass by," has far less impact than, "That Friday morning, Hal sat down on the front steps of the town hall with both middle fingers held erect for whoever passed him by." (It's also more likely.)

Generalizations are no less welcome when applied to dialogue:

> "What's the matter, kid, don't like blue stockings?" my father would say.
> "No," I'd answer. "And what's more I don't like stockings!"

The suggestion that the above exchange took place on several occasions is off-putting; unless it was part of an Abbott & Costello-like schtick, I'll bet it didn't. That the author puts the dialogue in quotation marks increases that dialogue's authority while doubling my doubts. Though occasionally narrators may prove unreliable, their unreliability should be germane to the story, not incidental to it.

When in your own work you find yourself using the conditional tense, be aware that you may be dramatizing routine. See if you can't substitute a specific event and let it stand for the routine.

Other words to watch out for: "always," "usually," "typically"—words that generalize about routines rather than offer us concrete, particular experiences from which routine may be extrapolated.

The same thing applies to nonfiction narratives. A student in a nonfiction class of mine told me how, as a young man, he worked as a "flagger" in his father's crop-dusting business. "A flagger," he explained to me, "is the guy holding a flag and marking off space—50 feet at a time, 17 steps (for me)—so the pilot can line up on something and not lose his place in the field. I did this every year for ten years." How, my student wondered, might he write a story about being a flagger?

My answer: not by generalizing about the experience, but by finding a specific event or incident to hang the story from. Focus on one day in your experience of being a flagger and let the experiences of that day stand for the overall experience.

Another example: A young woman visits her barely coherent father in the nursing home, as she has done daily for the past two years. Of such a plot readers may well ask, "What makes this day different from any other day?" On closer examination, we find that on the day in question, the young woman does indeed do several things that depart from her routine:

1. She stops on the way to visit the house where she grew up.
2. She reminisces with her father about her dead sister, Rose.
3. She talks to a young man working behind the counter at a bakery.
4. She meets the bakery young man for lunch at the hospital.

Though the story of a woman's routine visit to her father in a nursing home offers little hope for plot or catharsis, any one of the above listed specific events holds more than hope. For my money, I'd go with the bakery boy, and develop the relationship between him and the heroine, perhaps into a love affair, one that was never meant to be (as tends to be true of romances inspired by circumstance) and that ends badly—or not. Whatever event or incident is exploited, a story needs events and incidents: they are what put the status quo where it belongs, in the background.

In fiction as in life, exceptions prove the rule. Only through seeing characters put into extraordinary situations can readers fully appreciate their "ordinary" qualities.

4. Information vs. Experience:
Supplying Abstract Ideas and Conclusions in Lieu of Concrete Evidence

Information has its place in many kinds of writing, including fiction, personal essays, and memoirs; but when there is an experience behind or to go with the information, as storytellers we're obliged to provide readers with the experience, to create it as vividly and viscerally as we can, and with as few words as necessary or as space will permit.

Information:
I heard that lots of rumors about me were going around.

Experience:
"Everyone's talking about you," my friend Sheila leaned over my bed and whispered when she visited me in the hospital one day.

"They *are*?"

"You're the talk of the town. You should hear all the rumors. According to one you're paralyzed from the neck down and will never walk again."

Information:
That walk to the clinic with my broken hip was long enough to make me tear up.
Experience:
The distance from the curb to the front door of the clinic was only about forty feet, but without my crutches it might as well have been a mile. There was no railing, and every step came with an injection of molten lead into my left hip and a wish that I'd doubled up my dose of Percodan.

Information:
Mr. Benoit was unsuccessful in interrupting me.
Experience:
As I spoke, Mr. Benoit drummed his fingers on his metal desk and cleared his throat loudly; when I ignored him he took the yardstick from the chalk well and tapped it, louder and louder, against the blackboard.

Information:
My teachers were just as interested to hear my stories as the students were.
Experience:
As I regaled her third-period biology class with my adventures, Mrs. Szost stood proudly next to me in my shiny wheelchair, as if I were visiting royalty.

Information:
The picture taken was for my senior superlative (runner-up for best sense of humor). She, Joe Hinkle (the male best sense of humor runner-up), and I went out to the track field for the pictures. The picture chosen for the yearbook was of me running the guy over in my wheelchair.
Experience:
Sally walked and I rolled beside her to the running track behind the school. There—with the bright afternoon sun spilling down from a cloudless sky—she snapped a photo of me pretending to run over red-haired, pimply faced Joe Hinkle ("male best sense of humor runner-up").

Information:
While I waited, a kid in a wheelchair who was actually paralyzed rolled down that hallway.
Experience:
One afternoon, as I stood there waiting for my sister, something at the far end of the hallway caught my eye, a glint of sun from the window shining on a strip of chrome. The strip of chrome belonged to a wheelchair, and the wheelchair

belonged to Derek Meyers, a junior who'd been first-string quarterback on the Milledgeville Muggers football team until the previous winter, when he snowboarded into a telephone pole, paralyzing himself from the neck down.

Information:
That night, I felt guilty for enjoying my injury so much.

Experience:
That night, as I lay in my bed trying to fall asleep, I replayed the scene over and over in my head of Derek M. rolling past me down that hallway, only in this version I saw it all from Derek's point of view, and instead of a wheelchair, I floated in the throne of a gilded litter with isinglass curtains lofted by a quartet of swarthy Indian carriers in turbans and rags. Meanwhile a fifth bearer fed me peeled grapes, the seeds of which I spat onto his bare feet. At which point I realized I had fallen asleep and was having a nightmare.

5. Imitation Story:
Cliché at the Root of Conception

Someone has written a story about a police officer involved in a botched drug bust. The story is set in Spanish Harlem, where Emil, a rookie fresh out of the academy, and his partner Clyde stake out a bodega at the corner of 112th and Adam Clayton-Powell Boulevard. In the process Emil falls for Dulce, sister of the drug-dealing bodega owner.

Need I fill in the rest of this story? In the climactic scene Emil, seeing Dulce reach for her weapon, draws and fires. She was reaching for the love letter Emil wrote her the day before, or for a candy bar. She dies in the rookie's arms.

What's wrong? It all sounds familiar, doesn't it? If the characters and situation seem familiar, it's probably because they are. We've seen them, or something close, a hundred times before in as many TV cop shows. So what's wrong with that? Supposing the story is executed in brilliant style, so lucid and fresh that it can survive—if not surmount—its cliché origins?

That this story's problems are solvable may be true. It hardly matters, though, since they *shouldn't* be solved. Martin Amis tells us, "All good writing is a war against cliché." The first step to winning that war is to not charge hell-for-leather into a minefield.

The landmines are clichés and stereotypes, and the way to avoid them is to practice sincerity. "Sincerity," wrote Jorge Luis Borges, "is not a moral choice, but an aesthetic one." When we traffic in clichés, we're no better than a booster. Slap a fresh coat of paint on it, add a twist or two, change the boy to a girl: you're still dealing in stolen goods.

The way to avoid cliché at the root of conception is not to grab your idea from a TV screen, but from someplace deeper inside yourself. That sounds mushy, but how can you imagine work that has already been imagined for you? It's the difference between taking a bite out of a crisp apple and biting into applesauce.

When we produce work that's derivative, we aren't being honest. We're borrowing someone else's aesthetics and pawning them off as our own. We do it out of fear, calculating that whatever they lack in originality, used stories and characters make up for by being tried and true. This is like proclaiming a used tire more reliable than a new one, since it's been around longer.

Good stories and novels have been written about drug busts gone bad by people with fresh insights to offer. Maybe they've been cops themselves, or they've known cops or studied them long enough to tell their stories from a new angle, with a new twist. Or they have mined their imaginations for the essential truths of those characters in those situations. Keats wrote, "I am certain of nothing but the holiness of the heart's affections and the truth of imagination."[4] And though the truth of imagination may be accessed through other people's stories or derivations thereof, ultimately it reaches us only through our own sensibilities and experiences. Whether those experiences are real or imaginative doesn't matter, as long as they're ours.

Could it be that authors of imitation stories don't want to risk boring their audiences with material that's close to them, but that seems too ordinary, too banal, so instead they dish up melodramas spliced together from old movies? Yet for all the sensationalism, the result bores. It bores because the author's real material, the stuff that should really mean something to him, has been overlooked, disregarded, and dismissed in favor of a bunch of clichés.

"In every action," Marcus Aurelius wrote in *Meditations*, "make it a practice to ask yourself, 'What is the object of my doing this?'" If your object is just to tell a story, any old story, that may not be enough. It should be a story that only you can tell, as only you can tell it.

Am I saying you should write autobiographically? No. But write *personally*. Choose material close to you in spirit, that touches you where you live, that means something to you. Imagine the book or story you would most like to read and, as Seymour Glass advises his kid brother Buddy in Salinger's *Seymour: An Introduction*, "just sit down shamelessly and write the thing yourself."

---

4   Letter to Benjamin Bailey, 22 November 1817.

6. Disappearing Scenes:
Failure to Distinguish between Background, Flashback, Frame, and Present Story

Having been brought up on movies and television, we're used to having our stories shuffled and sliced, with flashbacks and flash-forwards turning time into a vertigo-inducing carnival ride. This shuffling back and forth in time has gone on since Homer. But in movies and TV shows, flashback is no longer spice or condiment, but bread and butter.

Understandably, fiction writers, not wanting to eat the dust of their show-biz brethren, feel compelled to play their own games with time. Hence the proliferation of stories and novels jammed with flashbacks, framing devices, and other time-manipulating machines.

Competing on any level with movies and television is, I think, a mistake. They have technology on their side; we don't. They have stars and multimillion-dollar budgets; we don't. They have passive audiences slumped in plush seats; we don't. They dazzle their viewers with special effects; we can't—and shouldn't have to. Readers, at least the sort I write for, read because they love written stories and the language that written stories are made of. They don't want substitutes for cinema; they don't *need* special effects. What they demand from works of literature they don't expect from movies, and vice versa. What can we give them that movies can't?

Well, for a start, good writing. And not just good, the best.

I don't mean to imply that screenwriters aren't brilliant. Of course they are. But language isn't their medium. Words are to screenwriters what love letters are to romance: not an end in itself, but a means to that end.

That said, gimmicks are seductive, and none are more seductive than the flashback. The very term suggests flashiness. The problem is that, like all bells and whistles and other shiny devices, they tend to be overused and abused. When, a page or two into a story, I'm yanked out of the present action and into a flashback, I tend to feel cheated. I feel cheated because I had begun to invest in a set of characters and circumstances, only to have my investment nullified. I have to start investing all over again.

With good flashbacks this doesn't happen. A good flashback increases and deepens my investment. If it sweeps me out of the present action, it does so temporarily, just long enough to add to my appreciation and understanding of the characters in their present situation. But give nine out of ten inexperienced writers a flashback, and they'll use it more or less as a pilot uses his ejector seat, to bail out of a story that's about to crash, or that can't get off the ground. Occasionally the ejector button parachutes them into a better story, begging the question: why open with a lousy story to begin with? Why not start out with the good one?

The answer is that most flashbacks aren't real flashbacks at all, but stories bookended by a scene or "framing device." And the trouble with framing devices is that they don't always work, and even when they do, they can frustrate and annoy. For example: a novel opens with someone named Hank getting up, getting dressed, brushing his teeth. As he stands before the bathroom mirror with his mouth foamy with toothpaste, Hank remembers his date the night before. White space: the scene shifts. We're in a restaurant in the Village. For the next eight pages we're with Hank on his date. What of the toothbrushing scene? *What of it?* It has been jettisoned, left to crash and burn as it so richly deserves to.

Even more annoying is the scene that doesn't tell us the character has gotten out of bed, namely because the character hasn't gotten out of bed; the character is still asleep, dreaming of hand-to-hand combat with colossal centipedes at the center of the earth, only we're not told that it's a dream until the end of the story, when Sally wakes up. Surprise!

Typically writers resort to framing devices and prolonged flashbacks for one of two reasons: a) because they don't know where their stories really begin; and b) because they aren't sure what story they're telling, or that they have one to tell. Note the symbiotic relationship to false suspense / withheld information (see Deadly Sin 2). Most if not all of a fiction writer's bigger problems tend to result from lack of faith in their material, which in turn results from lack of faith in the imagination.

On the other hand a writer who has a story to tell and has confidence in that story will tell it fearlessly, if possible by straightforward means, without resorting to flashy gimmicks or clichés, or padding the work with autobiographical clutter, or teasing readers along with false suspense, or neglecting to convey experiences from deep within a chosen point-of-view, or getting stuck in a holding pattern of routine as opposed to reporting singular events.

All these problems can be limited—if not eliminated—by writing from deep within character(s) in situation(s), rather than from outside, above, or beyond them.

In the end, all of these problems share one source: failure of imagination. As fiction writers, our job is to give experiences to our readers. And what you don't have yourself you can't give. Since we can't be expected to fully live the lives of all of our characters, we must let our narrators do it for us through the instrument of the imagination, by which we inhabit those experiences as fully, as richly, as deeply as we can. *I am certain of nothing but the holiness of the heart's affections and the truth of imagination.* Surrender to that instrument, trust its truths, and you'll write good fiction.

7. Sentimentality:
Implying or Describing Emotions in Excess of Experience

Merriam-Webster defines "sentiment" first as "an attitude, thought, or judgment prompted by feeling" and secondly as "emotion" or "feeling." For "sentimental" the same dictionary gives these two definitions: 1) "marked by or governed by feeling, sensibility, or emotional idealism," and 2) "having an excess of sentiment or sensibility."

Whether they are experienced by the characters in a work of fiction or by the reader reading about them, or both, emotions and feelings are the stuff of fiction; it can scarcely exist without them. Experience is fiction's stock in trade, after all, and experiences come with and generate feelings.

The issue of sentimentality arises when the emotions or feelings conveyed by a scene or by a sentence—either through the terms used to convey them or the actions or reactions of the characters—exceed the experiences that give rise to them. Sentimentality is *emotion in excess of experience*.

What causes sentimentality? How do emotions exceed experience?

The first and most obvious way is through exaggeration. If a character's emotional or physiological response to an event is overstated or sensationalized (the so-called "spit take"—a character spitting out his or her drink on hearing some news—is a classic example), we're entitled to label that response "sentimental." Characters bursting into tears, tearing out their hair, screaming and vomiting or punching each other in the nose—any of these responses may be sentimental, or not, depending on the experiences that motivate them.

Similarly, the terms used to express a character's emotional response to an experience may overstate that response ("he felt like he'd been stabbed in the gut," "her heart somersaulted with joy"). Another sentimental sentence (taken from one of the first pages analyzed in this book): "To release the pain of her next contraction, the woman screamed out an *agonized guttural bark*" (italics mine). The woman's scream could have spoken for itself; but no, the author felt compelled to color it with sentiment.

In a coming-of-age story (nonfiction) of a dirt road along a creek notorious for the illicit acts said to have occurred along it, we read, "The old roadway had become a thoroughfare of puzzlement, infested as if by termites by unknowns over every inch." The problem with such a sentence isn't that the sentiment it carries is inappropriate per se, but that it overshoots its target; it makes the point too aggressively. It uses a hammer to swat a fly on the windowsill. It does the job, but not without collateral damage. What's damaged is the reader's faith in the narrator, or conviction that we can go to the bank with his or her every word. Better to have let the facts about that old road speak for themselves.

Sometimes both actions and the language used to convey them may be sentimental. "A single, lonesome, diamond-like tear made its way slowly down Daisy's cheek." While it may be the case that Daisy cried, and it may even be true that a "single" tear "made its way slowly down" her cheek, it's also all too obvious that the author of this sentence didn't trust Daisy's crying to speak for itself, that he felt compelled to heighten her emotional response through the way in which he evokes it, to give it that much more pathos, to make it that much sadder. He didn't trust the action itself or the reader's ability to extrapolate emotion from an unadorned action. So he embellished, he exaggerated; he sentimentalized.

It's up to readers, of course, to decide for themselves whether or not such actions or terms exceed the events that go with them, and different readers will respond differently. All things being equal, however, it's better to understate characters' emotional responses than to exaggerate or pad them with hyperbolic language.

Another way for emotion to exceed experience is for the emotions to come either in absence of the experiences that give rise to them or ahead of those experiences.

A story begins:

> Slamming the stage door shut behind her, Sally slid herself down against it until her butt hit the floor, crying the whole way down. She knew she'd blown the audition.

Though we may accept that whatever happened at that audition has not only resulted in this response, but is worthy of it, still, not having had the experience ourselves—that is, not having lived through that experience with this character—we can't be expected to feel what she's feeling. We must either assume that her response is entirely warranted, or that she's being retroactively theatrical. Either way, the emotions that these opening sentences confront us with are *in excess of experience*—not Sally's experience, but *ours*. That the next paragraph supplies us with that experience helps, but it puts the horse behind the cart. Imagine how differently this moment would read were it to follow the description of the audition that gave rise to it, rather than precede it. In that case, instead of merely accepting them, we'd share Sally's emotions; we'd be right there with her sliding down that stage door.

It can be argued that confronting us first with Sally's emotional response, then backing into the event that caused it, creates more suspense by raising the question, "What went on at that audition?" True; it does. But it also confronts us with the specter of sentimentality at the onset of a story by having us bear witness to a character's emotional state as opposed to taking part in her emotions ourselves. Rather than uniting character and reader on that first page, those first lines separate them into two camps: victim and spectator. Is what is gained in suspense worth the cost?

8. (Bonus Sin) Grim Determination:
The Deadliest Sin?

To this gang of seven sins I'll toss in an eighth that may be the worst sin of all: *failure to have enough fun*. Bringing up the rear of the other seven injunctions, it may seem like contradictory advice. It isn't, really, since the injunctions are meant to be enforced not so much in drafting your narratives, but when looking over what you've written, in the process of revision.

While the demands of editing require that we approach our early drafts with calm and even icy detachment, writing those early drafts may require us to engage entirely different qualities, including the spirit of incautious, defiant, and even reckless playfulness. When he wrote, "Genius is no more than childhood recaptured at will,"[5] Baudelaire might well have been speaking in particular of an artist or author.

In a similar vein Heraclitus wrote, "Man is most nearly himself when he achieves the seriousness of a child at play." The key word here, I think, is "seriousness," since if it's to bear good results the game must be played hard.

Still, that said, lose the sense of play and all will be lost, since nothing will be left but grim determination. And though grim determination may produce results, those results aren't likely to give any more pleasure than was had in obtaining them.

---

5   *The Painter of Modern Life and Other Essays.*

III.

First Pages Analyzed

Introduction:
How to Use These First-Page Analyses

WRITING A NOVEL, A MEMOIR, OR A SHORT STORY ISN'T LIKE cooking a soup. Though the ingredients may be consistent (plot, situation, characters, language), every story we tell makes its own very particular demands on us as writers and comes with its own "recipe." One story (and as always when I say "story" I mean any work of narrative prose) may start with a character or characters; another with a broad concept or premise, a third with a sentence or an overheard snatch of dialogue that sets us off and running. There are no formulas. Well, there are, but none that work except occasionally or by accident.

For this reason the ordering of the first-page analyses that follow is, to a certain extent at least, arbitrary. Each page touches on an assortment of topics and raises a number of issues. The analyses can therefore be read and discussed profitably in any order.

Still, for convenience's sake, I've done my best to isolate and label the main issues raised by each analysis, and grouped them into the following categories:

A. Point of view: who speaks?
B. Structure: where to begin?
C. Plot/suspense
D. Characters
E. Genres
F. Memoir
G. Style

Unless otherwise stated, the first pages considered in the first five categories are from works in progress that qualify as "mainstream" or "literary" fiction, with mainstream fiction leaning more toward the commercial end of the spectrum—works that emphasize plot, action, suspense, and thrills—and literary fiction concerning itself more with language, style, technical experiments, and innovations, and plots that tend to comment on larger social issues and explore—in greater depth than average commercial fiction—the human condition. Literary fiction tends to be more character-driven and introspective.

Being the broader category, mainstream fiction embraces not only works of literary fiction, but other genres. All of Stephen King's oeuvre qualifies. So do *Gone with the Wind, Rebecca, To Kill a Mockingbird, The Hunger Games,* and *The Handmaid's Tale.* Once any book becomes a bestseller, it qualifies as mainstream fiction. (This is true even of books as formally innovative as George Saunders's *Lincoln in the Bardo,* a novel set in an intermediate realm between death and reincarnation and populated by ghosts that makes heavy use of *bricolage*: letters, snippets of historical texts and biographies, and other "found objects.")

Following each first-page analysis, I've provided exercises or prompts. Students are also encouraged to improvise. They can attempt their own revision of a first page under discussion, or apply insights gained to a first page of their own. Students might trade first pages of works in progress and critique, edit, and discuss them. Any exercise or prompt suggested for one page can most likely be applied to others. Teachers and students alike should take liberties.

Teachers are also encouraged to conduct their own first-page workshops. Have students bring copies of their first pages for every student in the class, redacting the students' names and any identifying matter. Teachers should collect and distribute copies. Have students volunteer to read the pages aloud prior to discussing them.

Finally, in considering any of the analyses that follow, and especially my suggestions and opinions, it's important to keep in mind that every decision we make as artists involves subjectivity. *There are no rules.* If I lay down a rule, it's with the understanding that any rule can be broken. There are two ways to break the rules: blindly, out of contempt or ignorance, or with conviction born of sophistication, in full awareness of the fact that we are breaking them. If this book has one main purpose, it is to produce more sophisticated writers and readers and thereby help them to follow *and* break the rules.

A. Point of View:
Who Speaks?

OF ALL THE DECISIONS WE FACE AS WRITERS OF FICTION AND
nonfiction, none is more fundamental than point of view. Who tells the story,
from what angle, attitude, or perspective, with what level of understanding?
Since they're telling their own stories, memoirists may assume they've got
the problem licked. They haven't. Establishing the narrative perspective of a
nonfiction work requires no less thought and effort than doing so for fiction.
In any case, narrators have to not only be chosen, but *created*.

In my years of teaching, I've encountered many definitions of point of view,
most of them faulty. "First person" and "third person" aren't points of view:
those are just handles by which a point of view can be grasped. Point of view is
something much deeper than pronouns; it's that crucial lens or filter through
which experiences are conveyed to us by a narrator, one who, unlike the author
(who inhabits a desk, typically), inhabits the world of the story.

Simply put: *point of view is the difference between the author and the narrator.*
For this reason it is sometimes referred to confusingly as a work's "voice." If
that is so, it's the voice—the awareness, insights, and diction—of the narrator,
not the author.

With first-person narratives, the narrator is a character central to or periph-
erally involved in the events described. He or she speaks to us directly, in
character. We get the story, as it were, straight from the horse's mouth. The
advantages of first person come down to intimacy and authenticity.

Third-person narrators, on the other hand, are more like God: present
everywhere, visible nowhere, without names or faces. They are more strictly
and obviously artistic contrivances.

The disadvantages of the first person are less flexibility and objectivity.
Being human and directly involved in the events described, a first-person
narrator can never be absolutely objective; there has to be some subjectivity to

his interpretation of events. If a first-person narrator says, "I walked out the door," we can probably accept that at face value. On the other hand, if the same narrator were to say, "Harvey Sedgwick was incompetent," we have to allow for the possibility of personal bias and unreliability. The exact same words spoken by a third-person narrator would have a more objective cast.

Third person has this advantage, too: greater flexibility of diction. Where a six-year-old first-person narrator can only speak with a six-year-old's vocabulary and syntax, in the third person that same six-year-old's experiences can be rendered in the language of an adult with an adult's wide-ranging vocabulary and all of that adult narrator's rhetorical, poetic, and interpretive powers brought to bear, not to mention their grasp of psychology, history, and other facts and perceptions with which adults are endowed.

Who narrates our stories? It's up to us to decide. Having decided, we must then create that narrator or those narrators: they don't come ready-made. Depending on who we choose to tell the tale, our job as writers will be made easier or harder.

Think of yourself (the author) as the owner of a hotel or some other small business. The narrator is the manager. As any business owner will tell you, hiring the right manager is half the battle. And no, you can't do it yourself.

Point of view is the difference between the author and the narrator.

1. Song of the Dust Bowl: 1936

(First Person / "Voice" / Style Born of Urgency / Child Narrator)

Puffy clouds skirted across the bright blue sky, mocking the parched ground. They offered neither rain nor shade. I poured another bucket of water over the turnips and straightened up to see how much further I had to go. At twelve, I was old enough to remember when the kitchen garden burst with tomatoes, cucumbers, and melons. When the ten acres to the west were full of corn and cotton. Now, the fields were ten acres of dust and the garden was a few scraggly rows of whatever we were able to keep alive.

Mama worked beside me, pulling sad tomatoes off the vines. Her blue dress, faded and twice turned, would not win a contest against the sky. She pushed her hair out of her face and sighed as a wail drifted out of the house.

"Julie, please go see to him. I'm about done with this row."

Glad to escape the sun if not the heat, I ran into the house and crossed through the kitchen. The crying got louder as I approached the front room. Baby Stephen had kicked off his covers and his face was as red as an over-ripe tomato. He waved his fists in the air and kept kicking against an invisible foe. I picked him up; fever came off him in waves. I added his diaper to the wash pile, dressed him in a clean one, and carried him out to Mama.

"He's burning up again."

Her attention snapped from the tomatoes to Stephen.

"Hush sweetie, Mama's here." She held him close and looked him over, pressing her fingers around his neck and thighs. His wailing became louder and harsher when she stuck a finger in his mouth.

Analysis

In first-person narratives, we get the story straight from the source, with the narrator typically an eyewitness to events, a participant, or both. At the very least, the first-person narrator has learned of the events he or she reports directly from eyewitnesses or participants. With first-person we get intimacy and immediacy. We don't get objectivity, or we don't always get it. To be sure we don't get absolute objectivity. The extent of close personal involvement in the events in question that makes for intimacy also limits objectivity.

With a first-person narrator we get one perspective colored by that individual's unique sensibilities and perceptions, as well as by her prejudices, hopes, fears, rationalizations, wishful thinking, and so on. All first-person narrators are, to some extent, subjective. That doesn't make them "unreliable," unreliable narrators being a category unto themselves. But they don't afford the same level of objectivity as third-person narrators.

This first page presents us with a strong first-person narrator. Under a bright blue sky riddled with "mocking" clouds, twelve-year-old Julie tends a parched garden, "a few scraggly rows of whatever we were able to keep alive." The year: 1936, the last year of the so-called Dust Bowl that ravaged a hundred million acres of farmland in the Great Plains. Even without those mocking clouds, that blue sky would be ironic, its teasing cheerful hue a stark contrast to the faded blue of the mother's (probably gingham) dress as she bends to harvest the garden with her daughter.

From the house comes an infant's cry. Julie is sent inside to tend to her baby brother, who has kicked away his covers and whose wailing face is "as red as an over-ripe tomato"—riper, for sure, than the "sad" tomatoes that have sprouted from the desiccated vines outdoors. Nothing on this first page escapes the Dust Bowl's merciless heat. Everything—sky, earth, vegetables, baby, mother and daughter—is baked and parched by it. The absence of adult males is noted. Where have they gone? Why? When will they return? The women are left to their own devices, to their powers of faith and endurance, at the mercy of the elements.

This first page offers what in writing workshops is often referred to as a "a strong voice." Though everyone talks about it, no one seems to really know precisely what the word "voice" means. Does it refer to the narrator's voice, or the author's voice? Are they the same? Is voice the same as style? If not, what's the difference?

I tend to tell my students to pay no attention to "voice," or—for that matter—to "style." Instead, focus on two other words: "clarity" and "precision." Choose your words as a surgeon chooses her instruments. Do that, and both style and voice will take care of themselves.

Some may protest that if we all swear allegiance to the same two gods— to clarity and precision—we'll all end up sounding alike, but I don't think so. There are, after all, many ways to be clear and precise. Even if that weren't so, we'd all be trying to be clear and precise about different things. Given these same two goals, each of us is sure to find our own way. Writer A needs only a sentence to be precise and clear; Writer B takes three pages.

When it comes to first-person narrators—to any narrator at all, actually— it's not our own words that count, but theirs. In the case of this first page, the words that matter are those of a twelve-year-old girl named Julie tending a parched dust bowl garden. To the extent that the author chooses *Julie's* words, honors her perspective, invests us in her sensibilities, the author achieves what some call a strong "voice."

My only quibble with this good first page is that I wish those first two lines engaged the narrator, and not just clouds and sky. Stories are about people, not about weather. Rearranged slightly to invest us immediately in the narrator's experience, the opening would read:

> I poured another bucket of water over the turnips and straightened up to watch as puffy clouds skirted across the bright blue sky. They seemed to mock the parched ground, offering neither rain nor shade.

Otherwise, I have no complaints.

As for the narrator's voice, there's something stark, dry, and dusty about it, something of the faded blue gingham cloth of which the mother's dress is doubtlessly made: something staunchly utilitarian, minus zippers and frills, yet not without its humble charms. Like water from a well dug deep into the parched earth and served in a chipped Spatterware cup, it may not be much. But considering the source, it's something to sing about.

Your Turn

Draft an opening scene, in the first person and from a young narrator's perspective, in which an event of some import is anticipated: a birthday celebration or reunion, someone returning home after a long absence, the sale of the family business or farm, or the sale of the home itself. Set the scene in a particular environment, the family room or on a porch or in some area of the yard or garden. Pay attention to the time of day and the weather. Also keep in mind the narrator's perspective on the scene being reported: does the narrator look back over a great distance of time, or from later that same day—or (in the present tense) from within the event itself? Note: some conflict should be introduced or alluded to.

2. The Logging Road to the Cabin

(Third Person / Information vs. Evidence / Default Omniscience)

The Suwannee River begins in a Georgia swamp and flows through northern Florida until emptying into the Gulf of Mexico. The real estate agent took Dan Horne up a logging road to a cabin about ten yards from a creek tributary of the river. "Is this far enough out of the way for you?" the agent asked with a knowledgeable smile.

"It will do. May I go inside," Dan replied as he stepped up on the ramshackle porch.

The agent unlocked the door and Dan followed him into a musty room. It was a large room with a fireplace and some furniture, rattan and bamboo predominating. There was also a kitchen, a bedroom and a bathroom with a shower. "It is hard to believe, but this place has central air and baseboard heating," the agent said as he completed the tour. "Come on, I want to show you the dock and the boat."

They tramped out to a sturdy looking pier where a small boat with an outboard motor was tied up. "If you go that way," the agent pointed downstream, "you will come to the village, two miles or so. The other way, well you don't want to go that way. It's a mangrove swamp."

"Any alligators?" Dan asked.

"Maybe some up in the mangrove. You ain't planning on going swimming are you?"

"A person could die out here and nobody would know it."

"You did say you wanted someplace out of the way."

Dan gave the agent a pat on the back and they went back to the car. On the way into town in the area they agreed on the financial requirements. In the real estate office Dan wrote a check for a down payment.

"That's what I like: a man who knows his own mind," the agent said.

Analysis

There's nothing wrong with this first page—nothing, that is, until we look at it more closely and see ways in which it might be improved.

First, let's agree that many things are working well. Grammatically, the writing is solid. Sentence by sentence, the opening conveys correct information in the right order. Dialogue is, if not superb, adequately handled. So, how to make it better?

Let's start by looking at that first paragraph, which informs us about the setting. John Steinbeck often begins his stories with setting. *East of Eden*, Steinbeck's magnum opus, begins:

> The Salinas Valley is in Northern California. It is a long narrow swale between two ranges of mountains, and the Salinas River winds and twists up the center until it falls at last into Monterey Bay.

Similarly, E.M. Forster opens his greatest novel, *A Passage to India*, with a paragraph that might have been lifted from a *Rough Guide*:

> Except for the Marabar Caves—and they are twenty miles off—the city of Chandrapore presents nothing extraordinary. Edged rather than washed by the river Ganges, it trails for a couple of miles along the bank, scarcely distinguishable from the rubbish it deposits so freely. There are no bathing-steps on the river front, as the Ganges happens not to be holy here; indeed there is no river front, and bazaars shut out the wide and shifting panorama of the stream.

Nothing wrong with opening a novel or story with a description of setting, even a static description, just as there is nothing wrong with the curtain parting to reveal the set of an opera before the characters have come on stage. Establishing the setting of a story goes a long way toward grounding us, the readers, in that story. We have a sense of place: now all we need is a specific time, a character or characters, and an event or a set of events.

That said, stories and novels have one subject: people, not geography. In *Aspects of the Novel*, his cycle of lectures on the novelist's craft, Forster himself says—or implies—as much. "Since the novelist is himself a human being," Forster writes, "there is an affinity between him and his subject-matter which is absent in many other forms of art." By "his subject matter" we may infer that he means people, not valleys, caves, or rivers.

Rather than lead off with a geography lesson ("The Suwannee River begins in a Georgia swamp …"), the author of this first page might have launched us more directly into the action, with Dan Horne being driven up a logging road by a real estate agent, and let the setting inform that event, making it part of an experience:

As the real estate agent drove, Dan Horne resisted looking over the side of the logging road, to where it plunged straight down the ravine.

To take things another step away from generalized description and toward concrete, active particulars, instead of having Dan escorted up a non-specific logging road to a non-specific cabin, why not give readers what they need to form a less generic, more specific and solid image of that logging road? Is it paved or dusty or muddy? One lane or two? Is there a shoulder or is it a sheer drop (as in my version)? We don't know; we aren't told.

A mistake beginning fiction writers often make is in failing to ground the material of their stories. When the real estate agent asks, "Is this far enough out of the way for you?" where is he? And where is Dan? How far from the cabin are they? Miles or yards? For all we know, they're still on that logging road, approaching the cabin in the realtor's car. What sort of car is it, by the way? Or is it a four-wheel-drive pickup truck? Does it matter?

The answer comes down to how thoroughly we want our readers to inhabit and invest in a character's experiences. Though the information provided by this opening paragraph is clear, the actions aren't always. When the real estate agent says, "Is this far enough out of the way for you?" I picture him speaking these words while still in the agent's vehicle, perhaps as they are pulling up to the property. In fact, they've already left the car or truck.

Again, does it matter? It does if the author wants me to experience that bit of dialogue as his protagonist experiences it—and not retrospectively, on a second read, but the first time around. Ultimately, I understood where the characters were; I figured it out. But for a moment I was confused. And my confusion had nothing to do with Dan's experience.

The problem comes down to point of view. The fiction writer's purpose isn't to convey information to the reader, but to create experiences for him. The point of view of a story or a chapter of a novel establishes whose experience we're sharing at any given time. Depending on what point of view is engaged, on who narrates, we may share one character's experience at a time, or the experiences of several characters. We may share those experiences from a distance, or up close, or even (as is most often the case) from inside the head of one or more characters—though not more than one head at a time, usually.

If that seems like too many choices, brace yourself: there are more. A third-person point of view can be located at a range of depths inside a character's head, so deep all we hear are the character's thoughts, or what is sometimes called their "stream of consciousness." Or it can be located less deeply. In fact, the number of possibilities for establishing a third-person viewpoint in a work of fiction is limitless, since the possibilities exist not as a discrete series of choices, but, as with the colors in a rainbow, along a continuum.

At one extreme of that rainbow is the point of view strategy used in this opening: one that is purely objective, that doesn't let us into any character's head. Like a video recorder, it sees and watches these two men, Dan and the real estate agent.

Yet the objective camera's point of view in this opening isn't always clear. In film this is never a problem, since the camera can only be in one place at a time, so we viewers never have to question our position with respect to what we are seeing on the screen. In fiction the equivalent of the camera angle has to be firmly established through language by the author. In this opening, not only do lines like, "The real estate agent took Dan Horne up a logging road to a cabin about ten yards from a creek tributary of the river" not tell us exactly where the characters are (just starting out up the road? halfway there? approaching the cabin?), they leave us clueless as to what vantage point we are seeing them from (in the car, sitting in the seat with Dan or the realtor, or seeing the car from a distance?).

Third sentence, third paragraph. "There was also a kitchen, a bedroom and a bathroom with a shower." Grammatically, informationally, a perfectly good sentence. But the sentence is inert, listless, dragged along by the passive "there was." Like many sentences on this first page, it squanders an opportunity to ground us in a particular character's experience.

The same sentence written from Dan's point of view:

Dan took in a kitchen, a bedroom, and a bathroom with a shower.

Now at least point of view has been engaged. Still, the sentence fails to avail itself fully of Dan's perspective, of his experience of those rooms. A sentence that truly conveys Dan's sensibilities would read something more like this:

Dan followed the realtor into a kitchen the size of his bathroom back home, and that smelled of mildew and dishrags; from there they passed into a bedroom the walls of which were painted a blue so dreary it could have passed for gray; next, the bathroom—though "room" hardly did it justice, since it was more like a closet, one equipped with a pull-chain toilet that ran and dripped.

Granted, these may not be the rooms that the author had in mind. Perhaps the bare-bones description of the original was intended. Perhaps the author wants us to experience these settings as generic, and chose the objective perspective to highlight their starkness, as Hemingway does for the small Midwestern town setting of his short story "The Killers":

> Outside it was getting dark. The street-light came on outside the window. The two men at the counter read the menu. From the other end of the counter Nick Adams watched them. He had been talking to George when they came in.

Still, there's a world of difference between intentional objectivity and an objective point of view that's accidental or arbitrary. In "The Killers," the brutal, ice-cold objectivity suits the subject: the story of two hired killers arriving in town to carry out a contract execution.

In the given first page, it's not clear what purpose the objectivity serves, if it's a matter of choice or omission. At any rate, we're denied the subjective content that is the greatest privilege offered by fiction, which, unlike movies, lets us in on not only what characters say and do, but what they see, hear, taste, smell, think, and feel—while given nothing of equal value to take its place. With the subjectivity filter absent, and no "cinematic" or "stark" filter replacing it, the result is simply bland.

One solution: from the start, plant this opening more firmly in the perspective of the character whose experience the author wants us to share: Dan Horne's experience.

This first page is just over 400 words long. It has taken me five times as many words to touch on some of the ways it might be improved. If that strikes fear into some hearts, don't let it. If problems in fiction writing tend to come in bundles, so do solutions. Fix one problem, and you've fixed a dozen. In this instance, with this opening, attend to the point of view issues, and all will be better than fine.

Your Turn

Make two revisions of a first page (your own or someone else's). The point of view strategy of the first revision should be thoroughly objective, void of subjective content. No feelings, opinions, or attitudes, just bare, objective facts from no particular character's perspective.

For the second revision, immerse us deeply and thoroughly in one character's perspective.

3. A Pair of Foggy Sisters

(Third Person / Default Omniscience / "Said")

As she took off her holiday apron, Mildred called out loudly to her fellow volunteer, "Rita, we're going to stop by on our way home tonight and look at your fall window display."

Her sister, Margaret, took off her St. Paul's green "Feed the Hungry" apron, wadded it up, and tossed it on the stainless-steel counter. She turned, faced Mildred, and silently mouthed, "What were you thinking? It is nearly nine o'clock."

Mildred was determined to ignore the disapproval in Margaret's eyes. Calmly she gathered up her umbrella and coat.

"Oh now, don't fuss at me. It's only a few extra blocks out of our way. The walk will be good for us."

As they left St. Paul's through the kitchen back door, a few of the homeless men were leaning on an iron railing smoking cigarettes. Mildred called out a chirpy, "Goodnight, see you next week."

The men avoided eye contact and just nodded as the sisters passed them.

The night was hazy, fog setting in. Her cataracts made the moon startlingly white and hazy. As she walked, she noticed most of the shop windows had faded "For Lease" signs up. The darkened movie marquee still had a "Coming Soon" sign.

Margaret was walking way ahead of Mildred. Mildred's speed was much slower than her sister. She'd stop every half block and step out of her shoes to rub her feet. She was wearing turquoise blue flats with red and blue rhinestones. They were her recent Goodwill senior discount day purchase.

Analysis

This passage from the opening of a short story exemplifies what goes wrong (or what doesn't go right) when point of view isn't thoroughly and consistently engaged.

In the first two paragraphs, the point of view is objective; we have not clearly engaged either character's consciousness. In the third paragraph we enter Mildred's subjective viewpoint, raising the question: whose experience are we getting here? If Mildred's, then why not engage her consciousness or viewpoint clearly from the start?

Subsequent paragraphs (starting with "As they left St. Paul ...") offer no particular perspective; they are objective by default. It's not even clear who speaks some of these lines of dialogue.

One reason for that particular problem may be the too common tendency among novice writers to avoid using "said." They do so, perhaps, under the false impression that whatever else good writers do, they avoid repeating the same word twice on a page (where do they get such advice?), with "said" the most likely perpetrator, since it's used repeatedly in dialogue exchanges.

Yes, "said" gets repeated ("he said," "she said"), but no, there's nothing wrong with it. In fact there's everything right with it, providing it helps make clear who is speaking. Alternatively, some writers go out of their way to substitute other attributions or "dialogue tags," with characters laughing ("Hello there," she laughed), chuckling, stating, barking, growling, and even replying and opining things as opposed to just saying them. In nearly all cases, the substitutes for "said" are more obnoxious than inspired. In any case, there's nothing wrong with "said." That "said" gets repeated makes no difference anyway, since it goes down like water; when reading dialogue, we barely notice it. That's as it should be. "Said" is the silent butler of good dialogue.

In the fifth paragraph down, the author has written "a few of the homeless men were leaning on an iron railing." Note how this avoids assigning the experience to either one of the two sisters. Instead it's presented as passive, objective. How different that experience would be had the author written, "Through her foggy cataracts, Mildred saw some homeless men leaning on an iron railing." Those foggy cataracts don't even get mentioned for two more paragraphs. Were this scene properly embedded in Mildred's perspective, we'd have watched it through that fog from the start.

Though it pays lip service to the viewpoint of one of the two main characters, the scene as a whole is, or may as well be, objective; it does not engage either character's consciousness with any degree of thoroughness or commitment: it merely states objective facts. There's nothing strictly wrong with that, but then there's nothing terribly right about it, either.

Written firmly from Mildred's perspective, the result might be:

Mildred watched as her sister sped up and walked ahead of her.
Margaret always had to go first; she couldn't help herself. Were it not for her silly habit of stopping every half block to step out of her equally silly

turquoise flats (with red and blue rhinestones) and rub her feet, Mildred thought, her sister would have left her far behind.

We get the same actions as in the original, but filtered through Mildred's sensibilities, so we get not only what is happening in the scene, but her subjective emotional response and her attitude. Here's the same scene rewritten from both sisters' perspectives:

Mildred watched as her sister sped up and walked ahead of her. Margaret always had to go first; she couldn't help herself. Were it not for her silly habit of stopping every half block to step out of her ridiculous turquoise flats with red and blue rhinestones and rub her feet (which wouldn't have needed rubbing had she worn sensible shoes!), her sister would have left Mildred in the dust. Meanwhile Margaret wondered (as she rubbed her foot, or made a burlesque of rubbing it, when really she was just killing time) why her sister had to be such a slowpoke. Why oh why does she always, always have to dilly-dally? Like walking with a ball and chain 'round me bleedin' ankle!

Your Turn

In the third person, do two revisions of this first page: first, entirely from Margaret's perspective, then alternate the perspective between both characters, so it switches with every paragraph. Make sure that the viewpoint of each paragraph is clear.

4. Where the Hernandezes Live

(Third Person / Subjectivity /
Information vs. Experience / Inhabiting Scene)

For two days no one answered the phone, so Saturday morning Bunker drove to the address listed in the school directory. The Hernandez family lived near the airport, in a residential pocket tucked beneath a thick canopy of power lines. Their home, a converted garage with window bars and a security screen, sat behind a clapboard triplex at the end of a stumpy driveway whose weather-beaten asphalt resembled the cracked top crust of an apple pie. Bunker rang the bell, energized by the autumn air as well as the task at hand. The middle school dean had discouraged him from going, saying teachers who got involved in their students' personal lives burned out quickly. He advised patience; education was a marathon, not a sprint. Bunker rang the bell again. The dean was a good man but a bit of a codger.

A skinny gray cat jumped out from a chokeberry bush by the side of the garage. It curled around a gutter pipe and scurried away just as Robert opened the door. The boy looked different out of uniform, like a wet dog without its fluff of fur, all muscle and bone. He wanted to know if he had done something wrong. Bunker assured him he had not and asked to speak with his parents. They were out. Robert's mother worked weekends at an auto upholstery shop and wouldn't be home until after five o'clock, but Bunker could wait inside for his father.

The home was a single large space with wiry blue carpeting that resembled an S.O.S. pad. Four mattresses lay tangled in sheets against a wall, flanked by a pair of space heaters whose humming orange glow did little to cut the chill. There was a kitchenette and a bathroom visible through an open door and a gigantic television set on a console. The TV's sound had been muted and a purple dinosaur cavorted on the screen. In front of the console, on a velour sofa, a small girl stared at Bunker. She had long black hair and pearls in her ears and wore purple leggings with a Red Sox shirt. She slithered off the sofa and over to Robert, tugging on his pant leg.

Analysis

This opening presents us with a character at odds with his environment. A teacher named Bunker arrives at the home of a troubled student. The author has a sharp eye for authentic, specific details; her command of language makes for entirely readable prose. On the sentence level the writing is accomplished. Still, this passage fails to deeply engage the protagonist's sensibilities on a subjective plane. Most of what makes it to the page is purely objective; we rarely access Bunker's thoughts and perceptions.

And though there's no rule of fiction writing that says you have to engage characters on that level (sometimes writers purposefully choose not to engage with characters on the subjective level), still, here the author does—occasionally, sporadically—engage her protagonist's inner thoughts. How else can we read, "The dean was a good man but a bit of a codger"? So I feel justified in wondering why the author hasn't done so more consistently and deeply, given that such an engagement would better suit this scene.

There are other ways whereby this opening could involve us more thoroughly in the character's experience. Let's start with the first sentence:

> For two days no one answered the phone, so Saturday morning Bunker drove to the address listed in the school directory.

Though this sentence gives us information about Bunker's motives and situation, it does not locate us in his experience. Is Bunker driving a car? Where? What time of day? Through what sort of neighborhood? In what kind of weather? Nor does the next sentence put me *into* the story:

> The Hernandez family lived near the airport, in a residential pocket tucked beneath a thick canopy of power lines.

More information, this time about the Hernandez home. It does not locate me in a scene with a character; it does not give me an experience. Am I with Bunker walking down a sidewalk approaching the Hernandez home? No. Where am I? What experience am I having? I don't know, since there is no engagement of scene/moment/experience here, just information. Next sentence:

Their home, a converted garage with window bars and a security screen, sat behind a clapboard triplex at the end of a stumpy driveway whose weather-beaten asphalt resembled the cracked top crust of an apple pie.

Here I get a more solid picture of this house, yet I am still not there in the scene. In order to be in the scene, I need to know where I (the reader by way of the author by way of the narrator by way of Bunker) stand in relation to this object being perceived (house). Am I (is Bunker) approaching from across the street? Does the house hunker dark against the dawn sky? Or is it a sunny morning? Is the air cool, or warm? The author has given me information about this house, but she does not give me Bunker's experience; she does not involve me in a scene in which this house forms part of the setting.

Next sentence:

Bunker rang the bell, energized by the autumn air as well as the task at hand.

Here for the first time a scene is truly engaged. I am with Bunker ringing this bell; I feel the crisp autumn air. I'm still not quite sure what time of morning it is, if the sun has risen fully or Bunker rings that doorbell at the crack of dawn. Other missing details make it hard for me to be fully in the moment. But at least a moment is being described; I am having an experience.

The first paragraph continues:

The middle school dean had discouraged him from going, saying teachers who got involved in their students' personal lives burned out quickly. He advised patience; education was a marathon, not a sprint. Bunker rang the bell again. The dean was a good man but a bit of a codger.

Though the author doesn't spell it out for us with the words "Bunker remembered" or "Bunker thought," I assume that what I'm getting here are Bunker's thoughts and memories. Since thoughts form part of his experience, then these thoughts are *experiential*; I am sharing Bunker's experience in this moment as he stands in front of that door. What sort of door, by the way? Are there any lights on in the building? Is the buzzer located inside a vestibule, or on the stoop? See how much of this man's experience has been left out of this paragraph?

This isn't to say that all fiction writers are required to recreate, blow by blow, detail by detail, every instant of a character's experience, but one does want to supply readers with enough information for them to feel themselves inhabiting key moments with a character or characters. Blow-by-blow photorealism isn't necessary or even desirable. By supplying just the right details, enough for the reader to form an impression, authors accomplish that purpose.

Yet too often—as in this opening—less experienced authors don't give us enough to put us into their character's experiences. The reason, I think, is that they fail to immerse themselves fully into their characters' experiences through their narrators. Being insufficiently engaged by way of their narrators, authors give us relatively dry reports from an outsider's—their own—perspective, informationally. It may be fine to write

> The Hernandez family lived near the airport, in a residential pocket tucked beneath a thick canopy of power lines.

provided the next sentence is something like:

> As he crossed the street toward the three-story brick home through the cool gloom, Bunker noticed a light burning dimly on the ground floor. He smelled smoke. A chill ran through him; he gathered his windbreaker tightly around his neck. In the near distance he heard a back-up signal and what sounded like garbage cans being thrown around....

so the information *informs an experience* rather than just sitting there on the page courtesy of an author who has failed to properly inhabit their own material by way of their narrator.

There's another more crucial reason for writing from within a character's experience rather than informationally: when we do so, instead of our having to decide or guess what our characters do or want, they tell us. They help write the story for us. By not immersing ourselves fully by way of our narrators into our character's experiences, we not only deny the reader those experiences; we deny them to ourselves and make the task of telling their stories that much more difficult, since we have to rely fully on our intellects—on what we *think* we know about the characters—rather than on their experiences and perceptions as communicated to us by our narrators, who live with them in the story.

This is why I say that point of view isn't a technical issue, as we have been so poorly taught. Pronouns are a technical matter; but a pronoun change is not, necessarily, a change in viewpoint. Point of view is what connects us psychically to our characters by way of a narrator or narrators, and what, in turn, connects our readers to their stories.

Your Turn

Draft an opening in which a character arrives in an intimidatingly unfamiliar setting. Give the character a good reason for being there, a significant goal. Example: a character who grew up poor and is entirely unfamiliar and uncomfortable with wealth paying a visit to the estate of a multimillionaire. Second example: a fastidious, prudish, or puritanical person—a monk or a priest—visiting a brothel (not as a patron, but for some other purpose).

5. On the Couch

*(Third Person / Free Indirect Discourse /
Dramatized Routine vs. Drama)*

Barry O'Neill let himself into the sunny hall of number fifteen and threw his school bag in the corner. He went straight into the lounge, and checked his watch to see how long he had, before anyone else came home. He was sure that he would have enough time. As sure as he could be in a house where most people had the decency to stick to a schedule. His Dad came home on the same bus every evening. His mother was always out somewhere learning to be even more creative. Liz, his older sister, was a bit of a loose cannon, often arriving back from some protest or other, just ahead of being arrested. He thought it was fairly safe. He could listen out. He could only relax doing it on his own.

Barry perched on the edge of the couch, which was covered in an old sheet, a very flowery sheet. It was not the flowers per se that worried him, but the general old and jaded nature of the sheet, now reinventing itself as a throw while the room remained briefly in transition. Again.

As long as he could remember, his mother had gone from room to room, decorating constantly. It was like an obsession. He remembered wanting to help her, but being terrified that anyone might find out he was interested in color schemes and fabric swatches, so he pretended she got on his nerves, which she did, a bit.

As he sat on the sheet-clad couch, channel-surfing with the remote control, Barry searched among hundreds of options for a Western. He scrolled down the endless lists of daytime telly programmes. Hospital dramas set in the outback, ads for funeral plans and incontinence pads, presenters whipping audiences into a frenzy over some ol' one sleeping with two brothers. He hadn't time for this, and wished there were a quicker way to find what he needed. Then he found one, barely started. He glanced at his watch again, and let the air slowly out of his lungs, and sat back. A whole hour of men and horses glistening with sweat, sweeping into town, taking care of the bad guys. Sweet....

Analysis

When we say of something that we've read, "Nothing happens!"—what, exactly, do we mean? What, in fiction and other forms of narrative, constitutes something "happening," i.e., an event?

In this opening passage from a young adult novel, Barry O'Neill—a not-so-atypical teenager (as conveyed by his sullen, petulant interior take on his own world, rendered deftly through the close third-person point of view)—arrives home to an empty house. Perched on the edge of the flowery-sheet-covered couch, he channel surfs in search of a Western "telly programme" (the setting is Australia or the UK). Having at last found one, he sits back to bask in "a whole hour of men and horses glistening with sweat, sweeping into town and taking care of the bad guys." And there our opening page ends.

Is a teenager watching television enough to lure us into a novel, or even a short story, especially given that—as is not only implied but stated—Billy's "telly" watching is routine, something he does regularly if not on a daily basis?

This opening is a good example of what I call "dramatized routine"—a contradiction in terms, since routines aren't dramatic. Whether the routine is channel surfing or mud-wrestling wild orangutans in the jungles of Borneo makes no difference, a routine is still a routine. When we read about routines in fiction, or in any kind of story, most if not all the pleasure we get from the experience derives from our anticipation of seeing the routine shattered, or, at the very least, disrupted.

That said, without routine drama can't exist. Unless underpinned by routine, dramatic events have nothing to disrupt, no context against which to flourish and stand out and apart from. They read like a white-on-white painting. Routine, you could say, is the canvas across which drama spreads its garish colors, the soil from which the roses and snapdragons of dramatic events flourish.

Authors are often told to start their stories as close as possible to an inciting incident or event, to plunge their readers directly into drama in the form of exceptional events, to not waste any of the reader's time with routine. But many good and great novels open with routine.

Mrs. Dalloway said she would buy the flowers herself.

That unspectacular first sentence opens Virginia Woolf's *Mrs. Dalloway*, in which the titular protagonist's decision to buy flowers for a routine dinner party leads to a long, stream-of-consciousness journey through her life and her past. George Gissing's 1891 novel *New Grub Street* likewise starts off with a routine—if somewhat baleful—breakfast conversation:

> As the Milvains sat down to breakfast the clock of Wattleborough parish church struck eight; it was two miles away, but the strokes were borne very distinctly on the west wind this autumn morning. Jasper, listening before he cracked an egg, remarked with cheerfulness:
> "There's a man being hanged in London at this moment."
> "Surely it isn't necessary to let us know that," said his sister Maud, coldly.
> "And in such a tone, too!" protested his sister Dora.
> "Who is it?" inquired Mrs Milvain, looking at her son with a pained forehead.
> "I don't know. It happened to catch my eye in the paper yesterday that someone was to be hanged at Newgate this morning. There's a certain satisfaction in reflecting that it is not oneself."

Though one can make the case that foreshadowing is at work here, strictly speaking this breakfast discourse has nothing to do with the plot that follows. Yet who would say that it's not engaging?

The challenge isn't to eliminate routine from our writing, but to render it in such a way that, while we anticipate its disruption, we're also—if not exactly gripping the edges of our seats—sufficiently entertained.

With the opening in question, through the evocation of Billy's character by way of the close third-person technique (known also as "free indirect discourse" or, in the original French, *discours indirect libre*) the author goes a good way toward accomplishing this.

Free indirect discourse is one of the most powerful tools in an author's trick bag. It lets third-person narrators dip freely in and out of a character's stream of consciousness, accessing their thoughts, feelings, opinions, even their syntax and vocabularies and other attributes of their speech patterns, without having to say (for instance) "Barry thought" or "Barry felt."

A fine example of free indirect discourse (there are many) may be found in the first page of *Ravel*, Jean Echenoz's 2005 novel[1] in which he imagines the life of the composer. It opens—routinely—with the composer taking a bath:

---

1   Translated by Linda Coverdale.

Leaving the bathtub is sometimes quite annoying. First of all, it's a shame to abandon the soapy lukewarm water, where stray hairs wind around bubbles among the scrubbed-off skin cells, for the chill atmosphere of a poorly heated house. Then, if one is the least bit short, and the side of that claw-footed tub the least bit high, it's always a challenge to swing a leg over the edge to feel around, with a hesitant toe, for the slippery tile floor. Caution is advised, to avoid bumping one's crotch or risking a nasty fall. The solution to this predicament would be of course to order a custom-made bathtub, but that entails expenses, perhaps even exceeding the cost of the recently installed but still inadequate central heating. Better to remain submerged up to the neck for hours, if not forever, using one's right foot to periodically manipulate the hot-water faucet, thus adjusting the thermostat to maintain a comfortable amniotic ambience.

The composer-protagonist's name appears nowhere in this passage, nor is there any direct indication that these are Ravel's thoughts (as opposed to the third-person narrator's). That we are being made privy to the famous composer's sensibilities is implied by the language and syntax by which the ideas are conveyed. Indeed, Echenoz's novel owes much if not all of its success to free indirect discourse, which allows us to inhabit the composer as he engages in quotidian activities. What's it like for a genius to take a bath? Now you know.

When, in our first page, we read of Barry's sister Liz that she was "a bit of a loose cannon, often arriving back from some protest or other, just ahead of being arrested," we know—anyway we sense—that these aren't objective facts about Liz, or purely objective, but facts colored by Barry's sensibilities, filtered through his consciousness. The same way a sliced onion left next to the butter in the refrigerator invests that butter with its essence, Barry's jaundiced personality infuses his third-person narrator's diction. We discover—subtly, slyly—that this same boy who relishes the opportunity to watch sweaty men on horses in secret is also "terrified that anyone might find out he was interested in color schemes and fabric swatches." These antipodal sides of his nature define him. The scene delivers more than just Billy's routine. It conveys his divided self—an internal drama, but a drama no less—and engages us accordingly.

Which isn't to say this opening can't stand improvement. Though it goes a good way toward evoking Billy's character through his interior take on things, it could go even further. What if, instead of merely being alluded to or listed, the glimpses of telly programmes he rejects while channel surfing were described—not neutrally, but from within Billy's jaundiced perspective?

The result would not only tell us more precisely what is "happening" (routinely) in the scene, it would provide an opportunity to color in Billy's personality more vividly, while occasioning some potentially delightful jaded humor.

Your Turn

Revise a first page using free indirect discourse, such that the third-person narration reflects the sensibilities and even the diction of the point of view character.

6. Drive-by Girl

(Dramatized Routine / Interior Monologue /
Free Indirect Discourse)

Dana wasn't a drive-by kind of a girl. Nope, she was more of a give-him-the-finger kind of a girl-woman. So, nix on the phone calls, no drunk dialing, no text messages, no emails, and certainly no driving by the house. Even now she turned right to avoid cruising by his school, her messy brain working overtime in an effort to avoid picturing him in his classroom. Jerry stayed until five, six, sometimes even seven, correcting papers, offering extra help, throwing baskets in the gym with a few of the jock kids. For a forty-six-year-old guy, he could move. Every day ended with free throws for those students who participated in discussions, part of Jerry's incentive program. Giving. That was Jerry. Dana wanted to throw up.

She took a left and another left, heading toward Stop & Shop. Grocery shopping was on her list of least favorite things to do after school, right up there with exercising and correcting freshmen essays.

At the supermarket, she was all business, plucking apples, bananas, strawberries, and raspberries—expensive, but she deserved them. A bad breakup meant feeling vulnerable. Dana wheeled her cart over to the deli counter for a garlic-roasted chicken. Oh, mashed potatoes. She looked over her shoulder, then realized that no, Jerry wasn't micromanaging her shopping cart with his disapproving look, the one he reserved especially for her and those occasions when she made bad food choices.

"Are you sure you want that?" Jerry liked to say.

And ten times out of ten, she'd put the offending item back on the shelf. Well, not this time, she wouldn't; she planned to enjoy those mashed potatoes. She might even eat some of the crispy skin off the chicken. She pushed her cart toward the checkout express line. Chicken with mashed potatoes and she'd watch an episode or two of Curb Your Enthusiasm, starring that idiot Larry David. Living on the edge. Her inner voice cackled with thoughts of an evening spent in unproductive bliss.

Analysis

A woman fresh out of a mixed-bag relationship is harassed by the specter of her ex-lover as she goes about her routine chores.

This opening scene finds Dana taking the long way to her supermarket to avoid the school where Jerry (her ex?) teaches, and where he's known to remain long after the last bell on behalf of his students, "correcting papers, offering extra help, and throwing baskets in the gym." One gets the feeling that Jerry's solicitous nature does/did not extend to his relationship with Dana—a suspicion confirmed later at the Stop & Shop deli counter, where Jerry's ghost berates her for buying mashed potatoes to go with her rotisserie chicken.

The technique employed here is *interior monologue*, also sometimes referred to as stream of consciousness, after the term coined by the psychologist William James. But while the stream-of-consciousness technique tends to encompass narratives as a whole (such that descriptions, setting, dialogue, and actions are all conveyed, as it were, by the flowing stream), interior monologue functions as a distinct device within a traditional narrative—as in the given scene, where Dana's thoughts enhance the narrative, but don't subsume it.

Compare with this excerpt from the most famous stream-of-consciousness passage of all in *Ulysses*:

> Mulveys was the first when I was in bed that morning and Mrs Rubio brought it in with the coffee she stood there standing when I asked her to hand me and I pointing at them I couldnt think of the word a hairpin to open it with ah horquilla disobliging old thing and it staring her in the face with her switch of false hair on her and vain about her appearance ugly as she was near 80 or a loo her face a mass of wrinkles with all her religion domineering because she never could get over the Atlantic fleet coming in half the ships of the world and the Union Jack flying with all her carabineros because 4 drunken English sailors took all the rock from them and because I didnt run into mass often enough in Santa Maria to please her with her shawl up on her except when there was a marriage on with all her miracles of the saints and her black blessed virgin with the silver dress....

With this sort of stream of consciousness, the author relinquishes—or appears to relinquish—control of the narrative to the mind of his protagonist. In fact that loss of control is entirely and cunningly contrived to give the appearance of spontaneity and randomness, much as the drips and spatters on a Pollack appear to be random and spontaneous (they aren't, really).

With interior monologue, the author never fully lets go of the reins. In the given example, the narrator (as distinct from the protagonist) remains behind the wheel, telling us, between forays into his character's thoughts, how, having choked back the bile inspired by a vision of Jerry shooting hoops with his charges, Dana "took a left and another left, heading toward the Stop & Shop." The narrator goes on to explain that in shopping Dana "is all business, plucking apples, bananas, strawberries, and raspberries—expensive, but she deserved them." Note how with that "but she deserved them" we are dunked, however briefly, into the protagonist's subjective stream, back into her interior monologue. That she plucks apples and strawberries is an objective fact; that she "deserve[s] them" is purely her subjective opinion, a sampling of her interior monologue.

This sly mixture of objective authorial narration and a character's subjective perspective goes by its own names. Called close third-person by some and free indirect discourse or method by others, it lets narrators move seamlessly between objective reporting ("Dana wheeled her cart over to the deli counter") and a character's thoughts ("Oh, mashed potatoes."), to where at times one can barely distinguish the two: ("she planned to enjoy these mashed potatoes").

Unlike the aggressive stream-of-consciousness technique, free indirect discourse gives authors full control over the degree of objectivity.

In this opening, the free indirect discourse method is well employed, though one might quibble that if Dana's brain is indeed "working overtime" in order to avoid picturing Jerry in his classroom, her effort hasn't paid off so well, as we are treated to the very images she's intent on avoiding. Better perhaps to have her inadvertently drive by the school (having neglected to take an alternative route), so the image of Jerry gyrating on the basketball court with his charges will be both better motivated and accidental.

It seems to me, too, that if indeed Dana is haunted by Jerry, better use might be made of his specter, who ought to be right there in the driver's seat beside her, telling her to change lanes and use the turning signal and that she almost cut that curb. The supermarket scene likewise feels stingy. Why not have Jerry's take on more than mashed potatoes? Why not see him micromanaging Dana's shopping list? Though not there physically, Jerry is a character in this scene—or should be. Under the influence of Jerry's ghost Dana might hesitate to drop that quart of mashed potatoes into her cart, and then defy him. Surely that beats telling us that this is what she would not have done in the past.

However skillfully rendered, a character's interior thoughts are seldom as telling as their actions.

Your Turn

Draft or revise an opening using free indirect discourse, so that the narration is colored by the point-of-view character's sensibilities as carried by her or his stream of consciousness.

7. A Woman Bedazzled

(Unreliable Narrators & Narratives vs. Unreliable Authors)

Even with their tint of hazy grime—swirled along the sides from hasty attempts at sponging—the sunlight radiated through the auto shop's wall-sized windows so intensely that Anna envied the blind man across from her, with his deep black sunglass lenses. The man's service dog slept soundly in an amber sunbeam. Anna wondered why she never saw blind women around town with their harnessed dogs. She supposed that even with a German Shepherd's protection a mugging or rape were still too real a possibility for the women—hardly worth the risk for a little shopping. She closed her eyes tightly against the light, the heat and starry red swirls glowing through her lids, dizzying her to sleepiness. She had often felt tired lately.

An air compressor rumbled in the garage behind her, a man's voice hollering over the noise in Spanish. Another man responded, "They're in. Came in today's truck."

Anna imagined a delivery of boxes containing complex bits of metallic machinery, with protruding gears and wires and thin hoses, like gleaming, steel organs in nests of shredded packing paper. She thought how vulnerable everyone in the waiting room was—at the mercy of the men with their greasy fingers and wrenches clinking under their car hoods. And if their work was shoddy, it was almost as if she deserved it—sitting helplessly in her vinyl seat, watching *Jeopardy*, instead of teaching herself mechanics and blackening her own palms with grease.

She picked up a magazine from the Formica table, leafed through it without focusing on any of the words, simply noting colors and shapes in the manner of an infant.

Analysis

A woman waits in an auto repair shop while her car is serviced. While waiting she is distracted by the glare of sunlight through the shop's windows, to the point where she envies the blind man waiting across from her, with his "deep black sunglass lenses." She goes on to ruminate about the lack of blind women in the town, at least in public places, and concludes that "even with a German Shepherd's protection" such women would be vulnerable to muggers and rapists.

Odd thoughts for a woman to have on an otherwise ordinary day at the auto shop. But then Anna is hot and tired ("She had often felt tired lately"), and even a little dizzy, and these oddly cynical thoughts might be ascribed at least in part to her exhaustion.

Then the litany of odd thoughts resumes, with Anna concluding that "everyone in the [auto repair shop] waiting room" is vulnerable, at the mercy of mechanics "with their greasy fingers and wrenches clinking under their car hoods." She's convinced that the mechanics are out to rip her off, and furthermore that she deserves it for "sitting helplessly in her vinyl seat, watching *Jeopardy*" instead of teaching herself mechanics (one wonders if at the dentist's office she berates herself for not having gone to dental school). One begins to suspect that these aren't merely the ruminations of an exhausted and wary woman, but the warped notions of a paranoid. At the very least Anna is deeply depressed.

The world as interpreted by a mind slightly off its tether is the subject of this opening. It's a good, if disturbing, read. I for one would read on to know more about this character with whom there is clearly something enticingly wrong, who compares spare car parts to human organs "in nests of shredded packing paper" and feels so undone by the sun's rays through a window she wishes herself blind.

In first-person fiction we call such a character narrator "unreliable." What makes a narrative unreliable isn't usually that he or she gives us the wrong facts, but that the facts are presented through the distorting filter or tinted lens of a psyche that has lost its grasp on reality, or anyway misses the point. From her perspective, Anna may see things very clearly, but she doesn't see them as you and I would see them. Unreliable narratives don't lie; rather, they provide us with perspectives that are far from objective or insightful.

A good example of this is the narrator of John Cheever's short story "Goodbye, My Brother," who tells us up front that his family "has always been very close in spirit," then goes on to eviscerate said family—and especially his brother, who by the story's end the narrator has attacked not only verbally, but physically, laying him flat on his back with a massive, saltwater-logged root. From the narrator's perspective this may qualify as filial devotion, but Cheever's readers know better, as we are meant to. The whole point of an unreliable narrative is that it makes us read *between the lines*.

Another good example of an unreliable protagonist is the butler in Kazuo Ishiguro's *The Remains of the Day*, a man rendered so emotionally comatose by his deeply ingrained sense of propriety that given one last chance at love he botches it. It's a terribly sad story, rendered sadder for being told by its victim, who doesn't even realize how sad it is, or even get that the story he tells us is a tragedy, and that he is its tragic hero.

> I made my exit, and it was not until after I had done so that it occurred to me I had not actually offered my condolences (on the death of my assistant, Miss Kenton's, aunt). I could well imagine the blow the news would be to her, her aunt having been, to all intents and purposes, like a mother to her, and I paused out in the corridor, wondering if I should go back, knock and make good my omission. But then it occurred to me that if I were to do so, I might easily intrude upon her private grief.

Though Ishiguro's butler-narrator reports the above scene accurately insofar as the facts are concerned, he misses the point: namely that he's in love with Miss Kenton, but his crippling sense of propriety prevents him from seeing this, so not only does he squander the opportunity to comfort her in her hour of need; he bungles his last chance at love.

But the protagonist of the first page presented here has more in common with Chief Broom, the narrator of Ken Kesey's *One Flew Over the Cuckoo's Nest*, a native American inpatient at a mental hospital in the Pacific Northwest, for whom events unfold through a hallucinatory fog as he pushes his broom back and forth down the hospital's corridors. Though his view of things is distorted, Chief Broom is the perfect narrator for Kesey's novel about a belligerent individualist (R.P. McMurphy) who fakes his way into the loony bin to avoid prison time, since he's been faking his own mental illness. Only after Kesey concocted Chief Broom (which event, we're told, occurred during one of the fledgling author's voluntarily drugged interludes) was he able to successfully write his novel.

Don't get out the peyote just yet. Unreliable narratives are rare, tricky birds, to be engaged only with the understanding that an unreliable narrative is what's intended, since the ultimate subject of an unreliable narrative is the narrator's unreliability. For this reason, though not altogether impossible, an intentionally unreliable third-person narrator is at best an odd duck. The writer who produces such a creature runs the risk of presenting readers not with an unreliable narrator, but with an unreliable author, for which there can be little if any excuse.

Unless there really does turn out to be something wrong with Anna—if her weird, unhinged perceptions are not just the author parading his or her descriptive prowess, being clever or cute—then this opening fails by making promises it won't deliver on, i.e., saddling us with an unreliable *author*.

But I suspect this author won't let us down, that these perceptions of Anna's are there for a good reason, to introduce us to the psyche of a woman on the verge of a mental breakdown. I suspect, too, that as the story progresses Anna's problems will get worse. How much worse will they get? And will Anna come through all right? These are reasons to keep reading.

Your Turn

Turn this first page into a true unreliable narrative. To do so, you'll need to do two things: first, change it to first person. Secondly, while not distorting or altering any of the facts, somehow make it clear that the perspective we are being offered is distorted or anyway not entirely accurate or objective: to get what's really going on, we must read between the lines.

8. The Curfew

(Second Person)

Ten shivering minutes pass on the balcony of your mother's condo before you realize that all cars look the same from a distance in the night: faceless grey bodies with brilliant bright eyes. You practice sucking in your gut and glance at your cell phone's clock, breathing a sigh that turns to smoke in the crisp November air. Winter's cold is fresh and new, but already you're bored with it, every ounce of your teenage being focused on the coming spring, the day in March when you'll shred your learner's permit to confetti and ride out with your mom to the Perrin-Beitel D.P.S. There, after you wait in line and pass a simple test, a man in a short-sleeved shirt and a clip-on tie will snap your photo and hand you a small, plastic card. In doing so, he will set you free. Your heart beats fast just thinking of it.

But for now you're fifteen and four hours from a midnight curfew, and every second lost waiting for your ride to show up makes the idea of getting to your first-ever party—a *real* party, with beer and liquor and girls—seem about as likely as a snowstorm in San Antonio. From the H-E-B lot across Broadway, thousands of jet-black grackles puff up their chests and yammer in the leafless live oaks, their static squawks a laugh track aimed right at your ears. Again you reach for your phone. You want to call Ari—not to annoy him, not to be that needy, car-less kid—just to touch base, to make sure he and Parker are still on the way. But as your fingers meet the keypad, a low rumbling and a series of honks overtakes the noise of the birds. You hustle back inside and shout that you're off to another Friday night movie at the Quarry. Your mom says to be careful, asks you to wake her when you get home. But you don't have time to reply; you're halfway down the stairs as it is, stumbling over yourself as you rush into the dark.

Analysis

There's a reason why few stories—and even fewer novels—are written using the second-person point of view. It tires readers out. It bosses them around. It says to them, in effect: you step into the protagonist's shoes, you play the role, you do what he/she does. Depending on who the character is, and what befalls them, readers may or may not want to play along. Even assuming that they're game, they may not be willing to play for hundreds of pages.

Which isn't to say that second person doesn't have its place. It has been used to great effect, more often in short stories, most notoriously by Lorrie Moore in what may still be her most famous collection, *Self-Help*, wherein many stories take the form of how-to guides, to wit (from "How to Be a Writer"):

> First, try to be something, anything, else. A movie star/astronaut. A movie star/missionary. A movie star/kindergarten teacher. President of the World. Fail miserably. It is best if you fail at an early age— say, fourteen. Early, critical disillusionment is necessary so that at fifteen you can write long haiku sequences about thwarted desire. It is a pond, a cherry blossom, a wind brushing against sparrow wing leaving for mountain. Count the syllables. Show it to your mom. She is tough and practical. She has a son in Vietnam and a husband who may be having an affair. She believes in wearing brown because it hides spots. She'll look briefly at your writing, then back up at you with a face blank as a doughnut. She'll say: 'How about emptying the dishwasher?'

Note how easily the second person viewpoint lends itself to comedy—far more easily and willingly than it lends itself to tragedy, since though we balk at being forced to endure, say, a heroin addict's withdrawal symptoms or gang rape, we don't seem to mind being the butt of a joke. At any rate, we don't mind for short intervals—say, the length of a short story.

That said, the second-person technique has proven extremely successful with longer forms, or anyway with one longer form, namely Jay McInerney's 1984 love letter to Yuppiedom, *Bright Lights, Big City*. Throughout McInerney's novel, "you" snort a lot of Bolivian marching powder. Here, too, the overall effect is comic, though by the book's end the comedy has turned to pathos and arguably to self-pity. But then, the self being pitied is, well, you.

Owing to the tortured metaphysical logic of second-person narrations, we readers have, in a sense, only ourselves to blame for whatever weaknesses endow their characters. We bear their burdens and their faults—and, to some extent at least, the faults of their authors. Call it guilt by association.

Then again many readers will cross their arms and say, "As a matter of fact, no, I am not in a nightclub talking to a girl with a bald head." And that will be that. In using the second person, you throw down a gauntlet. Supposing the reader doesn't pick it up?

In the given example, "you" (a teenage boy) wait on the balcony of your parents' home to be picked up by some friends for your "first-ever party." Just thinking of it "your heart beats fast," for you know it's not just a party that awaits you at the far end of that ride: it's a rite of passage, an initiation. There will be "beer and liquor and girls." You almost can't believe it. It even seems to you, as you stand there waiting, that the likelihood of your actually achieving this milestone is about as great as that of "a snowstorm in San Antonio."

The author does indeed put us into (or forces us, rather: for the second-person point of view is non-consensual) into the psyche of an adolescent boy, a psyche beside itself with nervous erotic energy and anticipation. The details are convincingly precise, down to the grackles whose cries make a laugh track of the night—fittingly, for here, too, though there's drama, it's underscored by comedy.

It makes for a strong opening to a story whose theme is the heady anxiety of adolescence—a story I, for one, wouldn't mind reading. Or playing the lead in.

Your Turn

Rewrite a first page of your own or another work in the second person.

9. Narrating from the Great Beyond

(Dead Narrator / Gratuitous Narrative Devices)

I should probably forewarn you, before we get into the story, that I'm dead.

That's why this story isn't about me, it's about my grandson.

Oh, I might pop up in conversations here and there but don't let that fool you. I am dead.

There, now that we have THAT out of the way, let's begin.

This story is about Noah Emmaus, the youngest and latest in our long family line, the oldest in Incanto. Our patriarch, "Dad" Emmaus, came to the island five hundred years ago on The Boat, and it was his leadership that helped the small group of settlers turn this little patch of dirt in the Gulf of Mexico into a nation all its own. Several generations later, it was Nicolas Emmaus who helped hammer out a treaty with the United States to add our island to their great Union as a territory.

My grandfather, Leslie Emmaus, founded our family business in 1923 as a little vaudeville show in downtown Incanto City, featuring the unique individuals that lived around that area. That little show was so popular, it inspired the tourism industry that has made the city so wealthy, and built Emmaus, Inc. into the leading entertainment and tourism business in the world.

That business now rests on the young shoulders of my grandson, Noah. He has been the CEO for just about a year, and is as good at that job at twenty-one as his father or I ever were.

But there I go rambling again. On to our story.

It began early one Friday morning at Noah's penthouse apartment. The sun was just barely peeking over the horizon, and the only light inside was the glow coming from the big television in his bedroom. Noah was starting his morning, like he did every morning, watching the news and doing yoga.

Analysis

I remember my first encounter with a dead narrator. It was at a screening of *Sunset Boulevard* at a revival house in Greenwich Village. Anyone who's seen Billy Wilder's classic film noir remembers the opening shot of a suited man floating face down in Norma Desmond's swimming pool. The voiceover meanwhile intones (slyly and cynically, as befitting a noir narrator): "Yes, this is Sunset Boulevard, Los Angeles, California. It's about five o'clock in the morning. That's the Homicide Squad—complete with detectives and newspapermen. A murder has been reported from one of those great big houses in the ten-thousand block. You'll read about it in the late editions, I'm sure."

The voice belongs to actor William Holden, and so does the floating body.

Since then I've had mixed feelings about ghost narrators. As narrative sleights of hand go, it strikes me as a little too easy, a bit too glib. It also requires suspension of all four laws of thermodynamics. "No fair!" is my first reaction. "Narrating from the dead—that's cheating!"

Though I've since become a fan of *Sunset Boulevard*, I'm still not sure that Wilder gets away with it—or, assuming that he does, that he *should*.

Since Bill Holden landed face down in that pool there've been no shortage of dead narrators in film and literature. Alice Sebold's *The Lovely Bones* offers a relatively recent example. Sebold's novel begins, "My name was Salmon, like the fish; first name, Susie. I was fourteen when I was murdered on December 6, 1973." Like the fish she's named for, Sebold's narrator swims against the current of mortality to expose the circumstances surrounding her rape and murder.

It's a gutsy gambit—or was, anyway, back in 2002 when Sebold's novel was first published to rave reviews. Since then, largely owing to its success, there's been an epidemic of dead narrators mostly in books for young people: Cynthia Rylant's *Heavenly Village*, Eoin Colfer's *The Wish List*, Gary Soto's *The Afterlife*. Each of these novels affords its young readers an opportunity to confront mortality, hell, redemption, and other issues that used to be the purview of churches, but without being bored to their own real deaths by sermons.

Then there are novels narrated by the Grim Reaper himself. I'm thinking, of course, of Markus Zusak's *The Book Thief*, an otherwise familiar-to-the-point-of-triteness Holocaust story rescued from cliché by its boldly original narrative approach. At least it seems boldly original, until one realizes that the Grim-Reaper-as-Narrator is merely good ol' omniscience wearing a cloak and carrying a scythe, which didn't prevent *The Book Thief* from becoming a runaway bestseller.

If dead narrators haven't yet worn out their welcome, they're perilously close to doing so. My guess is it won't be too long before they go the way of angels and anthropomorphic rabbits.

Apart from being yesterday's news, dead narrators also run the risk of being merely gratuitous. Here, the narrator himself seems intent on pointing out the superfluity of his author's attention-grabbing conceit: "Before we get into the story ...", "... this story isn't about me ...", "... now that we have THAT out of the way ...". How are we readers to treat such statements if not as disclaimers warning us against investing too deeply in a patently gratuitous device?

Still, the device does serve a purpose: it shocks the reader into a state of alertness in the hope of keeping him awake through what the narrator himself admits is a dull ramble of biographical names and dates. Indeed, up to the last paragraph, everything in this opening page apologizes for itself, leading me to wonder why—rather than commit said offenses in the first place—our narrator doesn't simply begin with the perfectly good final paragraph.

It may not grab readers by the throat; but from the reader's perspective it beats being grabbed by a gratuitous corpse.

Your Turn

Choose a novel or story you are well familiar with (it can be written in either the first or the third person). Write a new opening for it in which you introduce a dead narrator. For instance, write a new opening to *The Great Gatsby* in which Gatsby narrates his own story from beyond the grave. Or Holden Caulfield. Or Jane Eyre. Or any unnamed, unidentified narrator. (Note: it will be easier than you think.)

B. Structure:
Where to Begin?

THOUGH RELATED, PLOT AND STRUCTURE ARE TWO DIFFERENT things. The events of a story—the things that happen—along with their causal relationships—why they happen—form its *plot*. *Structure* is the order in which those events are conveyed. A story that ends with the protagonists' deaths may start with that event and work backwards (the strategy Peter Nichols chose for his bestselling novel *The Rocks*), or it may begin with the protagonists' first meeting and proceed from there. Similarly, a rags-to-riches story might start with its hero as a rich woman, then go back and tell the story of how she achieved her wealth from a state of poverty.

Or a story might begin somewhere in the middle, with some dramatic event that raises the question, "How did this event come to be? What circumstances propelled this character or these characters into this situation?" From the story's provocative middle we would typically be taken to a much earlier event, the event that started it all, otherwise known as the *inciting incident*.

The question of where to begin is among the most perplexing questions authors face. One way to answer is to ask oneself, "What question does my story mainly exist to answer?" Having arrived at that question, choose an opening event or moment that raises that same question in the reader's mind, compelling her to keep reading.

Chekhov said, "The writer's task is not to solve the problem, but to frame the problem correctly."[2] Of structure, Chekhov might have said something similar, especially as it relates to first pages. *The writer's task isn't to answer the question, but to frame the question correctly.*

As to the answer, that's what the rest of the story is for.

---

2   *Letters of Anton Chekhov*, translated by Constance Garnett (1920).

10. Megan's Life: A Surfeit of Beginnings

(Where to Begin? / Inciting Incident / Death)

Megan's life was set to reboot in ten days. She glanced again at the two tickets to New York lying on the nightstand. How would she make it through final exams, packing, saying goodbye to friends, when all she wanted to do was grab Luke's hand, hop a cab to the airport, and launch their grand adventure? Her mind still whirling, she crawled into bed and turned out the light.

At dawn her cell phone chirped five times, waking her from a dead sleep. When she answered, no one was there. She cursed the damn thing, then checked the call log. Luke. She dialed him back but he didn't pick up.

They sent two policemen to tell her. He'd swerved to avoid a young boy who'd wandered into the street and his car slammed into a lamppost. By the time help arrived, he was gone. Hers was the last number he'd dialed. They needed her to come down to the station.

The police sergeant led her through hallway after hallway, down stairs into a sparse room with a large curtain covering one wall, and asked if she was ready. Of course I'm not ready, you ass. This is the man I loved, the man I wanted to spend my life with. But she didn't say that. What she did was nod, then nod again when she saw the body, then throw up in her hands.

She caught a bus to his apartment and let herself in. She packed up the things she'd left there—a change of clothes, her toothbrush, a ratty pair of slippers. She took the picture of the two of them on the beach in Sausalito, his favorite Miles Davis album, and his unfinished screenplay. His mother and stepfather, who'd never even met her, could take care of the rest when they flew in.

The plan had been to move right after graduation. He'd found a studio apartment and put down a deposit. He'd work at *Huffington Post*, she'd revise her novel and look for an agent. They'd eat ramen noodles, drink cheap wine, bike through Central Park on Sundays. Turned out that wasn't going to be her life after all.

Instead she boarded American Flight 6023 and flew to Chicago. To her childhood home. To her mother Helen. To the last place on earth she wanted to be.

Analysis

"Whatever you can do, or dream you can, begin it. Boldness has genius, power and magic in it. Begin it now." These famous words, usually attributed to Johann Wolfgang Goethe, are in fact from William Hutchinson Murray's 1951 book *The Scottish Himalayan Expedition*. Whatever its source, the quote doesn't tell us *where* to begin, let alone *how*.

Where to begin? The question comes down to *structure*. Not what happened, i.e., the series of events that make a story, but the order in which those events are conveyed. Should we start with the beginning, or at the end? Or should we cherry-pick a dramatic scene from somewhere in the middle, and backtrack from there, filling in all the things that lead up to that dramatic moment, then continue to the end?

Assuming we've chosen to tell a story from the beginning, *what* beginning do we start with? Writing guides often use the term *inciting incident*, meaning the event or incident that propels a character or characters out of their status quo existence, igniting the plot.

But locating that inciting incident isn't always that simple, since often there's more than one. In fact there's *always* more than one, with an inciting incident lurking behind every inciting incident, a breadcrumb trail of inciting incidents leading back to the birth of the protagonist and beyond, to her conception, and the birth of her parents, and the birth of *their* parents, and, finally, ultimately, by logical extension, the creation of the universe.

But unless you're writing the Bible (or a James Michener novel), you probably want to begin your story as close as possible to the event that sends your protagonist off on her dramatic journey—a journey of exceptional struggles and fresh opportunities.

This first page of a novel about a woman whose dreams are shattered by her boyfriend's sudden death confronts us with a plethora of beginnings. It's as if the author, unwilling to decide between several opening strategies, has left them all on the table. Rather than enhancing and building on each other, the multiple openings compete with and weaken each other, resulting in an indecisive, jerky, wishy-washy opening.

The first paragraph gives us Beginning 1: As Megan, the protagonist, prepares for bed, she contemplates her upcoming trip with boyfriend Luke to New York City, and the new life they plan to lead there.

The problem with this beginning is that it's static, with the action, such as it is, consisting of Megan envisioning (the strongest verb applicable) her future with Luke, an "event," if it can be called that, that has doubtlessly happened in the past and will as doubtlessly occur again over the course of the ten days that remain before the actual journey: a routine event, in other words.

And as I've pointed out before, routine is of interest to readers only insofar as we expect it to be disrupted or upset. So why not begin with the thing that upsets it?

Which brings us to Beginning 2: Luke's unanswered phone call. Arguably this, too, is routine. Presumably it's not the first time Luke has called Megan, or the first time that, having missed his call, Megan phones back and gets no answer. So as an inciting event, something that clearly disrupts routine, this beginning likewise leaves something to be desired.

The same can hardly be said of Beginning 3, in which Megan opens her front door to two policemen who have come bearing the news that her boyfriend has died. That this qualifies as an inciting incident, a moment or event that shatters routine, can hardly be denied: making it, if not the obvious choice for a beginning, a strong contender.

The next paragraph, in which Megan identifies Luke's corpse at the morgue (Beginning 4), implies Beginning 3, while taking it one step further, to a moment no less dramatic. This, too, would make a strong beginning.

But then so would Beginning 5 (next paragraph), which finds us with Megan in Luke's apartment, gathering her belongings a day or so after his death. Though less intrinsically shocking than Beginnings 3 and 4, this scene, unlike them, allows for memories and other reflections aroused by the objects in that apartment, providing the author with an opportunity (unexploited here) to convey to us through those memories the dreams that have been shattered by Luke's death (which this scene, too, leaves to implication).

Finally we come to Beginning 6, which puts us aboard a passenger plane with Megan, bound for Chicago and her childhood home, "the last place she wants to be." Though it lacks the drama and urgency of the previous four openings, it's also nearest and dearest to the presumptive plot, which isn't about a woman whose boyfriend has died, but about the journey which that event sends her on, a journey that (also probably) begins with this plane trip to her childhood home. So why not start there?

In starting decisively with any one of these possible beginnings rather than rushing us through all of them, the author might slow things down and take more time, exploiting their dramas—whether those dramas are external and dynamic (police officers at front door; identifying corpse) or internal and reflective (sorting through objects, memories, imagining what might have been; ditto aboard childhood home–bound plane).

Given the attention it deserves, each of these possible beginnings could easily fill a first page.

Your Turn

Choosing one of the suggested starting points for this first page, revise it accordingly. Whatever moment or event you choose to begin with, it should be expanded to take up most, if not all, of the revised first page.

11. Flying with Mum and Dad

(In Medias Res / *Framing the Question*)

I was sitting on Mum's lap in the front seat of the small single-engine airplane as we accelerated down the bumpy overgrown grass strip with Dad at the controls.

Just over halfway into takeoff, we unexpectedly hit a deep pothole. Instantly I was tugged upwards out of Mum's arms, thrashing my head against the instrument panel above.

I thumped heavily back down again, landing askew on Mum's lap. Blood gushed from my head and Mum was frantic. Dad was shocked too, but remained composed, still needing to focus on the takeoff.

"I've got to keep going," he yelled above my cries and Mum's terrified shouting.

"I can't stop now, I'm too advanced. I can get airborne, come back 'round again and land,"—all the while nearing the end of the grass strip, pulling back on the controls and dealing with the hysteria inside the cabin.

He banked the aircraft to the left and looked back at Mum. "Is Taylor OK?"

Mum had used a length of her dress to wipe away the blood and saw a deep, long gash to my head which would need stitches. Being a nurse, she scrunched up her dress and pressed it firmly against my head as she pulled me tight against her.

She peered over her shoulder at my little sister, Giovanna, who sat bravely; quiet and frightened, watching all of the drama as it had played out.

"Are you all right, darling?" Mum asked anxiously.

Giovanna nodded dumbly as she clung tightly to her seatbelt.

"It won't be long now, love," Mum reassured, despite her own panic.

As we headed back to the airstrip it wasn't long before we had landed and Mum was attending to my head wound; just another sticking plaster.

Dad had flying in his blood and you would never have known to look at him; to witness his obvious prowess and experience with his flying, that he had once been a young, small, unfed and neglected boy from Uruguay who had been miraculously rescued by elderly Irish missionaries.

Analysis

By starting "in the middle of things" or *in medias res,* authors avoid the long and potentially tedious expositional climb to exciting scenes and dramatic events, while at the same time plunging readers headlong into a story's central issues, themes, and conflicts. By starting *in medias res,* they frontload their tales with action and suspense.

But when starting *in medias res,* it's important to choose a moment or scene that not only gains a reader's attention, but is relevant to the work as a whole, providing a tantalizing glimpse of what's to come, while also raising the right questions—namely, those questions which the book as a whole exists to answer. An opening that's sensational but with only a tangential or tenuous relationship to the book's overall theme may pull in readers, but it will also lead them to disappointment and, possibly, frustration and resentment.

The Duke of Deception, Geoffrey Wolff's brilliant memoir about his con-artist father, opens not in the middle but near the end, with Wolff learning of his father's death.

While Wolff and his family are summering in Narragansett, a telephone rings. The telephone belongs to the friend on whose "shaded terrace" Wolff is relaxing, "sitting in an overstuffed wicker chair ... glancing at sailboats beating out to Block Island ... smelling roses and fresh cut grass" and drinking rum "with tonic and lime." His soon-to-be four-year-old son Nicholas is with his mother-in-law, out for a ride in her black Ford sedan. Nicholas's little brother Justin is with his mother at the beach.

"It was almost possible to disbelieve in death that day," Wolff writes, "to put out of mind a son's unbuckled seat belt and the power of surf at the water's edge." The opening continues:

> In my memory now, as in some melodrama, I hear the phone ring, but I didn't hear it then. The phone in that house seemed always to be ringing. My wife's brother-in-law John was called to the telephone [...] John returned [...] As I stared down the terrace at him, Kay and her children quit talking, and John's cheeks began to dance. I looked at the widow Kay, she looked away, and I knew what I knew. I walked down that terrace to learn which of my boys was dead.

In fact neither of Wolff's sons has died. The bad news has to do with his father. "Your father is dead," John tells him. To which Wolff replies,

"Thank God." That "Thank God" is what Wolff's book exists to explain. That "Thank God" frames the tale that follows, puts it into context, while at the same time raising a pertinent question: why, on learning of his father's death, would a man say "Thank God"? Had one of Wolff's sons indeed died, it would still have made for a powerful prologue, but for a different memoir.

Here, in this opening page of the story of a woman whose father was a pilot, we begin with her in her father's plane as it accelerates down a grassy runway. The airplane's wheels strike a pothole and the narrator's skull is bashed against an instrument panel. Too late to abort takeoff, the father lofts his injured daughter into the sky while her mother "wipe[s] away the blood" from the "long, deep gash to [her] head which would need stitches." Since Mom is a nurse, she tends her child's wound with expert calm, "scrunching up her dress and press[ing] it firmly" into the gash.

All of this is described well, and it is certainly dramatic. Yet the scene is misleading, since it conveys nothing essential about the father or his relationship with his daughter (nor does it illustrate his piloting skills; anyone can hit a pothole). What's best demonstrated here are the mother's nursing skills. Yet my sense is that these are not central to the memoir. Ultimately, since it fails to point to the crux of the story, this opening scene feels anecdotal, a curious event, but not an exemplary, or relevant, one.

The last paragraph of the opening crash-lands us into pure summary exposition about the father's impoverished Uruguayan past.

Might it not be better to choose an opening scene wherein somehow that past intrudes on the present: where, for instance, the father flies his daughter over the land of his birth? Then we would have action, drama, exposition, and relevance all at once.

Your Turn

Draft an opening in which a character revisits the scene of a life-changing event. It can be fiction or nonfiction (in which case the event will have happened to you). Example: with his spouse, partner, or lover in tow, a character visits the former home of a now-dead college professor who, for better or worse, changed his life. Note: the partner or lover isn't keen in this pilgrimage.

12. A Fateful First Encounter

(First Glimpse / Atmosphere / Framing Device / Authorial Intrusion)

Working Title: "Prelude to a Kiss"

The first time they met was in Atlantic City.

She had a small and shabby apartment above a run-down cigar shop across from the marina, the rows of neat white boats bobbing and clacking in the wind, the evening hot and sultry, water whispering at the bay. She parked her little old white Ford Cortina in the little parking space in front, the thudding of the car door and the click of the lock interrupting the silence of the evening. Her sandals echoing loudly on the pavement in the peaceful azure of the early evening, she slowly made her way to the back door, clambering over the overflowing rubbish bins and listening to the calming rushing of the bay that was just a few hundred yards in front of her. She fumbled with her keys in the lock, before stepping into the cool dimness of the storage room behind the main shop; taking the stairs two at a time, she finally reached her destination, a cheap and thin door that led into a poky and sparsely furnished apartment.

The familiar calming scent of tobacco wafted lazily through the still open windows, thrown wide in the stifling heat of the day. The sun was beginning to sink on the New Jersey coastline and she breathed in the sticky, salty sea air with relish. A gentle warm breeze played on the faded burgundy curtains, fluttering flirtatiously with the windowpanes, the sounds of the lapping and onrushing of waves lulling her mind; for all her worries, all her past and future misdeeds, this city would always live long in her heart, longer than the ones she had left behind—the others, those that held memories she would rather not recall.

She stepped out onto the tiny balcony, a glass of cheap chilled white wine in hand, and sat down on an elderly chair and table ensemble that nearly filled the petite balcony, her feet up on the dusty table. She watched the clear waters of the bay for a while, sparkling in the receding daylight, and the lights blinking on the coastline.

Analysis

An unnamed woman of indeterminate age—having either survived a broken love affair or preparing to embark on one—settles into her shabby beachfront apartment. Based on the title, we may reasonably assume the latter.

Titles are microcosms, miniatures of the stories or novels they stand for. Though titles aren't protected by copyright, and though there's no law requiring them to be original, you want to consider whether a title has too much wear and tear on it. A quick search at Amazon's book holdings reveals no fewer than 49 products titled "Prelude to a Kiss," best known as that of Craig Lucas's 1988 drama. The title "Prelude to a [fill in the blank]" is even more common, so unless used ironically it may strike some readers as trite.

Even if it isn't trite, the title is abstract; it suggests no image or metaphor.

The direct, inviting first line promises a love story. By making this sentence its own paragraph, the author increases its portentousness, suggesting that this meeting has been fateful and resulted in at least one broken heart, and possibly in tragedy.

The implied point of view in the second paragraph is that of the protagonist about to park her car in front of the cigar shop housed in the building in which she lives. But the sensory details provided here are not, or don't seem to be, part of her experience of the present moment. Can she simultaneously be parking her car and hearing the "clacking [of] the wind"? Does she see "neat white boats bobbing" as she maneuvers her Ford? If one of the purposes of fiction is to create experiences for the reader, it's important for the author to know whose experience is being reported at any given time. Is the experience of "neat white boats bobbing and clacking in the wind" that of the heroine parking her car, or that of an omniscient, objective narrator? Or has information about the setting of this opening scene leached into it by way of an intrusive author?

In the same paragraph the point of view settles into that of the female protagonist. We enjoy a wealth of sensual sensory details—the clicking of sandals against pavement, the color of the evening sky, the calm rushing of the bay. Sounds, sighs, and smells—all generously and judiciously evoked. The moment is richly atmospheric. At the end of the same paragraph, however, the viewpoint shifts again, with the reader being told about the quality of the apartment beyond the "cheap and thin door"—despite the fact that the protagonist has yet to open that door and enter into that experience. This, too, may be an instance of authorial intrusion: the author's knowledge leaking into the narrator. But when reading a work of fiction, it's not the author whose perspective we're interested in sharing, but that of a narrator or narrators created by the author. In the case of a third-person narrator, at first the difference may seem purely semantic or hair-splitting. In fact, the difference is a crucial one, since while the author exists outside of her story, the narrator inhabits the world of the story.

Since by and large this third-person narrator shares the perspective of the protagonist, why not describe the inside of her apartment from her viewpoint, once she has entered it, rather than before, when it's not (yet) part of her momentary experience?

The third and fourth paragraphs of this opening build upon the mood and atmosphere established by the second paragraph. Here the details of setting are firmly grounded in the character's experience: she sees the sun setting, smells the salty air, hears waves lapping.

So far, beyond the vague and coy reference to "all her worries," nothing in the way of a conflict or plot is suggested, let alone engaged. Which is fine, provided the writer does indeed have a story to tell us concerning this woman, and provided that the status quo of her daily existence, so well established here, is disrupted within the next page or two—as readers have every right to expect, being uninterested in routine except to see it broken.

On that note, a few questions. Is this where the story begins, or where it ends? Has the fateful meeting alluded to in the first sentence already occurred, or does it lie in store? The opening sentence suggests that we will bear witness to the fateful encounter by way of a dramatic scene. It promises a demonstration, a dramatization.

In view of which, unless the front doorbell is about to ring (while our protagonist sips Chablis on her balcony), perhaps it would be wiser for the author to state more specifically in that first sentence the circumstances of the fateful meeting ("They met in a bar in Atlantic City") and begin her story accordingly—not with the protagonist wallowing routinely in her apartment, but at that bar the evening in question.

In any case the author should be clear about what's being offered in this scene—a fateful first encounter, or a woman's routine existence in her shabby Atlantic City digs? Or has that fateful meeting already taken place, along with the love affair engendered by it, in a past to which this scene is more prologue that prelude? In that case, what we're presented with here is the frame of a story rather than the story itself. The story is what happened in the past; the opening scene merely contextualizes or opens the door to it. What follows in that case will, in essence, be a flashback—one that will take up the rest of the book or story. The proper term for that is a *framed narrative* (as opposed to a regular flashback, which fits inside a scene and does not become the story).

Whatever this author intends, based on the quality of this first page, I would keep reading. Would you?

Your Turn

Draft or revise a first page/scene that serves as the frame for a story set in the past, i.e., a framed narrative. (Note: though they have much in common, a framed narrative differs from starting *in medias res*, since a framed narrative begins with a moment or event that follows or comes at the very end of the story, and not from the middle or anywhere within the story.)

13. Living with Lyle

*(First Glimpse / Mistaken Identity / Whose
Viewpoint? / Implication vs. Statement)*

I had only been out of jail two days when I met Eleanor. I was sneaking around Cost Mart hoping to pilfer any amount of money from an unsuspecting, leisurely Sunday grocery shopper. But it's hard to blend into one's surroundings when a young lady is staring, mouth agape, in the produce section. She had a green purse flung over her right shoulder, a shopping basket in one hand hanging with quite a weight at her side, and a pink grapefruit jittering in her other hand. There was no denying her attractiveness but the freaky trance-like fixation with me had its hazards.

I could tell she was about to say something. Her look was one of disbelief, excitement and paranoia. Who does she think I am, I wondered? Because it sure the hell can't be me she's this interested in.

A good twenty seconds passed. Even though I was starting to feel more than shifty—is she stuck in a standing coma?—I didn't move. I had committed myself to this uncomfortable situation and I had to see it through.

I locked her gaze, hoping to prompt her to action. Nothing. I ran my fingers through my hair and took a step towards her. She jumped a little and the grapefruit fell to the ground. She didn't flinch when it hit her foot. Having reached my daily awkward encounter limit, I turned to leave.

"Lyle?" she asked softly.

Wrong. But at that point in my life, I would have answered to anything an attractive female called me. I looked over my shoulder at her.

"Yeah?"

"It is you!" she shrieked. Both her purse and the shopping basket reunited with the grapefruit on the floor as she launched herself into my arms. She squeezed my whole body with more strength than she looked capable of possessing. She hesitantly pulled herself back from the embrace to look me over again.

"I can't believe it; after all these years. I saw you walking towards me and thought it can't. It just can't. But it is. How insane is this?"

"More than you know."

Analysis

A young woman runs into an old friend in a grocery store—at least she thinks he's an old friend. In fact the man Eleanor mistakes for Lyle is fresh out of prison, sent there for what crime we don't know. But rather than correct her, "Lyle" lets the mistake stand.

"I can't believe it," Eleanor responds. "After all these years ... How insane is this?"

"More than you know," the narrator answers, and means it.

This opening has a lot going for it; in fact it's hard to find fault with it. The first line thrusts us into the heart of the story, with the paragraph that follows setting the scene for the inciting incident—the unique event that will wrest the character or characters out of their status quo and into a story. Here, that unprecedented event is the meeting of not-Lyle and Eleanor, an encounter that turns on a case of mistaken identity. Not one but two lives are about to be derailed from their routines—or, in not-Lyle's case, from whatever passes for routine in the life of an ex-con fresh out of the slammer.

The question framed is: what's going to happen with these two? It's the right question, the very question that will propel us through this narrative. Will he take advantage of her? Will she fall in love? Will she uncover his criminal past along with his deception? Is he a petty thief, or a murderer? Will he love her in turn, or will he rob, beat, or kill her? Or a combination of these things? The possibilities are, if not limitless, rich.

I wonder: how would this story read from Eleanor's point of view? As a point-of-view character, pseudo-Lyle has his charms. But then he also knows he's an ex-con, just as he knows what sent him up the river in the first place. It will be much harder, and may require manipulation on the part of the author, to withhold his knowledge from the reader so as not to give a big part of the game away. If she manipulates too much, the author exposes herself to the charge of creating false suspense—suspense achieved artificially by withholding information from the reader that the character is fully aware of. In that case, it may be better to experience this relationship from the point of view of the character who's totally in the dark: Eleanor.

In that case, the author faces another challenge: namely, how to plausibly render a case of mistaken identity from the viewpoint of the person making the mistake. Will we be treated to Eleanor's perspective after she has already survived her experience, such that, as she begins the tale, she knows it is one of mistaken identity and deception? If made, such a choice would result in a great loss of tension and suspense. For one thing, we'll know from the start that she survives to tell the tale.

Hmm, maybe our author had the right idea. Maybe it's better to stick to Lyle's viewpoint.

You see the sort of decisions writers wrestle with. There are no absolute or easy solutions. In the end, it may be best to rely on gut instincts.

Here, so far at least, those instincts seem to be paying off.

Your Turn

Write a "first glimpse" scene in which two people with a shared troubled past meet again for the first time after a long interval. Example: a former high school star athlete now fallen from grace and down on her or his luck, and someone from the same high school—with whom he or she had a brief romantic or sexual relationship and then dumped—and who has since achieved much success. Be careful; avoid cliché and sensationalism; treat both characters with respect.

14. After the Fire

(Nested Scenes / Russian Doll Syndrome /
Past Perfect / Dialogue Tags)

I sink deep into Scott's couch and travel back thirty years to the duplex townhouse above the freeway. The one Sam and I rented after our house in Santa Cruz burned down.

The committee asks me about the fire. I guess I need to talk about it. I haven't spoken out loud since the limp hoses were reeled back onto their drums, and one of the big sweaty firemen told us we were lucky to be alive.

"We expected to be pulling corpses outa here," he says.

"Thank you for coming," I whisper.

Just when we think we are so special. So smart. So lucky. Sam is on his way to a PhD in literature; I am scheduled to interview for a teaching job. Dad's wedding gift buys us a very hip little Fiat Spyder convertible, British racing green. We live in the guesthouse attached to the garage of a popular English professor. His wife takes me under her wing, shows me how to bake her signature New England sandwich bread. Harriet is a solid 5'11", towering over the dough as she kneads and punches it into the proper consistency.

"Now, your turn," she smiles.

I take her place at the counter. I try to bully the dough the way she does. I glance around for a step stool. Worn out with squeezing, I step aside so she can finish up. She chatters about baking bread from scratch since she was a little girl. Chop wood. Carry water. Take notes.

After the fire, these rooms are reduced to a six-hundred-square-foot pile of smoldering stuff we used to care about. The walls are still standing, but blistered and black. My mother's first batch of original oil paintings claim a spot in one of the layers of stinking rubble. She left them with us on her sudden return to Spain. The charred canvases curl like French crepes.

We tour the Salvador Dali landscape of our former digs. The floor-to-ceiling shelves of classic writings are now soggy blackened globs of pulp. They have toppled into a jagged heap of literature. Humpty Dumpty.

The rotary telephone is solid again now after melting into the silverware drawer. Spear-shaped timbers have pierced through quilts and mattresses and are lodged in the dog's favorite spot under the bed. Clothes are welded together in the closet. My beloved navy peacoat is slumped over my leather boots, until we poke it with a curtain rod. Then it disintegrates.

The stench is everywhere and deep. Burnt wet carpet. Burnt wet books. Burnt wet upholstery. Grotesque bricks of fabrics and nasty plastics. High on the kitchen counter, two scorched and petrified loaves of New England homemade bread.

We don't have a thing to wear, literally.

Analysis

As children most of us had them, a nest of little painted wooden dolls that opened, one after another, to reveal an ever-smaller doll within, until we arrived at the ultimate doll—typically an infant carved from a single piece of wood. Russian ("matryoshka") dolls, they're called. Beyond reiterating themselves, they serve no purpose, which is what makes them so delight-fully droll.

With one crucial difference, this first page of a memoir is structured like one of those Russian dolls. Here the hierarchy is reversed, with the nested "dolls" (read: scenes) becoming bigger and more substantial as we pass through them, starting with the least substantial scene of all, the one conveyed by the first sentence that finds us sinking "deep" into a couch with our narrator. No sooner am I settled into that cozy couch than it's pulled out from under me, with the narrator (and me with her) transported "back thirty years to the duplex townhouse above the freeway. The one Sam and I rented after our house in Santa Cruz burned down." As transitions go, it's as jarring as the one that turned poor Gregor Samsa into a giant beetle in his bed.

But there are more transitions—more Russian dolls—to come. In fact, no sooner are we relocated to that townhouse than we've left it for another setting in which the narrator responds to questions posed to her by a commit-tee—presumably at an inquest of some sort occasioned by the fire. Though the venue of the inquiry isn't given, it's not likely to have been in that townhouse. Leaving me to wonder—where are we now?

The bread-baking scene itself is no sooner introduced than it gives way to a scene shortly after the fire, when the narrator (accompanied by someone, presumably Sam), surveys the destruction, with its "blistered and black" walls, the charred canvases of her mother's oil paintings "curl[ed] like French crepes."

The description of the aftermath of the fire is extremely vivid and effective. I see those charred walls; I smell the sour ashes. Anyone who has lived through a house fire never forgets what it feels like to sift through the remains, the evidence of lives reduced to soggy ashes. With its acrid stench and burned sodden upholstery, this scene is so well rendered (the charred clothes welded together in the closet), so sensuously specific in its inventory of tragic loss, it easily overwhelms all the halfheartedly engaged quasi-scenes that came before—the bread-baking, the committee/inquiry, the dialogue with the "big sweaty" fireman, moments that pass too quickly to leave much of an impression. As for the narrator sinking into that couch, who—having reached the bottom of this page—will still remember that?

The difference between this smartly written opening and Russian dolls is that ultimately it does give us something substantial. It's the scenes leading up to the fire-aftermath scene that feel (relatively) empty. Why not plunge us straight into that aftermath scene, the one fully engaged scene offered by this opening? If the author wants to nest that scene in a more recent one in which the event is recalled—to *frame* it—that's fine. But then there should be a greater investment in the frame (narrator sinking into couch or responding to questions at an inquest) as well.

A final note and a nitpick:

If for whatever reason you're determined to transition readers quickly through various scenes occurring at discordant times, skillful handling of tenses, and particularly of the no-longer-taught past perfect or pluperfect tense, becomes vital. If the primary scene—the moment from which the past is being looked back from—is present tense, then all moments being looked back upon should (probably, logically) be written in the past or the past perfect. Otherwise we court confusion as in this opening, where all scenes past and present are flattened onto the same present tense plane.

Nitpick: As mentioned earlier, often writers tag dialogue with something like "she smiled" or "he laughed," as if dialogue can be "laughed" or "smiled" (it's not; it's spoken). That it's done all the time by reputable writers in published books makes it no less objectionable—to me.

"Now, your turn," she said, smiling.

Your Turn

Write a first page that plunges us into the aftermath of a tragic event: a fire or a natural disaster, the shutting down of a factory, school, or business. Let the scene be an occasion for an inventory of meaningful objects: a father's abandoned work shed or toolshed; the camp where, as a child, the protagonist spent many a happy summer; the school destroyed by a tornado.... Filter the scene through a single character's perspective (first or third person).

15. The Unwritten Masterpiece

(Sleeve Rolling & Throat Clearing)

It was midnight when I sat down to write my masterpiece. I would include everything and nothing. In so doing, I would transform my personality, distilling it into some immortal work of art, created by me, for me. I would be the vatic chronicler of my own mind-windings, the perambulations of a brain seeking egress from banality. Either it (my personality) would flower, bloom and expand like some kaleidoscopic balloon, or it would vanish entirely from the earth, allowing whatever creativity was trapped inside my brain to surge forth unchecked like a rabid river. Either way, I would sooner or later have on my hands something worthwhile, a collection of letters, words and phrases that meant something, meant something powerful, did justice to all my dreams, longings and hopes.

Of course, I didn't really believe in anything that was immortal. Nor did I think that anything I wrote would somehow supply me with a final, terminal quenching of my desire. But a part of me wanted to believe in such a possibility, the same part of me that wanted to believe in God, even though I knew it was only a morbid consolation. I wanted to believe in these myths, while at the same time I was skeptical of them.

But, either way, I poised my pen above the paper. I was prepared to strike, to draw fresh blood, to finally write the masterpiece whose possibility and potential gnawed at the gnarled roots of my soul, even while I mocked the hope and set it on a realistic table to see its worried corners and haunted dents. My experience, I said to myself, in all its mortifying banality, would serve me now. How, I wasn't so sure. But it seemed to me that experience was like a landscape; that the sun shone on it and the moon flowed down it like anything else, and it was up to me to capture those moments when something interesting happened, when the flowers bloomed or the tulips cracked.

So then and there, I wrote down the first words, the unremarkable, terrible words. These words were profoundly un-sublime. They were mired in the juice of the mundane, fairly squeaking with a lack of originality. I will not repeat them here, but suffice it to say they were mawkish and uninspired, which I found confusing, for the fit that produced them seemed to me then to be very inspired, somehow forceful and effervescent.

Analysis

Older readers of this book may remember *The Honeymooners*, and Ed Norton, Ralph Kramden (Jackie Gleason)'s sidekick, the vest-and-tee-shirt wearing municipal sewer employee played to a fare-thee-well by Art Carney. In one of his better schticks, Norton would confront some trivial undertaking with extravagant overtures, rolling up his sleeves, loosening his shoulders, licking his lips, approaching the task like a pool player trying for a three-ball shot the hard way, until at last a frustrated Ralph would bellow, "Will you cut that out!"

Reading this ornately empty opening, I feel a bit like Ralph Kramden, or—to borrow another analogy, this one from Hollywood—like Dorothy confronting the man she thinks is *The Wizard of Oz*, when in fact she's confronting a sham operated by a humbug.

In *The Wizard of Oz* the illusion is achieved via smoke, flames, a thunderous basso profundo, and 1939 cinema's equivalent of a hologram. In this opening it's obtained through language as oozing and pungent ("gnawed at the gnarled roots of my soul," "a landscape that the sun shined on," "juice of the mundane") as an overripe camembert, language that doesn't convey content so much as it camouflages and conceals a lack thereof.

In the absence of a story, we get a narrator narrating—rolling up his sleeves, clearing his throat, wetting his lips and rubbing his hands together ("Will you cut that out!"). It's all wind-up with no pitch. The prose, though metaphorically overripe, is amusing. A strong voice is achieved, but in service of what?

This first page reminds me of another:

"Listen to me. I will tell you the truth about a man's life. I will tell you the truth about his love for women. That he never hates them. Already you think I'm on the wrong track. Stay with me. Really—I'm a master of magic.

"Do you believe a man can truly love a woman and constantly betray her? Never mind physically, but betray her in his mind, in the very 'poetry of his soul.' Well, it's not easy, but men do it all the time.

"Do you want to know how women can love you, feed you that love deliberately to poison your body and mind simply to destroy you? And out of passionate love choose not to love you anymore? And at the same time dizzy you with an idiot's ecstasy? Impossible? That's the easy part.

"But don't run away. This is not a love story.

"I will make you feel the painful beauty of a child, the animal hominess of the adolescent male, the yearning suicidal moodiness of the young female. And then (here's the hard part) show you how time turns man and woman around full circle, exchanged in body and soul.

"And then of course there is TRUE LOVE. Don't go away! It exists or I will make it exist. I'm not a master of magic for nothing. Is it worth what it cost? And how about sexual fidelity? Does it work? Is it love? Is it even human, that perverse passion to be with only one person? And if it doesn't work, do you still get a bonus for trying? Can it work both ways? Of course not, that's easy. And yet—"

The more this narrator of Mario Puzo's *Fools Die* exhorts me to "stay with [him]," to not "run away," the more inclined I am to head for the hills. That the author's earlier novel was the mega-bestselling *The Godfather* changes nothing. Like the first page under analysis, this one is all foam and no beer. Both narrators have what in the theater is called *stage presence* (picture Orson Welles stepping out of a Viennese shadow in *The Third Man*, or Vincent Price peeking out from behind a velvet curtain with raised eyebrow). All both narrators need is a good story to tell. Of that—alas—both of these first pages offer scant evidence.

It would help to know what's at stake for the protagonist of our first page as he prepares to pen her or his masterpiece. Supposing he or she can't write it—or writes it only to be told that it's anything but a masterpiece? Clearly it matters to this person. The question is: what would make it matter to *us*?

Not that sleeve rolling can never be effective. Remember the opening of *The Crimson Petal and the White*?

> Watch your step. Keep your wits about you; you will need them. This city I am bringing you to is vast and intricate, and you have not been here before. You may imagine, from other stories you've read, that you know it well, but those stories flattered you, welcoming you as a friend, treating you as if you belonged. The truth is that you are an alien from another time and place altogether.

Here's another familiar bit of sleeve-rolling that works:

> If you really want to hear about it, the first thing you'll probably want to know is where I was born, and what my lousy childhood was like, and how my parents were occupied and all before they had me, and all that David Copperfield kind of crap, but I don't feel like going into it, if you want to know the truth.

From there, having acquainted us with his attitude, within a sentence or two, Salinger's Holden Caulfield gets his story going ("I'll just tell you about this madman stuff that happened to me around last Christmas"). One tip about effective sleeve-rolling: a little goes a long way.

Your Turn

Draft a first page in which the narrator speaks directly to us about the story he or she is about to tell. Make it matter to us that the story gets told. Don't just make vague promises. Give us a good reason to keep reading.

16. Strawberry Fields

(Starting Off with a Dream)

It was a lonely sound. A sad lament in the early morning. It was the quivering, somber sound of a wind organ. At least that's what it sounded like to me. A man with a blue voice was singing and the quiet drumming followed. Plodding lethargically, and vacant ... and a slow jangly guitar. The day was cloudy and grey, and there I was, in a bright sliver of sun, peeking through the clouds. I had no idea where I was, but I wasn't scared. All around me were odd flowers. Startling rich nonagons, bright with color. Searing red, blazing yellow and lavish blue. I wanted to ask, "Why so sad?" but I couldn't. I opened my mouth to speak and nothing came out. The man with the blue voice sang these words, "nothing is real." How can that be? Nearby, a herd of horses escaped from a carousel, and headed towards a convertible train. I hopped on, and the sadness went away. The music of a backwards calliope accompanied the ride while hurtling through rolling hills, on loops and curls, like a roller coaster. The train blew its whistle to alert the horses. But the whistle was more like a siren not intended to warn, but to delight. The wind was blow-ing through my hair and I was smiling so big, my face hurt. It wasn't a dream. I had been invited to this place through a song playing on the radio. I was really there, I went to Strawberry Fields.

I opened my eyes and I was in my bedroom lying in my bed. The radio next to my bed was playing, softly. My mother gave me the radio, because she knew it would help me sleep, and I was permitted to have it on through the night as long as it wasn't too loud.

Analysis

Two of the most common admonitions delivered to fiction writers are 1) Never begin a story with a character getting out of bed; and 2) Never write, "And then she/he woke up" (or the equivalent).

As with all rules, not only can these two be broken, but we can leave it to a genius to break them brilliantly. "When Gregor Samsa woke one morning from uneasy dreams, he found himself transformed in his bed into a giant beetle." With that first sentence of "The Metamorphosis," Kafka strikes a definitive blow not only against both rules, but against realism, establishing a parallel universe in which such things happen. No explanations; take it or leave it.

Similarly, in what has been credited as the world's shortest story, Augusto Monterroso signs the death notices of rules 1 and 2. Here are all seven words of "El Dinosaurio," or "The Dinosaur":

> *Cuando despertó, el dinosaurio todavía estaba allí.*
> (When he awoke, the dinosaur was still there.)

As with "El Dinosaurio," this first page gives us a protagonist waking up from a dream, but instead of a dinosaur, what's "still there" are the haunting strains of John Lennon's most famous song, "Strawberry Fields Forever," playing softly on the radio next to the narrator's bed. In her music-inspired dream, the narrator is transported to a place where "nothing is real," a realm of "odd flowers" in blazing, searing color, of horses "escaped from a carousel" hurtling toward a train "to the music of a backwards calliope."

Dreams have their own logic, one that doesn't play by the rules and is therefore hard to argue with. The same can be said of the best fiction: it makes its own rules by spinning (in John Gardner's words) a "vivid and continuous dream."[3] And since a work of fiction is already its own dream, reading about a fictional dream puts us at a two-step remove from our own lives. It's like kissing through *two* screen doors.

That said, dreams have played crucial roles in literature. Without Scrooge's nightmare, Dickens could hardly have written *A Christmas Carol.* Before he murders the pawnbroker, in a dream symbolizing the soul's dual nature, torn between bloodlust and compassion, *Crime and Punishment*'s Raskolnikov revisits a time when as a boy he watched a group of peasants beat an old horse to death. And what is Alice's looking glass but a doorway to her dreams? As Francine Prose writes in "Chasing the White Rabbit," her fine essay on fictional dreams:

> Literature is full of dreams that we remember more clearly than our own. Jacob's ladder of angels. Joseph saving Egypt and himself by interpreting the Pharaoh's vision of the seven fat and lean cows. The dreams in Shakespeare's plays range as widely as our own, and the evil are often punished in their sleep before they pay for their crimes in life.

---

3   *On Becoming a Novelist.*

And who says good stories can't start with dreams? Tell that to Daphne du Maurier, whose most famous novel, *Rebecca*, starts:

> Last night I dreamt I went to Manderley again. It seemed to me I stood by the iron gate leading to the drive, and for a while I could not enter, for the way was barred to me. There was a padlock and a chain upon the gate. I called in my dream to the lodge-keeper, and had no answer, and peering closer through the rusted spokes of the gate I saw that the lodge was uninhabited.

The problem with dreams is that, translated into lucid, rational prose, they often sound artificial. Whatever "stuff" dreams are made of, words aren't it. As Francine Prose goes on to say in the same essay: "What's [hard] to recreate on the page is anything remotely resembling the experience of actually dreaming, with all the structural and narrative complexities involved, the leaps, contradictions, and improbable elements." This may be why poets write the best dreams: they're better at making those improbable leaps.

But a bigger problem with fictional dreams is that they ask us to invest emotionally in an experience only to have that investment rendered null and void when it turns out not to have been—by waking standards, anyway—"real." Just as in life I tend to grow restless when someone buttonholes me with their dream, whenever I come upon a dream in a novel or story I read it with my emotions in check. Heck, it's just a dream.

On the other hand, if the dream presents itself as real (as this one does) and I invest in it accordingly only to learn that it never *really* happened, like any bait-and-switch victim I feel cheated. Depending on how much I invested, I may want to strangle the author. Here the dream itself is quite well rendered, replete with the sorts of sensuous, specific details that make for a vivid fictional experience (the "quivering" wind organ; the man who sings in a "blue" voice, those escaped carousel horses hurtling over hills). Though vivid, it's also rife with the jump cuts and non sequiturs that characterize real dreams. So I can't help feeling disappointed when I learn that, as the song says, "nothing is real." There are no carousel horses; there is no "convertible train" (whatever that is). It was all just a dream prompted by a song playing on a radio.

Maybe the dream has symbolic import; maybe it will resonate and/or recur throughout the rest of the story, thus earning back my initial investment. I hope so. I hope, too, that whatever story follows, this dream is the best place to enter it. Perhaps the point of the dream—and the radio that (softly) plays the song that inspires it—is to underscore the protagonist's fear of the dark and—possibly—of the dreams she'd been having, not good dreams like this one, but nightmares that scared her so much she was afraid to sleep. How else explain a mother letting her child play the radio all night long? Raising the possibly pertinent question: *What happened to this kid?*

But if the dream was just this author's carnival barker way of luring us into her fictional world, I don't know about you, but I'll want my emotional deposit back.

Your Turn

Start a story with a dream. Do it so we invest not only in the dream, but in the dreamer, and in the story that the dream somehow portends.

C. Plot/Suspense

IN THE LAST SECTION I DISTINGUISHED *PLOT* FROM *STRUCTURE*, with plot defined as the series of causally related events that make up a story, and structure as the order in which those events are related. Plot is a matter of substance, structure a matter of form. They can be discussed separately, but they can't be separated.

Many attempts have been made at formulating or providing authors with a recipe for plot, including this popular ABC formula (credited to both Anne Lamott and Alice Adams, though I suspect it preceded them both):

> **A**ction
> **B**ackground
> **C**onflict or Crisis
> **C**limax
> **D**evelopment
> **D**enouement
> **E**nding

However memorable and neat, the formula fits most stories only insofar as its ingredients are in unspecified quantities and can be combined in any order. In other words, it's pretty useless.

Though there's no one-size-fits-all formula for plot, plots may be broken down into two varieties: Plot A and Plot B. With Plot A, a character's status-quo condition of discontent (Melvin is lonesome) is challenged when opportunity presents itself (Melvin meets Doris). With Plot B, a character's status-quo contentment (Melvin enjoys evenings of quiet classical music) meets with an obstacle or an irritant (a rap DJ moves into the apartment below his).

With most novels and even most stories, Plots A and B do a sort of opportunity/irritant tango with each other, with opportunity leading to irritant (the lover met at the coffee shop turns out to be a serial killer), and irritant leading to opportunity, and so on.

Plot is what generates *suspense*, i.e., the itch to learn answers to questions raised by what we've read—questions that keep us reading to gain answers. Like plot, suspense also takes two forms: *true suspense* and *false suspense*. But unlike Plot A and Plot B, each of which is equally desirable, false suspense is, as we'll see, a poor substitute for the genuine article.

17. A Stubbed Toe in the Library

(Plots A & B, Inciting Incident / Retrospective Narrative)

New Haven, October 1952

When I was a boy I used to wake up thinking today could be the day when everything changes. When something miraculous happens. What it would be I couldn't articulate but I knew it would catapult me from the life I had into the one I was destined for. Everything I wanted would be mine for the asking. Power, fame, riches and glory would fall glittering from the sky like a meteor shower. After thirty-five years of waiting, some part of me still hasn't given up.

But a day that began with a two-hour commute from New York to New Haven in a rocking overheated carriage that smelt of damp overcoats and inadequately deodorized armpits wasn't one that augured well for miracles. And now, second in line at the desk fronting Yale University's Rare Books and Documents Reading Room, I'd begun to think the only miracle coming my way might actually be getting inside the Reading Room. My field of vision was filled by the bearlike back of the patron in front of me. Whoever he was addressing, presumably the librarian, was totally obscured by his linebacker shoulders canted at an angle that suggested a head-on tackle.

"I'm asking you to look again. Is that so hard?" The voice matched the posture, belligerent, boorish.

"I'm sorry sir. I've checked and rechecked but I can't find any record of your request. If you'd just like to step over there...." A pale long-fingered hand emerged from behind his right shoulder and pointed to a desk against the wall, "and fill in another request form, I'll be happy to...."

"Fuck that," came the reply and the shoulders straightened. "I've got better things to do. I've got a dissertation to write, lady. If you even know what that is." With the snort of an aroused bovine, he thrust into reverse, rammed into me and planted the Cuban heel of his right size twelve solidly on my toe.

Analysis

On this first page we are treated to a sly blend of Plots A and B, with the nameless first-person protagonist reaching all the way back to 1952 to tell us of a day in his life that started out less than auspiciously, first with a damp, "inadequately deodorized" train ride from New York to New Haven, and then with a fellow library patron stepping on his toe. Neither of those events would seem to suggest "opportunity presenting itself," or Plot A; if anything, they land us in Plot B territory.

But wait: what about that first paragraph—those devoutly wished-for miracles falling "glittering like a meteor shower" from the sky? Thanks to that opening paragraph, by frontloading our expectations with miracles, or anyway the hope for them, the narrator performs a kind of alchemy whereby smelly armpits and stubbed toes become the stuff of dreams. We know—anyway we're given good reason to believe—that somehow or other this will turn out to be a "miraculous" day in the narrator's life. And so before our very eyes Plots A and B are joined in matrimony. Which isn't to say that they are going to live happily ever after. However strong it may be, our belief in miracles doesn't extend to them lasting forever. Still, we sense that this rude snorting bear who has injured our narrator's toe will be important to him and to his story, that he'll play—if not the lead—a key role in this miracle in the making.

As inciting incidents go, a stubbed toe may seem like a paltry event with which to launch a whole novel. Yet literature offers many examples of trivial events having epic consequences. *Appointment in Samara*, John O'Hara's most famous novel, owes much if not all of its plot to a single fateful act: the moment when Julian English, the protagonist and owner of a used Cadillac dealership, throws a highball in the face of one Harry Reilly, a major investor in his business.

Similarly, were it not for an errant snowball, there would be no Deptford Trilogy, Robertson Davies's novel sequence set in a fictional Ontario village. Instead of it striking its intended pubescent target, the snowball hits a pregnant woman, sending her into premature labor and precipitating a series of mostly tragic events. That incident opens *Fifth Business*, the first novel of the trilogy. As with the opening page in question, it, too, plants us firmly in a particular year:

> My lifelong involvement with Mrs. Dempster began at 8 o'clock pm on the 27th of December, 1908, at which time I was ten years and seven months old.

The whole plot of Paula Fox's 1970 novel *Desperate Characters*, the story of an upper-middle-class couple living in a Brooklyn brownstone in the 1960s, is set in motion when Sophie Brentwood is bitten by a cat—an innocuous event, it would seem, but one from which Fox extracts a grippingly persuasive portrait of a white, privileged, middle-aged couple whose hermetically sealed existence succumbs to the pressures of change.

More typically, stories whose openings catapult us into the past are apt to land us at the brink of a momentous event. From *Endless Love*, by Scott Spencer:

> When I was seventeen and in full obedience to my heart's most urgent commands, I stepped far from the pathway of normal life and in a moment's time ruined everything I loved—I loved so deeply, and when the love was interrupted, when the incorporeal body of love shrank back in terror and my own body was locked away, it was hard for others to believe that a life so new could suffer so irrevocably. But now, years have passed and the night of August 12, 1967, still divides my life.

Apart from being well strategized, this first page is also well written. From its yearning first paragraph through those odoriferous commuter armpits through its rendering of the bear-like, boorish, toe-stomping library patron, it invests us vividly in its narrator's world. (That the Rare Books bear metamorphoses into a linebacker and subsequently into a bovine we might take issue with, but we would be nitpicking.)

Given this opening page, I would keep reading.

Your Turn

Draft or revise two different openings. In the first opening, engage an A plot (an unhappy or dissatisfied character presented with an opportunity). In the second opening, engage a B plot (content character encounter an irritant or obstacle).

18. Clouds Across the Moon

(False Suspense / Trusting Your Narrator / Prologues)

Prologue:

The report read, "August 20, mid-afternoon. River Road. Medium pony attacked, now deceased. Two goats gored and gutted, deceased. Owner reported sighting of a large black mammal, possibly feline."

August 20, 11 pm

The clouds rolled across the moon, making it intermittently dark and light. Douglas Travis waited, hidden by the trees. He looked around, listening to the eerie silence, and shuffled his feet on the ground.

Leaves rustled and he heard the snap of dry branches. Footsteps fell from behind him approaching fast. As the clouds cleared and the moon shone bright, he caught a flicker of a shadow and turned.

No one there. He squirmed and looked at his phone for messages for the ninth time. Shaking his head in frustration he turned on his heels to leave, only to face the figure in the black slicker.

"What took you so long? I've been waiting. Did you bring it?" Douglas said, nervous. "Never mind, this ain't right. I changed my mind," he continued, looking down at the ground.

When he looked up, the figure was holding a syringe.

"Whoa, that's not what I ...," Douglas said taking a step back. "Wait—I'm going to call my mom." He held up his phone.

The assailant plunged the needle into the boy's neck. Douglas Travis jerked backward and slammed against a tree, fighting against the branches that seemed to try and catch him in a web of their grasp.

The boy was beginning to turn a bluish color, snorting sounds exploded from his mouth. The figure in the black slicker fled through the woods while the boy made a desperate clutch for his cellphone.

Ashen and weak with barely a pulse, he had meant to push the keypad to dial for help, but pushed the button for the camera instead, and began filming his last breath while catching a distant fleeing shadow. Other eyes then glowed in the dark night.

Analysis

We read fiction largely to learn two things: 1) what has happened, and 2) what's going to happen next. Question 2 is the one raised by the condition called *suspense*, the state of anxiety produced by uncertainty. In real life, suspense is often unpleasant. In a work of fiction, however, it's both desirable and pleasurable. It causes a mental itch that can only be scratched by turning the page.

In my years of reading works in progress, I've identified two main kinds of suspense, the good kind and the not-so-good kind. The good kind (true suspense) is the kind of suspense that raises the question, "What's going to happen next?" and arises organically and authentically from characters and their actions as conveyed to us through a firmly established, consistent viewpoint. The other kind of suspense I call "false suspense": suspense generated by an author who, intentionally or otherwise, withholds information.

On this first page of a mystery novel the author generates both kinds of suspense.

Putting the police report paragraph aside, on a quick first read the rest of this page goes down well. The writing is sensuous, engaging our eyes first (those clouds rolling across the moon, painting the scene in noir shadows and light), then our ears (rustling leaves, snaps of dry branches). True, the author might have appealed to other senses as well (the musty forest smell, its chilled dankness), but two out of five isn't bad. And no one can argue that the scene lacks mystery, surprise, or suspense. Indeed, this first page packs plenty of all three into a very small space.

But with my second closer reading a nagging suspicion is confirmed: namely, that this skillful author has subverted her narrator and imposed her own cherry-picked view of things, one that disengages me from her protagonist's perceptions and, as a result, from the fictional world that I had inhabited through his perceptions.

This opening page has no consistent narrator, no clear point of view. How can that be?

Let's read it closely, starting with the sentence "The clouds rolled across the moon, making it intermittently dark and light." So far the ostensible point of view is neutral or objective, with the experience belonging to no one (or to the clouds). Presented as the character's experience, the sentence might be combined with the next to read, "Hidden behind trees, Douglas Travis watched as clouds rolled over the moon, casting the forest into alternating shadow and light." As for "Douglas Travis waited, hidden by the trees," it, too, is neutral: it could be from Douglas's perspective, or not. However the sentence after that ("He looked around, listening to the eerie silence, and shuffled his feet on the ground.") plants us firmly in Douglas's sensibilities, as does the next paragraph, through Douglas's ears (the snap of branches) and his eyes (the flicker of a shadow).

Our engagement with Douglas's perspective continues with the next paragraph, up to the point where Douglas "face[s] the figure in the black slicker." Though it seems as if we're still sharing Douglas's perspective, we aren't, really. As we will soon discover, Douglas knows the identity of "the figure in the black slicker"; he may even know the man's name. Anyway, it's clear that Douglas and the man are familiar with each other and have arranged this meeting in the woods ("Did you bring it?"). Though these things obviously inform Douglas's perspective, they don't suit the author's wish to withhold said knowledge from us. Hence "the figure in the black slicker," and not "Joe" or "the man Douglas had spoken with two days earlier."

With the last two paragraphs, increasingly jarring shifts in perspective occur, with (in the third-to-last paragraph) Douglas referred to as "the boy"—a designation that carries an outsider's perspective, but not his, and then, in the penultimate paragraph, us watching "the boy" turn "a bluish color" (that he cannot see) and hearing the "snorting sounds [that] explode from his mouth." The last paragraph drops the boy's perspective entirely, with the scene's final moments relayed from a neutral, objective distance per the clouds in the first sentence. We've gone from Douglas's subjective experience to the objective experience of "the boy" to camera-like objectivity. At the moment when my investment in Douglas's subjective personal experience is greatest, I'm no longer in Douglas's shoes, but in the equivalent of a movie theater, watching him. Not only does this void my investment, it suggests that it wasn't sound to begin with: that there never was a clear point-of-view strategy to this scene, that what I've been getting all along isn't a genuine narrator with a firm perspective, but the author's point of view, omniscience by default. *Point of view is the difference between the author and the narrator.*

The last paragraph ("Ashen and weak with barely a pulse ...") tries to reclaim Douglas's perspective, but it does so too little and too late. By then we've already lost faith in that investment and sold our shares. In case we haven't, the last sentence ("Other eyes then glowed in the dark night")—which, given that Douglas is presumably dead, conveys an experience well beyond his grasp—puts the final nail in this narrator's coffin. Though it resembles a fictional experience, that last sentence is pure information doled out by an astute but obtrusive author.

Does point of view have to be consistent? Yes, which doesn't mean it can't move around; it can, consistently, through the authority of a narrator who, for whatever reason, is able to move from one perspective to another, and does so in ways that don't disorient and are never arbitrary. In any scene the perspective may change; but the *narrator* doesn't. When point-of-view problems occur, it's usually either a case of the author not having properly engaged a narrator, or failing to surrender fully to that narrator's authority. Writing teachers are known to say, "Trust the reader." I say, "Trust your *narrator*."

For comparison:

He ran in the early morning, floating like a specter amid the tall, wet pines of the Wisconsin forest. His thick hair curled from the mist. His lungs burned. His breath stank of beer and cigarettes. At the road, he stopped and swiped his glasses on his baggy sweatshirt. Late June, and the damp, cold spring had yet to give way to summer.

Three months earlier, Dave Cubiak had left Chicago, steering a small rental car north along the Lake Michigan shore, across the Illinois state line, and up two hundred miles to the Door County peninsula. He was forty-two, a former cop undone by the deaths of his wife and daughter, who had been killed in an accident he believed he could have prevented.

The move was supposed to be a fresh start.

Instead, it was a mistake.

Grief stricken, guilt ridden, and often drunk, Cubiak felt like a blot on the tourist landscape, a reclusive misfit among the friendly locals, people who waved even to strangers. He had committed to staying one year and had nine months to go. The time it took to grow a baby, to figure out what next.

Cubiak adjusted his glasses and bent over, his hands on his knees. For a moment, he thought of his mother and felt ashamed. He had failed her; he had failed everyone.

A sharp wail shattered the stillness, and through old habit Cubiak straightened, trying to pinpoint the source. A seagull wheeling over the bay? In his new job as park ranger, he'd sometimes watch the plump birds dive-bombing the water, full of avian bravado. Perhaps the sound had been made by a red fox on the prowl. Or the wind. Silence again. The forest gave away nothing.

The opening of Patricia Skalka's *Death Stalks Door County* has much in common with our first page, but with a crucial difference: It invests us swiftly by way of its narrator in a character's perspective. Having done so, it honors that investment. I'll leave it to you to discover what fate has in store for Mr. Cubiak, but to be sure this opening arouses suspense.

Were the first page written as deeply from Douglas's perspective it would shed some false suspense but gain more of the genuine article and intensify our sensory immersion in the scene.

Other notes: prologues are quaint and can be cheesy. The police report topping this one is effectively the prologue of a prologue, and makes for a stammered opening. I'd cut it and call the rest Chapter One, or make the report the prologue without calling it such.

Your Turn

Draft the opening of a horror or crime novel or a thriller in which a murder takes place. Write it two ways: from a neutral, objective perspective, and from the victim's perspective.

19. A Stranger Approaches

(False Suspense / Artificially Withheld Information)

Janice watched as he crossed the road, seemingly oblivious to the traffic. He leaned forward slightly, as if buffeted by a strong wind. She would recognize that stuttering gait anywhere, despite all the lost years. She'd told him to meet her at Jaipur's on Liverpool Street. No one knew her there. Her hand had trembled when she replaced the receiver.

His long arms hung slackly at his sides; the too-short sleeves of his tightly buttoned jacket exposing his bony wrists. Inches of vivid red sock above each dusty shoe, and her heart constricting with love and pain.

At the door his eyes darted across the tables and she saw relief flood his face when he saw her in the corner, arm raised. Unmindful of the chairs, he stumbled down the aisle and fell into her, his grip hard and hungry. His body shuddered as he held her. "Shhh. Shhhh," was all she trusted herself to say for now. They had attracted some attention, she saw over his shoulder. Some looked away when they caught her eye, others, unabashed, continued to stare. Finally he let her go.

"Hello, sis." An attempt at a smile.

"Hello, Luke," she greeted her brother.

The day before, she and Delilah had watched a wattlebird feeding on a grevillea bush in the garden. The cat had paused, mid-toilet, then slunk along the path, all senses alert. Kate had thrown a half-eaten mandarin at her.

"Honestly, Jan, why do you keep feeding that mangy cat? She's a killer and a tart."

She'd laughed: "You may be a tart but you're not a killer, are you, old girl?" She reached down to rub the tattered earlobes. Delilah had tricked three families in their street into thinking she belonged to them alone. It was only when the Kennedy children, three doors down, posted missing cat posters complete with photograph around the neighborhood that they discovered her duplicity.

"She's a survivor. Her own mistress. No one owns her. That's what I like about her."

Kate had rolled her eyes. "You two—made for each other."

Then the phone rang.

Analysis

In works by less experienced authors, suspense tends take one of two forms. The first kind of suspense, the good kind, raises questions such as the following:

What will happen to X when Y happens?

How will Character X solve Problem Y?

With the second type of suspense, the questions raised for the reader tend to fall more along the following lines:

Who is X?

What is Y?

Where is this?

What's going on?

What in blazes am I reading, and why am I reading it?

Both kinds of suspense create tension in the reader, but in the first case the tension created is desirable. Though eager to arrive at answers to the questions raised, the reader of a narrative that generates true suspense is willing to be teased, knowing that the answers will come in due time, and confident that when they do come they'll be satisfying and worth the wait. While waiting for answers to genuine suspense questions, readers are provided with enough answers to inhabit the world of the story, to fully appreciate and experience its characters, settings, events, moods, and themes.

With false suspense, many if not all of the virtues of true suspense are sacrificed. Instead, readers are treated to the extremely circumscribed and dubious thrill of wondering, for instance, in what part of the world a scene is taking place, and in what year, and who are the characters involved, what are their names, how old are they, how are they related to each other? Such questions are rotten fruits of the practice of withholding information: denying readers access to basic facts perfectly well known both to the writer and his characters.

That practice is hard at work in the opening scene of this novel, in which a woman named Janice watches a man cross a street toward her. From his "stuttering gait" to "the too-short sleeves of his tightly buttoned jacket, exposing his bony wrists" to the "inches of vivid red sock above each dusty shoe" the man is carefully and vividly rendered. Though syntactically awkward in places ("she saw relief flood his face when he saw her in the corner"), on the whole the prose is solid, the actions—albeit laced with melodrama—duly observed.

And yet because the scene raises and answers the wrong questions, because its author is bent on false rather than real suspense, it falls flat. Instead of asking, "Who is this strange, raggedy man walking toward the protagonist?" (a false suspense question, since the protagonist knows perfectly well who it is), we should be asking, "Why has this woman not seen her brother for so long? Why does he look like a bum? Why is he shuddering? And what brings them together now, after so many years?" These genuine questions—the answers to which may justify the rest of the novel—are undermined by that one question, "Who is he?"—a question with no relevance to the situation at hand, and one no sooner answered than the scene ends, as if it had nothing better to accomplish.

Why do writers generate false suspense? Possibly because, in reading works by other authors, they confuse real suspense with a state of confusion, or because even in the works of celebrated authors they encounter the same phenomenon. *Stephen King does it, why can't I?*

The more likely explanation is that they lack confidence in the ability of their material to generate its own true suspense, so they try to help it by capriciously withholding something here and there, in this case, the fact that the man crossing the street toward the woman is her brother.

Unfortunately, this explanation often points to a deeper problem, namely the reason why authors lack confidence in a story's ability to generate authentic suspense: they don't yet know, or aren't sure, where their stories are going, or if they have a story to tell.

I'm willing to give this author the benefit of the doubt. In fact, I'm sure that Janice and Luke have had an intriguing past, and are headed for an even more intriguing future. I just wish their creator were as confident of it as I am.

Your Turn

Revise this first page so it holds less false suspense, while true suspense is enhanced. Feel free to invent and supply any information needed.

Second prompt: look at one of your own first pages and see if you can identify any false suspense in it.

20. Conducting Olivia

(False Suspense / Grounding Scenes / Context /
Accident as Inciting Incident)

August, 2006 Henry winced and lowered his hands like a conductor shushing the strings.

"You're talking too loud."

Olivia adjusted the volume and continued to talk; it didn't really matter what about, most likely a new poem, or a story she was working on, something she'd read in the paper that got her blood boiling; or maybe a juicy bit of gossip she thought he'd appreciate.

She knew she should have stopped after the wincing, definitely after the shushing. But she hoped that if she told the story just right, he would laugh, see the irony, share her outrage or amusement. As always, she hoped this time would be different; that something other than pathology would engage him.

Olivia had been told by experts to bury this hope, that Henry would never enjoy the give and take of conversation again, even though he was quite talkative himself, but this felt too much like a death. She allowed herself to be sucked in, say too much. She did her best to speak in simple sentences, to keep herself from spinning the stories he once cherished, the sort of thing the rehab people routinely told families to avoid. She resented the notion that a successful patient was one whose partner suppressed her personality for the good of the other.

"Calm down," he said, glaring at her.

"I am calm," she said, "just animated."

"You do that to torture me."

"My talking is torture to you?"

"You know it is."

"Why don't I just control my heartbeat?"

She hadn't meant to snap at him; she never did. It wasn't his fault. Still.

As long as she could separate Henry from the angry stranger inhabiting him at times like this, she was okay. Brain injury didn't give a damn that it was a summer day and she wanted to enjoy a walk with her husband, hold hands, maybe stop somewhere nice for lunch, preferably al fresco. It didn't leap out of bed and bound into conversation, especially with a wife who'd been up for hours, a writer who lived to tell stories....

Analysis

This novel opening presents us with a man and a woman bickering. The man's name is Henry, the woman Olivia. Although eventually we learn that they are husband and wife, for the better part of this first page their relationship is mysterious, and we don't know in what setting their bickering occurs. Indoors, outdoors? At a restaurant? In their living or bedroom? What we do soon come to realize is that Olivia, whose perspective we share, is frustrated by her inability to converse as she used to with her husband, who—we also discover—has suffered brain damage.

Among a novelist's chief challenges is that of determining what information to supply when and where: how to balance the desire to arouse suspense with the need to prevent confusion. In this opening the balance tips toward confusion. The nature of the relationship, the setting, even the precise subject of the conversation (something to do with Olivia's writing) are withheld from us, as is the cause of Henry's disability, how long he has been ill, and how long he and Olivia have been together.

Our ability to invest emotionally in the given scene, to care about these people, depends on our being supplied with at least some of that context. Otherwise we're left with a couple of indeterminate conjugal status bickering in a vacuum owing largely to the husband's unspecified mental condition.

What information to supply, and when to supply it: it's a question not of plot, but of structure. Often as authors we *know* our plot; we've got all the causal-relation puzzle pieces. We just aren't sure how to put them together, in what order. Supply too much information too soon, and you destroy suspense. Supply too little and you create false suspense, i.e., confusion.

To put to rest some of the nagging false suspense questions raised by the given opening, and establish the necessary context for it, might it make sense to enter this story earlier, with the inciting incident, the event that resulted in the circumstance at the story's center—namely, the incident or accident that caused Henry's brain damage? Whether Henry's affliction was the result of a tumor, a stroke, a car or sporting accident, or something falling from the sky, doesn't matter. What matters is that we don't have a question hanging over us when that question isn't the point of the opening scene.

That's the strategy taken by Ann Packer in *The Dive from Clausen's Pier*, her bestseller about a woman's conflicted sense of responsibility toward her fiancé after he breaks his neck and becomes paralyzed as a result of diving off the titular pier into a too-shallow reservoir. Packer's novel begins, "When something terrible happens to someone else, people often use the word 'unbearable.'" Though the accident itself is alluded to rather than dramatized, by the end of the first page Michael is comatose in a hospital bed: the inciting incident has been supplied to us.

Tom McCarthy's *Remainder* likewise begins with an accident—indeed, one that alters his first-person protagonist's brain. It begins:

> About the accident itself I can say very little. Almost nothing. It involved something falling from the sky. Technology. Parts, bits. That's it, really: all I can divulge. Not much, I know.

Though skimpy on details (excusably if conveniently, since the protagonist's memory was affected), we have all the context necessary to proceed. Another novel that opens with memory and an accident is Stephen King's *Misery*.

> Memory was slow to return. At first there was only pain. The pain was total, everywhere, so that there was no room for memory.

Here, too, the accident that delivers author Paul Sheldon into the guest room (and the clutches) of a pathological fan is merely alluded to at first; we learn of the car accident only as Paul remembers it, through a fog of pain. If we're confused, it's Paul's confusion that we share. The suspense is organic: it isn't false; it's *real*. King gives us everything we need to inhabit the moment of that opening scene from the protagonist's point of view.

Ian McEwan's *Enduring Love* presents us with another writer (of scientific subjects) whose emotional equilibrium is shattered by an accident—in this case, a stranger's death in a freak hot-air balloon accident.

> The beginning is simple to mark. We were in sunlight under a turkey oak, partly protected from a strong, gusty wind. I was kneeling on the grass with a corkscrew in my hand, and Clarissa was passing me the bottle—a 1987 Daumas Gassac. This was the moment, this was the pinprick on the time map: I was stretching out my hand, and as the cool neck and the black foil touched my palm, we heard a man's shout. We turned to look across the field and saw the danger. Next thing, I was running toward it.

Though not a work of fiction, Floyd Skloot's *In the Shadow of Memory* recounts his experience of disability as the result of brain damage caused by a virus. Skloot wastes no time getting to his inciting incident:

I used to be able to think. My brain's circuits were all connected and I had spark, a quickness of mind that let me function well in the world. I could reason and total up numbers; I could find the right word, could hold a thought in mind, match faces with names, converse coherently in crowded hallways, learn new tasks. I had a memory and an intuition that I could trust.

All that changed when I contracted the virus that targeted my brain. More than a decade later, most of the damage is hidden.

Here, the author takes a less dramatic (scene-oriented) approach, with the point-of-view character confronting us directly, through exposition, with his situation. I can imagine a similar opening for the novel in question. But I can also imagine one in which, one way or another, we either *experience* or *learn of* the cause of Henry's brain injury. It might be a brief prologue or a new first chapter or even a sentence, one that sets up the given opening wherein we re-enter Henry and Olivia's marriage however many months or years following the event.

However different, with each of the above examples, directly or indirectly, via summary or scene, the novelist gives us the inciting incident, the event that caused the conditions that set the plot in motion, framing the question[s] that, presumably, the novel will go on to explore and possibly answer.

Instead the given opening frames the questions, "What's going on with this relationship? Why do these two people speak to each other this way?" By not mentioning Henry's brain injury until after we've spent some time with these characters, and keeping us in the dark as to its cause, the author directs our focus to the quality of this couple's relationship, its rhythms and nuances. It's as if we are being forced to listen to and learn a new language without knowing yet which country we've landed in. Disorienting or not, the approach is undeniably effective.

Whether or not we approve of the particular approach taken here, the writer's job remains the same: not to give answers, but to frame the question[s] correctly.

Your Turn

Draft the opening of a story or novel in which an accident of some sort functions as the inciting incident, with the main events of the story occurring *after* the accident. Example: Driving drunk one evening after a party, a young woman strikes a pedestrian—an old man—as he's crossing an intersection, blinding him (or causing him some other permanent injury or debility). The story is set weeks, months, or years after the incident, with the young woman visiting the old man. Note: in describing the accident, avoid sensationalism and sentimentality. Let bare facts do most of the work.

21. Taking the Yoke

(Foreshadowing / Implications vs. Statement)

September 1942

I crawled forward from the cargo hold after the plane stopped throwing us around. I made sure to find handholds at each point in case the plane jolted again. Only when I reached the cockpit did I pull myself upright, grabbing the doorframe for support.

Lieutenant Robert Jones, our pilot, smiled when he saw my reflection. "Glad you came up, Lieutenant Bowman. Sit there." He motioned to make sure I heard him over the grating noise. The engine must have swallowed a huge amount of sand as we went through the storm, which would explain why it was now so much louder than when we'd left Malta.

I twisted into the other seat, behind a half-wheel like the one he gripped. "Find the two ends of the seat belt and fasten it around you."

A belt held him to his seat. Ah, seat belt. I found the ends of mine and fitted the prong into an eyelet.

"Take the yoke."

"Yoke?"

"That half-wheel in front of you."

I threw up my left hand between us as if it could block his words. "But. But I can't fly an airplane." I shouted as loud as I could although he wasn't much more than a foot away. I wanted to be sure he heard my objection.

"Can you drive a car?"

"Well...." I didn't want to admit it, but I could hardly lie.

For some reason, he took that as a yes though few women had driven before the war. "The yoke moves in more directions than a steering wheel, but you'll just be keeping it steady. You do have to remember not to move it forward or back while you keep it steady side to side. I'll be here to make slight adjustments."

He took one hand off the yoke to hold up a swollen finger, looking at it accusingly as he continued to speak loudly. "I jammed my finger between two levers as I flew through the sandstorm. My own fault. I'll be fine, but I want to take my hands off the yoke for a few minutes. So, if you'll hold it."

I swallowed stomach acid, put my hands on the half-wheel in front of me, and tried to suppress my worry about making some mistake that would kill us all. I still believed—even though I was on my third flight within the last two days—that the laws of physics would reassert themselves at some point since these machines were obviously too heavy to really fly.

Analysis

In the cockpit of a cargo (?) plane flying from Malta to an unspecified destination, a passenger joins the pilot. The passenger is a woman; the pilot a man. Both are officers, lieutenants, in whose army we aren't told. The ride has been bumpy. One of the plane's engines (presumably it has several) grumbles loudly, having "swallowed a huge amount of sand" while flying through a sandstorm.

The time stamp tells us the world is at war. The Battle for Stalingrad has been joined. The US is poised to deploy its 1 Corps to the Pacific theater. Meanwhile, RAF bombers armed with incendiary bombs target Düsseldorf, Munich, and Saarbrücken. As these epic battles rage below, a smaller battle unfolds in the cockpit, with Lieutenant Bowman, the passenger, fighting her fear as Lieutenant Jones (the pilot) asks her to take the wheel—or the "yoke," as it's called.

This scene has its intrinsic drama. First of all, we are in an airplane during a war; that in itself is dramatic. That the ride has been (and will likely go on being) bumpy increases that drama, as does our knowing that at least one of the plane's engines is unhappy and complaining loudly. On top of these things—or riding along with them in that cockpit—is the drama of strangers, a man and a woman, meeting under strained and/or unusual circumstances. In Hollywood they call it the "meeting cute" scene: the scene in which the romantic leads first encounter each other. Since the late 1940s it has been a staple of romantic comedies.

To those who may object that the mere fact of two opposite-sexed people sharing the first scene of a novel (and a cockpit) doesn't, necessarily, imply a romantic future between them ... well, it does. Not that they will—necessarily—have a romantic relationship. But the possibility has been raised and can't be ignored. Given that, the connotations of the word "yoke" likewise can't be ignored. Though the applicable definition here is "an airplane control operating its elevators and ailerons," according to the *OED* it's also "something that connects two things or people, usually in a way that unfairly limits their freedom." The phrase "unequally yoked" suggests a team in which one ox is stronger than the other. The expression "to pass under a yoke" comes from the Latin *passum sub iugum*, to "pass under a beam," a ritual humiliation practiced by the ancient Romans on their enemies and from which we get the verb "to subjugate." Will our two lieutenants be yoked together in an uncomfortable or unequal relationship?

But supposing the purpose of this opening isn't to establish a romantic relationship, or a relationship of any kind, between its two characters? In that case I have to ask myself: what *is* its purpose? Why start this novel here?

Maybe its purpose is to *foreshadow* the novel's larger drama. Foreshadowing is a fairly common device in fiction and especially in novels. Sometimes it can be subtle, as in this bit of foreshadowing that comes in the first line of Hemingway's *A Farewell to Arms*:

The leaves fell early that year.

Hemingway's novel isn't about autumn or leaves. It's about war and death, specifically the death of nurse Catherine Barkley, who cares for Frederick Henry, the hero who has been injured in a mortar attack, only to die prematurely herself following the stillbirth of their child.

Foreshadowing can also be done less subtly but no less effectively, as in the opening of Sylvia Plath's *The Bell Jar*. It begins:

It was a queer, sultry summer, the summer they electrocuted the Rosenbergs, and I didn't know what I was doing in New York.

Before the novel ends, Esther Greenwood, its protagonist, will undergo electric shock therapy as part of her treatment for mental illness.

An even more pointed example of foreshadowing can be found in *Native Son*, Richard Wright's 1940 masterpiece about a young African American man doomed by destiny and circumstance. Wright's novel opens with the sound of an alarm clock, shortly after which a rat appears in the one-room home shared by Bigger and his family. The ensuing chaotic scene ends when Bigger, having chased and cornered the terrified rat, executes it with an iron skillet. In much the same way, Bigger Thomas will himself be chased, cornered, and sentenced to death.

With the opening in question, the "taking the yoke" scene may foreshadow the novel's main story, that of a woman officer who finds herself faced with challenges she never imagined or anticipated—as she never anticipated flying a plane. It would help, in that case, to be given at least a clue to the plane's destination and (possibly) the nature of Lieutenant Bowman's assignment.

Two other issues raised by this opening page. The first is *implication*. As a general rule with fiction—and with narrative writing of any kind—if a thing is implied, it's best not to state it. Trust the reader; let implication do its work. Here, in this scene, I find many moments when the author relinquishes that trust, starting with the dialogue, "Glad you came up, Lieutenant Bowman"—a line obviated by the pilot's smile. Other implied statements that could be cut: "I wanted to be sure he heard my objection"; "I didn't want to admit it"; "and tried to suppress my worry about making some mistake that would kill us all." Whenever we authors state things that are or might be implied, we rob our readers of an interactive moment, of the chance to infer those implications: among the great pleasures offered by good writing.

Lastly, this intriguing and otherwise nicely written opening suffers from the common ailment known as *backwards sentences*, sentences in which the emphasis is misplaced. Take the opening sentence here:

> I crawled forward from the cargo hold after the plane stopped throwing us around.

Nothing grammatically wrong with that sentence, but it puts the punch line first rather than saving it for last. Just as novels have plots, so do sentences. The climax of this one isn't—or shouldn't be—the turbulence coming to an end, but the protagonist's arrival in the cockpit.

> After the plane stopped throwing us around, I crawled forward from the cargo hold.

That sentence points toward, rather than away from, the scene that it heralds. There are more backward sentences to be found in this opening, but I'll let you find them.

Your Turn

Revise this first page so nothing is stated that is or can somehow be implied (through action, gestures, or by other means). While at it, look for and correct any backward sentences. Do the same for a page of your own or that of a fellow writer.

22. Hanging from a Cliff

(In Medias Res / *Premature Climax*)

Ruby strained to keep hold of the narrow ledge in the rock wall. Her fingertips scraped to bleeding, the tips of her shoes clinging to shallow crimps, she gripped the looming wall like a spandex spider. A sweating, grunting spandex spider.

"Sal, I'm kicking your ass when I get up there." Risking a glance to the top of the ridge, she growled at the wide grin waiting for her.

"Only a bit more. C'mon, you can do this," he said. "Hell, you've climbed taller men than this."

He laughed as a variety of muttered curses wafted up to him, and then readjusted his grip on the belay line leading to her harness. The thick treads on his boots gripped the sandy rock as he braced himself against the line tension. He adjusted a few inches, and then cursed aloud as his front foot slid, skimming through the loose grit and hitching up against a larger rock. Ruby yipped from over the cliff edge. He was stuck, groin muscle straining as he narrowly avoided tearing it in his wide straddle. A dark chuckle escaped from him as his arms and legs trembled with Ruby's weight in his awkward position.

"Hey, Rubes?" He wrapped the belay line around his arm again, yanking it up an inch behind his back. "You all right?"

"Shit," Ruby hissed. She'd dropped about a foot, and her fingers had slipped. The skin on the inside of her wrist throbbed raw as she scrabbled for purchase against the porous rock. She ground her teeth. Even breaths. Focus. She scanned the rock face above her and found her path. She bumped with her left hand, secured the hold, and then edged her feet into new jags, feeling her way between visual checks. Breathe. In, out. "Yeah. Peachy."

Her eyes narrowed, her vision centered. She no longer noticed the trickle of sweat between her breasts, the raw skin, the gnat cloud orbiting her head. Nothing mattered but the wall, and climbing it. Part of her mind noted the remaining distance, the slant of the sun, her growling stomach, but Ruby ignored it. Her body took over, seeking workable holds, lifting her own weight from crack to nub to grip. Sal egged her on, but his voice faded to the background. She heard nothing but her own breathing.

Analysis

Near the end of *North by Northwest*, Alfred Hitchcock's careening suspense comedy starring Cary Grant as Roger Thornhill, a divorced ad executive mistaken for a CIA counterespionage agent, Cary Grant grips Eva Marie Saint (another CIA plant) by the hand as she dangles off one of the faces of Mount Rushmore. The movie literally ends on a cliffhanger. (Spoiler alert: he not only rescues her, but vaults her straight into the arms of marital bliss in a train couchette.)

Instead of ending with a cliffhanger, this novel opens with one. Unlike Cary and Eva Marie (who've been pushed to the brink of Mount Rushmore by James Mason and his band of spy-thugs), Ruby and Sal are voluntary "cliff-danglers"; they climb rocks for fun, though with this cliff they've apparently met their match. As Ruby's "fingertips bleed" while she "strain[s] to keep hold of the narrow ledge," she looks up at her partner Sal, who adjusts the belaying rope and eggs her on, saying, "You've climbed taller men than this."

The mixture of comedy and suspense is something else this piece shares in common with Hitchcock's masterpiece. As they dangle in tandem from Thomas Jefferson's nose, Eva Marie Saint asks Cary Grant why his previous wives divorced him. He replies, "They said I led too dull a life." A similar repartee binds these two protagonists together as surely as their belaying line.

In *North by Northwest*, by the time we arrive at this blend of nail biting and quip tossing, we know the protagonists well enough to invest equally in both the suspense and the humor of their situation, to laugh out loud while biting our nails. Sal and Ruby, by contrast, are strangers to me. Their dangling from a cliff means no more or less than would the peril of any two perfect strangers. The same goes for their sarcastic banter.

I'm reminded of another movie, *Butch Cassidy & the Sundance Kid*, in which the two outlaws sling affectionate barbs at each other ("You just keep thinking, Butch. That's what you're good at."). With respect to their banter, thanks to the above-mentioned movies (and also to TV shows where paired sleuths share sarcastic repartee), the dynamic feels a bit too familiar. On the one hand, I don't know these people, really; on the other, I've seen and heard them a dozen times before. I know them as cardboard cutouts.

In the interest of grabbing the reader's attention, writers often choose to open with a sensationally dramatic scene from somewhere in the middle (*in medias res*) or near the end of the story. The trouble with that strategy is it can result in a *premature climax*, one for which we have not been sufficiently prepared, arrived at with little or no plot or character development. Though that climax may still deliver a dramatic jolt, and though we may care whether or not Ruby falls, we care less than we ought to.

Supposing we met these two characters earlier, under less dramatic circumstances, so we might get to know them a bit better first before they arrive at this dramatic summit?

However well done, affectionate repartee and authentic descriptions of rock climbing can't substitute for character development.

Your Turn

Draft an opening in which we first encounter the main character or characters at the figurative (or literal) summit of a climactic scene: a soldier facing a firing squad; an escaped prisoner or fleeing suspect at the point of capture; someone who has just been handed a fateful verdict or some other life-altering piece of information (example: they learn that the man they thought of as their father isn't; or that someone else—a total stranger or the next-door neighbor—*is*). Pay attention to small, authenticating details while avoiding clichés.

23. Romance & Fireworks

(False Suspense / Pointed First Sentence)

She stretched out lazy in the hot night. She wasn't particularly interested in the colorful display overhead, but her attention kept returning to the diffused splash of color reflecting on the water's surface. With each splash followed another loud BANG as the fireworks exploded in the night sky. She closed her eyes and couldn't remember a Fourth of July this humid for years. It was hard to tell the smoke of celebration from the haze of summer.

"Kate, catch," a voice called out. She didn't hesitate. Her instincts hadn't slowed much despite the weather. She nodded her thanks and held the cold can up to her forehead momentarily before opening it and drinking greedily. She'd have to be careful how many of these she drank, she reminded herself.

She returned her attention to her own private celebration, aware of the sounds and the laughter going on around her but lost in her own thoughts. One firework explosion dragged into the next one. She'd never been much of a fan of the Fourth. She wasn't even sure how Neil had convinced her to come out here. Her thoughts were interrupted with the presence of someone sitting down beside her. The warmth of another body so close felt like a personal intrusion. She wanted to move away but decided against it to avoid giving the wrong impression.

"Quite an impressive display," he said.

"Sure," she responded, but clearly she wasn't as impressed.

"Are you having a good time?"

She looked up into his face and saw the glow of blues and reds reflecting in glittery showers in his glasses. The brightness in contrast hid the expression in his eyes but she was fairly certain she knew what was going on behind the mirrored celebration. The vibration of her phone saved her from lying as she excused herself and got up to put distance between herself and Neil, probably much more than was necessary.

She sighed once she was satisfied that she'd allowed herself enough privacy and looked at the display number on the phone. It wasn't one that she recognized, but that wasn't important right now.

Analysis

The first page of a novel can and ideally should accomplish many things. It may tell us something of the nature and background of the characters whose dramas we'll experience with them, or it may describe the setting or settings in which those experiences are to occur and that may even give rise to those experiences (as John Steinbeck's dust bowl setting of *The Grapes of Wrath* gives rise to the Joads' and other sharecroppers' struggles).

A first page also forges a tacit understanding between reader and author as to how the material is to be presented, in what voice, by means of what technique and style. First person? Omniscient? Subjective? Epic or lyric? Based on a book or story's first page, the reader forms certain expectations. Assuming they are met, said expectations will give rise to consternation, disappointment, or—assuming the reader has an appetite for surprises (which appetite will likewise be whetted or not by the first paragraphs)—amusement.

Ideally, though, whatever else a first page accomplishes, it holds out the promise of a story. And since stories are always about one thing—people—a first page that successfully evokes character(s) goes a long way toward not only making, but keeping, that promise.

Here, the author introduces us to Kate, who, on a muggy Fourth of July evening, lies stretched out (on the grass, on a chaise lounge?), aware of but not all that interested in the fireworks exploding in the sky overhead, and whose mental reflections are rendered as splashes of color diffused over the surface of a body of water (lake? ocean? river?).

And though the fireworks and their reflections are lovingly and capably described, beyond her being jaded about both the Fourth of July and Neil (the young man watching them with her), what do we know or learn about Kate?

The answer to the question points to the weakness of this otherwise well written opening. The answer: very little. How old is Kate? What is her relation to Neil? Why—since she seems indifferent and even hostile to him—did she accept his invitation to the fireworks display? What town are we in, in what part of the country (we assume it's in the United States, since people don't celebrate July Fourth elsewhere). We learn more about the fireworks, the weather, and Kate's mood than about who these two people are and the nature of their relationship and situation. That Kate's feelings are expressed negatively, in terms of what *doesn't* preoccupy or interest her (fireworks; Neil), makes it all the harder to get a handle on her.

In the penultimate paragraph Kate's cellphone vibrates, rescuing Kate and her readers from this anti-scene that seems to fulfill no purpose other than to be interrupted. Possibly the phone call will present us with something more dramatic or to the point; perhaps the fireworks display is merely a setting for—and the set-up for—the phone call. In that case, the author might want to frontload the scene with this as a first sentence:

> They were watching the fireworks display when Kate's cellphone vibrated.

From there, the author might go on to establish that Kate's mind isn't on the fireworks or on the young man watching them with her, but on that phone call, one she's been longing for or dreading. By being even more specific, the first sentence might thrust us more deeply into the crux of a story ("Kate was watching the fireworks display with her fiancé when the casting director called.").

By means of a cunningly chosen first sentence, readers might enter this story with just the right expectations raised, with curiosity and tension, rather than with a series of bored sighs set against a backdrop of colorful explosions.

Your Turn

1. Starting with the sentence, "They were watching the fireworks display when Kate's cellphone vibrated," revise this opening following the suggestions provided in the analysis.

2. Introduce a pointed first sentence to a first page of your own or that of a fellow writer. Revise the rest of the page as necessary.

D. Characters

"SINCE THE NOVELIST IS HIMSELF A HUMAN BEING," WROTE E.M. Forster in *Aspects of the Novel*, "there is affinity between him and his subject matter which is absent in any other forms of art." The "subject matter" referred to here is *people*. Whether we're writing fiction or nonfiction, our task as storytellers is to render—or recreate—human experiences. Good stories are, first and foremost, about people.

Since stories are about people, evoking characters is high on, if not at the top of, our list of priorities. As storytellers, just about anything we do that evokes character in some way is almost certainly to the good. On the other hand, whatever we do that fails to evoke character in *any* way, that merely describes something or provides information without either imbuing that description or information with some quality or trace of human nature, without infusing it by one means or another (by *how* it's said, for instance) with some quality or aspect of character (wit, for instance), should be held suspect and either revised or given the axe.

When writing your stories, whatever else you're up to, get character into your sentences and onto your pages. Including—and maybe especially—your first page.

24. Meeting Ewan

(First Glimpse / Evoking Characters / Memoir)

I have always seen my life as a movie directed by Gus Van Sant, starring me as me, and characters of my picking to do my bidding throughout scene after scene after scene. Is it boring? That is why I have chosen Gus Van Sant to direct the happenings, so it doesn't become boring. A good director keeps things moving along plot-wise. Gus Van Sant as God in the movie that is my life. Would Matt Dillon be in it? I think that everyone has their *Own Private Matt Dillon* in their lives.

During the summer before my last year of graduate school in a small town in Illinois there wasn't much to do and even fewer people to do it with. During the summer is when this guy named Ewan began to latch onto me. He was at Quarter Round even more than me. I found Ewan to be quite annoying the first time I met him. He always played devil's advocate. And I hate people that do that. It's such a waste of conversation.

"Are you for or against pro-choice, Lilli?" he asked me one afternoon from where he sat at the counter of the coffee shop. There were only a few people in there that afternoon. Ewan at the counter, Mike Vonnegut playing chess with Thurston while Karl watched, and a very large freshman guy smoking a pipe on the front couch while reading a newspaper.

I looked up from the books and papers on the table where I was and said, "Huh?" I had been up to my ears in revolutions, peasant upheavals, and guerrilla warfare at the time and didn't hear what he said.

"Pro-choice, Lilli, or are you a Bible-beater?"

Analysis

If plot is the backbone of fiction, that which ignites fiction and gives it its forward movement, scenes are plot's vertebrae. A concatenation of causally related scenes adds up to a plot.

Beyond their technical function, scenes are what we're most likely to remember about a story and discuss, with enthusiasm or dismay, with others. Think of a memoir, novel, or story you loved and what you remember most about it, and odds are you'll remember a scene. I'm thinking of *Catch-22*, of the scene where Yossarian rips open wounded Snowden's flak vest to uncover the "secret" that Snowden has hidden and that spills out of him in the form of shredded intestines. Or the scene in *Anna Karenina* where Vronsky rips his shirt open. Or the scene in Toni Morrison's *Beloved* where Sethe kills her own baby.

If scenes are what we remember, characters are what make them memorable, explaining why, of all the types of scenes in stories, few are more memorable than first-glimpse scenes, in which key characters encounter each other for the very first time. Examples spring readily to mind. From *Moby Dick*, here is Ishmael's first encounter with Ahab:

> He looked like a man cut away from the stake, when the fire has over-runningly wasted all of the limbs without consuming them, or taking away one particle from their compacted aged robustness ... His bone-leg steadied in that hole; one arm elevated, and holding by a shroud; Captain Ahab stood erect, looking straight out beyond the ship's ever pitching prow.

Another first glimpse, from *Zorba the Greek* by Nikos Kazantzakis:

> [T]he stranger opened the door [of the cafe] with a determined thrust of his arm. He passed between the tables with a rapid, springy step, and stopped in front of me.
>
> "Traveling?" he asked. "Where to? Trusting to providence?"
>
> "I'm making for Crete. Why do you ask?"
>
> "Taking me with you?"
>
> I looked at him carefully. He had hollow cheeks, a strong jaw, prominent cheekbones, curly gray hair, bright, piercing eyes.
>
> "Why? What should I do with you?"
>
> He shrugged his shoulders. "Why! Why!" he exclaimed with disdain. "Can't a man do anything without a why? Just like that, because he wants to? Well, take me, shall we say, as a cook. I can make soups you've never heard or thought of...."

And another, this one from Elizabeth Smart's novel (extended prose poem?) *By Grand Central Station I Sat Down and Wept*, where the first glimpse is of the wife of the man with whom the narrator is hopelessly in love as the wife de-boards a bus:

But then it is her eyes that come forward out of the vulgar disembarkers to reassure me that the bus has not disgorged disaster: her eyes, soft as the newly-born, trusted as the untempted.

The first-glimpse scene offered in this author's first page presents us with Ewan, a fellow student at the narrator's university "in a small town in Illinois." By the end of this first page we know very little about Ewan. That he is a fellow student we can only assume, since we're not told as much; in fact we're hardly told anything. We don't know what he looks like, or how he walks, or—when he speaks—how he speaks. We're told that he's a "guy"—something we can surmise from his name, and that at some point he will "latch on" to the narrator, but that point exists in the future, and has no bearing here.

If Ewan emerges as a character, it's mainly through his dialogue. "Are you for or against pro-choice, Lilli?" he asks the narrator one afternoon as she sits at the counter of her favorite coffee shop. If these aren't Ewan's first words to her, they're close to being so; anyway, they successfully evoke a man who, to put it nicely, has little patience for decorum. Those less generous would call him tactless.

If only we could see Ewan as clearly as we hear him, the way we see Zorba strutting into that cafe. Since Ewan's words are what characterize him, my inclination would be to lead off with his in-your-face inquiry, and take it from there.

As for the first paragraph, I would cut it. It indulges the author's gratuitous wish that her novel were already a movie—and not just any movie, but one directed by Gus Van Sant. But this fantasy gives nothing to us readers: in fact it discourages us. Not only is the wish doomed; it's the wrong wish to hold out to lovers of fiction. If the novelist is really so intent on Gus Van Sant and Matt Dillon, she should be writing the screenplay.

Your Turn

You've already written a first-glimpse scene. Rewrite it so that at least one character is evoked strictly through action. Then rewrite it with the emphasis on the character's dialogue. In a third revision, combine action and dialogue with a physical description of the character.

25. Painting the Nude

(Stereotypes / Fictional Artists)

Here I was with my first naked woman ever, not a stitch on her. She kept squirming closer, and I kept jabbing paint into her eyes.

"Or maybe, 'Crippled Innocence?'" she suggested. "Something like that?"

"Uhhh, yeah...." My lips and jaw worked around for a while, but only that one word edged out. Trying to think of something charming or eloquent to say is like digging around through cooling street tar with a straw wrapper. In a borrowed white tux. I'm guaranteed to make a mess of things.

Well, at least I'd managed more than a grunt this time; I'd dredged up one whole word. Though maybe I should have said yes, rather than yeah. Or yes, ma'am.

No. Too formal. Yes, that is a patently good idea, Ma'am, although I generally don't assign titles to my various artistic renderings.

She flipped her hair away from the front of her shoulders. Freckles surfed the soft white swells of her shimmying breasts.

Stop! Don't look down there! I jerked my eyes back up.

Say something, moron, maybe she didn't notice.

Dang it; open your mouth. Say something. Anything. You know a ton of words; pick out any three. Everybody else can talk.

By the time I can think of anything to say, I've been rummaging around for days, and the other guy's gone home.

"Hello; are you in there?" she asked. "You don't talk much, do ya?"

I started crushing more paint into the canvas, shooting a quick sideways look at her nose. Then back at the portrait. I studied her neck. As I braked against letting my gaze drift any lower, my breath bottled up in my ears. I felt even more exposed than she was. Fully clothed, I felt like I was the one who was naked. Like she could see I had nothing on under my armor.

Analysis

I remember the first time I was confronted with a nude model. I was a freshman at the Pratt Institute, in Brooklyn, New York, nineteen years old. The drawing studio was on the top floor of an old brick building with arched windows. I stood behind my drawing horse—a wooden platform with a graded surface—with my newsprint pad ("penny paper," we called it) and charcoal sticks and pencils. This would have been in September, but I remember the studio being cold, perhaps because come November it would be an igloo, with us all huddled in winter coats and scarves, our breaths fogging an atmosphere already murky with charcoal dust. Ms. Helmann, our instructor, forbade us from drawing faces or genitals. "Distractions," she called them. "No lines," she used to say. "There are no lines in nature, just planes and shadows; a line is a concept. We're not here to draw concepts. You can do that at home."

One thing I remember about those drawing sessions: they were not the least bit sexy. No matter how good-looking the model was (and some of them were quite good-looking), after staring at them long enough through curtains of dust, with eyes aching, feet sore, and fingertips blackened with charcoal, you grew blind to abstract judgments like "beautiful" or "handsome" or "attractive," which was the point. You got so you only saw light and dark, shapes and values, negative and positive spaces. That these shifting patterns of light and dark added up to a beautiful woman was beside the point; anyway, you were too busy drawing to notice.

When writing about visual artists—what they do, and how they think while doing it—most writers get it all wrong. For one thing, they assume that the artist is consumed with the significance and meaning of his subject—maybe so, but not while he's working. While painting or drawing, he's concerned with one thing only: with *seeing*. He's measuring shapes, shadows, proportions. Labels don't exist. This is as true whether the subject is a haystack or the *Mona Lisa*.

Of course, the artist may be an amateur, or a charlatan. That is the conclusion pointed to by this first page, since first of all no serious artist tackles his very first nude in oil on canvas: he'd have sketched her first, many times. That he's already gotten around to "jabbing paint into her eyes" likewise raises suspicions. By then our tongue-tied Picasso would have had to at least sketch in the rest of her, giving him some time to calm down. As for his speechlessness, it seems as suspect as his art. To have talked her into posing for him in the first place, he must have a way with words. Or is his affliction triggered only by those "surfing" freckles?

Much that seems forced here might be alleviated given the proper context. But since we're given no context, we can't be blamed for imposing our own. Are they in his studio, or her boudoir? Is he a professional, or an imposter? Whose idea was it to paint her in the nude? Nor do we know, apart from his stupor and her freckles, who these two are, let alone what they mean to each other.

Imagine how much better all of this might have worked were we told from the start that he met her the week before at the Brass Jail, a local bar where, under the influence of one tequila shot too many, he passed himself off as a portrait artist (N.B. vocationally he installs mufflers for Meineke, but he has doodled on a napkin or two). Over a few more drinks he talked her—and himself—into a commission, for which in the intervening days he has invested a small fortune in paints, brushes, easel, etc., and even squeezed in an art lesson or two. And now—

Well, you get the idea. And you get the scene, too, which isn't so bad after all, now that it comes with some context.

Your Turn

Draft an opening scene involving an artist or writer at work. Provide authenticating details and avoid clichés. Note: though they may be frustrated, your artist should be competent.

26. A Balcony Overlooking the Bay

(Dramatized Routine / Fictional Artist)

The balcony of the small villa overlooked the undulating turquoise waters of the bay of Girona, the waves of the Spanish side of the Mediterranean rolling lightly and unfurling as they reached shore, frothy and shimmering with light that splashed against the houses and shops of the village by the sea.

Nicu Macek watched as a few people, probably visitors, walked the narrow black-railed promenade by the water, women with hands raised struggling to keep hair in place. He had long given up battling his, preferring to brush the wiry strands back and let the thickness keep it in place. It was still easier for a man to do this than a woman, he thought, recalling how impossible his daughter Ana had found it to tame the black kinks she lamented inheriting when the style was long and straight.

A light salt breeze blew off the water as Nicu wrapped another piece for the show at the Museo de Arte Contemporáneo in Barcelona, a coup for a Romanian in a region of the world known for its glassworks. Yes, he had something certain others didn't, an ingrained knowledge of what it meant to not have light like this and the kind of security that didn't dissipate with every wind. His critics, who were many and vocal, had begrudgingly begun saying as much. "His work does have a certain ethereal yet substantial quality—and he manages to use all that color in a way that doesn't mask flaws or degenerate into kitsch." Kitsch, in these circles, must be avoided like disease, though he still played with the glass in the studio, making objects for local shops, like the paperweights that still sold in bookstores though paper had been sentenced to a torturous and slow death.

Another gust whisked up from the shore, sprinkling particles of sand onto the russet tiles under the long table that was reserved for dinners with friends where he was typically banned from working. He usually did these chores in his studio, a comparatively short walk down the stone steps across the uneven cobbles of the alley to the hilltop.

Analysis

At the outdoor table of his Spanish villa overlooking a Mediterranean bay, a glass sculptor prepares his works for an important exhibition. Normally, he would perform such chores in his studio, but for reasons unstated, he's chosen to work outdoors, on a blustery day, and against the wishes of friends who have enjoined him not to use the table as a workspace.

There are some lovely qualities to this opening scene. As a lover of anything to do with the Mediterranean, I can't help being drawn into the setting. I'm also drawn to this artist by his Romanian background and the distinct nature of his art. In works of fiction I've encountered many artists working in oils or chiseling marble. Until now I've run into no glass sculptors.

The setting and the artist are engaging; the scene less so. In terms of action we have a man wrapping things while watching tourists walk along a windy promenade. The tourists' struggle to shield their hairdos from the wind reminds the protagonist of his daughter, Ana, and her struggle to "tame the black kinks of her hair"—a quest that Macek (who also has black kinky hair) gave up long ago. From there Macek's ruminations turn to past critical appraisals of his work. Ultimately the scene is more about a man's thoughts than about his wrapping or the people down in the street below. Indeed, until the third paragraph we don't even realize he's wrapping a sculpture. By then we've already formed an inaccurate image of a man standing idly on a balcony gathering in the view.

Which brings me to the biggest problem with this otherwise well-written opening: Mr. Macek's ruminations—assuming that they're really his ruminations and not the interjections of an intrusive author—feel unmotivated.

Let's start with the first rumination, the one about Macek's daughter and her struggles with her hair. What motivates it? True, a series of mental leaps might carry him from the people down in the street to his own "wiry strands" and from there to his daughter's hair, but even mentally this seems like a long way to travel for a man wrapping sculptures on a windy Spanish balcony for a major art exhibition. For me the rumination feels arbitrary—or worse, contrived for convenience, there for the author's sake, as a means to introduce to us the fact that the protagonist has a certain racial background as suggested by his hair.

In the third paragraph, as the artist wraps "another piece for the show at the Museo de Arte Contemporáneo in Barcelona" (so we're told, somewhat intrusively), we're treated to something like a Wikipedia entry summarizing past critical receptions of his artwork, including a snippet review. The contrast between this and the earlier stream-of-consciousness passage where the protagonist dwells on his daughter's kinks could not be greater. The first takes us into the character's psyche; the second is dryly objective. Yet both feel more convenient than organic. They exist to supply us with information.

The biggest question raised by this scene—and one not confronted by the character in his ruminations—is why, on this blustery day, does this man forsake the relative safety of his nearby studio and choose instead to wrap his sculpture on the "forbidden" dining table on his balcony? What urges him outdoors, or deters him from his studio? Surely there must be compelling reasons. These reasons point to an event that would seem to be fodder for his ruminations—more than his daughter's hair issues or past critical receptions of his work—and might form the spine of a stream-of-consciousness narrative.

As it so often does, the issue here comes down to point of view, to the extent to which an author has inhabited the perspective of her character through the agency of a close third-person narrator. Assuming that character's stream of consciousness has been faithfully and genuinely engaged, none of his thoughts would be out of bounds or off-limits. But between dipping faithfully into a character's stream of consciousness and taking advantage of it as a convenient excuse to supply information to the reader, there lies a world of difference. And in this opening scene certain information feels more convenient than genuine.

Were this scene written more thoroughly, deeply, genuinely, and consistently from the protagonist's point of view, his resistance to his studio might form the substance of the scene—which, as written, though set as carefully as a jewel, lacks a thematic center or focus.

Your Turn

Draft or revise an opening scene in which we confront a character at his or her place of work or business. Evoke both the setting in which the work is done, and the nature of the work (process). For instance: a jeweler repairing a watch in the back room of his store. Note: for the opening to work, it mustn't be static. We must encounter your character on a workday in which something important occurs (the jewelry store is robbed—but no; that's too predictable). The non-routine event need not be engaged on the first page. You just need to know what's going to happen.

27. An Opening in Search of Itself

(Unreliable Narrator / Mental Illness / Abstraction / Metaphors)

If I could know what I am, if I could see myself plainly, if there were a place that I could fit into like a bolt into a nut, if I wasn't on this knife not knowing if the knife could go right though me, slicing me in two, if only I were not standing on this cliff about to fall right off into the flames below, then perhaps I could feel that I fitted into my skin, filled the cavity of my skull with my brain, but I know that these ifs are not about to be turned into certainties, I am not about to be one thing or another, not about to be circling complete as a person. Christ, this is all too Kafka for me, seeing myself as a turtle or the famous cockroach, I have to put all this shit aside and think of normal, everyday things.

Matti lifted a saucer and turned it over to examine the base. Not bad. Doulton Stellite, a reasonable restaurant product. Before she got married, she had worked as a buyer in a restaurant supply wholesale warehouse and she knows her china, does Matti. She placed the cutlery in precise order and folded and unfolded her napkin, while a slight breeze teased the terrace tempting her to lift her face into it.

It's essential to present herself as especially elegant, chic, fashionable, sophisticated etc. for birthday lunches. Oh, God, her life is full of fucking clichés. Her butter-yellow silk suit glowed in the shadows as if her body was lit by a lamp inside it and for a change, her long, gold hair, just colored and streaked yesterday in a four-hour hair appointment....

Analysis

Within the eleven lines of its first paragraph, this opening scene presents readers with a mélange of no less than ten metaphors for the narrator's frustrated desire to belong fully to something, to "fit in." The writing is passionate, poetic, full of spit and vinegar—but what is it *for*?

"If I could see myself plainly," the narrator laments at the inception of this hyperextended metaphor, then proceeds to describe her spiritual condition in terms of a) a nut in a bolt, b) a knife blade, c) a cliff's edge (overlooking flames), d) an empty skull, and e) something that "circles." Having exhausted nearly every available metaphor, the narrator throws her hands in the air, declares the whole affair Kafkaesque, tosses two more metaphors our way (one reptilian, one insectile), then ditches the metaphor parade in favor of "normal, everyday" thoughts—something some readers will wish she had done so sooner.

As a nosedive into a neurotic narrator's distraught thoughts, there's something to be said for this opening with its manic energy. Who can read it and not think of this other tale told by a less-than-stable narrator?

True—nervous—very, very dreadfully nervous I had been and am; but why will you say that I am mad? The disease had sharpened my senses—not destroyed—not dulled them. Above all was the sense of hearing acute. I heard all things in the heaven and in the earth. I heard many things in hell. How, then, am I mad? Harken! And observe how healthily—how calmly I can tell you the whole story.

However, unlike the opening of Edgar Allan Poe's "A Tell-Tale Heart," which provides me with solid, concrete information ("Above all was the sense of hearing acute") and seems to me accurate and even reliable despite the narrator's unhinged state, I find the first page in question vague, abstract, and sentimental, brimming not only with mixed metaphors, but with feelings thrust at us with no basis, i.e., *emotion(s) in excess of experience*. Whatever else this befuddled opening achieves, it convinces me, if I need convincing, that this narrator can't see herself clearly. Which is probably the point. Still, even assuming the narrator is unreliable and this is the opening of an *unreliable narrative*, I need some measure of reliability, something solid to hold onto, not just a barrage of distraught metaphors.

I suspect that the real purpose served by this opening may be even more basic. Stated by means of another serial metaphor: it's to get the author's pen rolling, to blow some warmth onto the icy blank page, to get the narrative blood flowing. Others less charitably inclined will call it "throat clearing." In any case, for all its energy and passion, it should probably be cut, all of it. It's there for the author, not for the reader.

The real beginning starts with Matti inspecting a piece of restaurant china at an event, a birthday lunch. Perhaps she's an event planner of some kind. We don't know, but she has a vested professional interest in the affair at hand and its dinnerware. To be sure, she is dressed to the hilt in her suit that "glow[s] in [its] shadows as if her body was lit by a lamp inside it"—making me wonder how much it would glow were it exposed to full sunlight.

Here the writing is comprehensible and much more effective. Still, we don't quite know what's going on; we have to guess. And some information provided seems misplaced. Do we really need to know that, before she married, Matti worked as a buyer for a restaurant supply wholesaler? Maybe, but within the context of so much more that remains unknown, that bit of information seems more coy than generous, more like a tease than enlightenment. Most readers will prefer to know who Matti is and what she's doing, rather than who she was and what she did.

In the final paragraph, again the author seems to throw her hands in the air: "Oh, God, her life is full of fucking clichés"—a comment that doesn't seem to attach itself to anything, unless birthday lunches are a cliché, or butter-yellow suits, or certain types of restaurant china. But my guess is that the charge of "cliché" is a preemptive strike by the author against her material, as if by the end of this first page she's grown disenchanted and declares defeat even before the first battle lines have been drawn.

In each of the sections that pattern is repeated, with the author undertaking a bold initiative, then questioning it, then surrendering before the reader can engage in hostilities. This reads more like a talented author's exploratory draft than like a finished manuscript.

Your Turn

Draft the opening of a story told by a mentally disturbed narrator. Decide for yourself whether the narrator is reliable or not—but you must decide. Remember: an unreliable narrator isn't a narrator who knowingly or purposely distorts the truth or gets the facts wrong. On the contrary: he or she has command of all the facts. It's the narrator's sincere interpretation of the facts that isn't reliable.

28. Finding Jenny

*(Indolent Character / Mental Illness / Sensational
Event Conveyed by Torpid Scene)*

Somehow, when Robert heard the report on the eleven o'clock news he knew that they had found Jenny, even though the police had not yet identified the woman discovered in that motel room just outside Hemet. The newscaster recounted the circumstances with a touch of sadness in his voice, which made her barbiturate overdose tragic rather than tawdry. Robert imagined the rest: medication washed down with vodka, the bottle lying next to her on the bed, the remaining pills scattered across a knotty pine floor.

It had been a year since she had disappeared—for Robert, a year of feelings shut away like furniture crated in some dark, musty warehouse. He lay down on the couch, clutched a pillow to his chest and stared at the television screen, which minute by minute seemed to lose its authority, melting into a blur of images without connection to his life. The pungent smell of leftover Thai food—pineapple, shrimp and Massaman curry—drifted from cartons on the dinner table. *It couldn't be Jenny*, he told himself. The living room suddenly seemed too cold for April in Los Angeles. He felt he had to call the Hemet Police Department, to learn if they really had found his wife, but instead could only hug the pillow more tightly.

In the morning Robert Leonard Singer, Jr. knew he had to put on his navy wool suit, tie the tight Windsor knot in his tie and spend the day reviewing documents and depositions, all in the name of billable hours. He had dropped the *Junior* years ago, just after graduating from college, and now was Robert Leonard Singer, *Esquire*. The sound from the television became a low drone. Warmth diffused into his hands, his arms and legs, and for a minute the world receded into numbing silence.

He didn't know how long he had been asleep, but when he awoke to the chatter of a late-night talk show, Robert realized he was too tired to work. The papers he had intended to study would have to stay in their manila folders locked in his briefcase.

Analysis

While watching the evening news, a lawyer—Robert Leonard Singer, Esquire—learns of a woman found dead in her motel room, the apparent victim of a drug overdose. Authorities have yet to identify the body, but Robert thinks he knows who she is. In fact he's sure.

Her name is Jenny, and she disappeared a year before, "a year of feelings shut away like furniture crated in some dark, musty warehouse." From this we infer that Robert and Jenny were close—involved in a prolonged passionate affair, perhaps, or just a fling? At the next paragraph's end we learn that Jenny was his wife.

Whatever relationship Robert had with Jenny, we know that her disappearance—and now her apparent suicide—have both affected Robert deeply. Overcome by his emotions, or numbed by them, he collapses onto his sofa, hugging its pillow "tightly" as the evening news murmurs on and "the smell of leftover Thai" takeout food drifts his way from the dining table. Instead of attending to the depositions in his briefcase, Robert drifts off to sleep. The page ends with him waking "to the chatter of a late-night talk show," still in a torpid state and unable to work.

Though the events conveyed by this passage are sensational—a woman's unexplained disappearance, the sudden discovery of her body in a motel room, her apparent drug-overdose suicide—the opening scene itself is as torpid as its main character. Robert listens to the evening news, lies down on his sofa, and goes to sleep. That accurately summarizes the action here.

And though Robert's descent into indolence is, presumably, triggered by grief, one gets the feeling—I do, anyway—that on his best days Robert is not exactly a man of boundless energy (witness the takeout cartons on his dinner table). He seems to have been depressed long before he switched on the television news. The news of his missing wife's death plunges—if that's not too active a verb—Robert into ever-greater depths of indolence. The question is: how far did he have to drop? Measured on an emotional altitude meter, my guess is an ear-popping two-and-a-half feet.

Though not all that common, paralytically torpid characters can make for good fictional protagonists. Melville's Bartleby ("I would prefer not to") springs obviously to mind, as does Tom Sawyer, who gets Ben Rogers to white-wash the fence for him, and Jacob Horner, the apt-named protagonist of John Barth's second novel, *The End of the Road*, a character figuratively "cornered" by indecisiveness.[4] And let's not forget Hypnos, the god of Greek mythology, who, when not putting people to sleep, spends his time drowsing in a cave in the underworld. Perhaps the best example of an indolent hero is *Oblomov*, the protagonist of Ivan Goncharov's eponymous 1859 novel, about a young Russian nobleman so incapable of making decisions or taking any significant action he spends most of the novel getting from his bed to his chair. *Oblomov* begins:

> One morning, in a flat in one of the great buildings in Gorokliovaia Street, the population of which was sufficient to constitute that of a provincial town, there was lying in bed a gentleman named Ilya Ilyitch Oblomov. He was a fellow of a little over thirty, of medium height, and of pleasant exterior. Unfortunately, in his dark-grey eyes there was an absence of any definite idea, and in his other features a total lack of concentration. Suddenly a thought would wander across his face with the freedom of a bird, flutter for a moment in his eyes, settle on his half-opened lips, and remain momentarily lurking in the lines of his fore-head. Then it would disappear, and once more his face would glow with a radiant *insouciance* which extended even to his attitude and the folds of his night-robe.

Returning to our first page, Robert's emotional torpor goes beyond numb-ness into oblivion, to where, moments after learning of his wife's death, having made up his sluggish mind to call the authorities and verify things, his thoughts drift into getting dressed for work the next morning, and from there to tying "the tight Windsor knot on his tie and spend[ing] the day reviewing documents and depositions." From there his thoughts wander even farther afield of imme-diate circumstances, to ruminate upon his name and title, having recently shed the "Junior," replacing it with "Esquire."

What in blazes has any of this to do with the shocking news of his wife's dismal and unsuspected suicide? Nothing, which may be the point. We are, I take it, witnessing the full extent of a man's disconnection from his emotions. We're dealing with an emotionally unhinged character, with a man losing, or who has already lost, part of his sanity to grief.

Be that as it may, since Robert's feelings (along with that measure of his sanity) were already "shut away like furniture ... in a dark, musty warehouse,"

---

4   So indecisive is Jacob, he vacillates over his own name. "In a sense, my name is Jacob Horner." So he introduces himself in the novel's first sentence. A far cry indeed from "Call me Ishmael."

what we're met with here in this opening scene is the spectacle of his musty, crated feelings sprouting a fresh layer of dust, mold, and mildew. Even when the mold is fertilized by dramatic, sensational events, watching it grow isn't all that exciting.

I would suggest one of two alternatives: either an opening scene that finds the main character deep in his torpor, or one that confronts him with shocking, disturbing news. I would resist doing both things at once.

Your Turn

Draft your own opening of a story or novel featuring an epically indolent or indecisive character.

29. A Self-Conscious Queen

(Judgments, Labels, and Epithets / Dramatized Routine)

Often, during the transformation, the Lady Javana found herself considering the word "glamor." It was no wonder, she thought, as she sharpened an eyebrow pencil, or elbowed past another queen to peer in the mirror, that the word rhymed with "clamor." She had to plaster down those eyebrows with the glue stick, beat her face with the powder, chisel new features out of her face with foundation and blush. There was the brutal art of the tuck. Then she wrestled into her pads. Then the dress. Last the wig.

The Lady Javana—who spent most of her days as Joseph Ryan Gainer, library assistant—hated the tired metaphor of the caterpillar and the butterfly, but could not dispute its relevance. Because the holometabolism of the butterfly was a complex transition. It was sticky, confusing and savage.

Javana, whose job in the Bridgeport library's nonfiction room brought many science books through her hands, once looked "metamorphosis" up during her lunch break. She didn't eat that day. The self-mutilation that happened inside the chrysalis horrified her. Drag could be just as confusing, and just as painful. But the payoff? Sublime.

The Lipstick Lounge's dressing room was filled with queens. Queens. Javana smiled at herself in the mirror, straightened her wig, and dabbed the lipstick off her teeth. She had always been taken by the idea of being a queen. Not just a boy in a dress. Not a man. Not a woman. Not a female impersonator, because what female wears glitter on her eyelids, pink beehives and six-inch heels? But a *queen*.

She straightened her bodice and checked herself in the mirror. All was as it should be: Nose straight like a razor under tiers of caramel curls, angular face faceted like a....

Analysis

In the dressing room of the Lipstick Lounge, the Lady Javana "straighten[s] her wig" and "dab[s] the lipstick off her teeth." Lady Javana, we're informed, is neither a man nor a woman, nor "a boy in a dress" nor "a female impersonator": "What female wears glitter on her eyelids, pink beehives and six-inch heels?" (More than a few, actually, but never mind.)

No, in her own over-determined estimation, Lady Javana is a *queen*. I've italicized the word, since the author goes to such great lengths to emphasize it.

Rather than present us with a character, instead the bulk of this first page is taken up with a series of terms and metaphors by which Javana either identifies and labels herself, or that she refutes (Note: when someone is in drag, etiquette requires that they be referred to by the opposite pronoun, and so a woman in drag would be a "he," and a man in drag a "she"). What starts out promisingly as an evocative, concrete scene ("She had to plaster down those eyebrows with the glue stick, beat her face with the powder, chisel new features ... with foundation and blush") in which the particular (drag queen putting on makeup) stands for the general, breaks down into an exercise in denotation, such that, by the end of the page, what we've read feels more like a jacket blurb than a scene.

Too bad, since the writing is quite strong:

> Lady Javana—who spent most of her days as Joseph Ryan Gainer, library assistant—hated the tired metaphor of the caterpillar and the butterfly, but could not dispute its relevance. Because the holometabolism of the butterfly was a complex transition. It was sticky, confusing and savage.

As prose this can't be faulted, but the issue here isn't so much whether or not the metaphor of the caterpillar transforming into a butterfly aptly conveys the experience of a drag queen. The metaphor may or may not be apt; but the harping on it here conveys a self-consciousness that would seem to apply more to the author's fascination with his subject than to the character in question. Though hatched from its "self-mutilating" chrysalis, this butterfly never takes flight. Like a lepidopterist's specimen, instead it has been pinned to the page and pasted with labels.

Butterflies don't go around self-consciously inventorying their butterfly-ness. Nor do readers of fiction especially want labels, and if they do want them they prefer to supply their own. Nor do readers want judgments imposed by the author on a character or by characters on themselves. What readers want is experience evoked concretely through action or dialogue, or through a character's internal responses to particular events, challenges, and situations—illuminated, perhaps, by a sympathetic and/or wise narrator, and possibly by the character's own reflections, but not sewn up and boiled down into the shrunken heads of judgment and epithet.

Here, the only behavior exhibited aside from the application of lipstick and eye-glitter is the character's self-conscious pursuit of a label for him/herself. Even accepting that this pursuit is real—that is, belonging to the character and not to an author overly fixated on the presumed novelty of his subject—still, it's hard to imagine such self-conscious soul-searching taking place, as suggested here, on a regular basis for any duration. Surely this queen doesn't spend his/her days (or nights) mulling over what to call him or herself? If so, one wants to say to him/her, "Get over it, already."

What's sacrificed here for the sake of a story about someone "being a queen," is a better story about a unique human being—a librarian—who, apart from all the other qualities that render him unique, *happens to be* "a queen."

Your Turn

"Begin with an individual, and before you know it you find that you have created a type; begin with a type, and you find that you have created—nothing." With this opening sentence of F. Scott Fitzgerald's story "The Rich Boy" in mind, draft an opening in which you introduce us to a character who, though he or she clearly qualifies as a *type* (tweedy professor, gourmand, rock star, ambulance chaser, adventurer, preppie, pool shark, nerd … you get the idea), is also a unique individual.

30. Up a Tree

(Child's Perspective / Blunt Sentences)

1962

"Hey, do you like your mom?"

I was in my tree, the dogwood in the island of grass that divided Covewood Drive into two lanes. I climbed that tree nearly every day. Halfway up, on the perfect branch, the one where I could perch with my feet dangling free, steadying myself with the smaller branch just above, at perfect arm's length. From my tree I could keep an eye on everything that happened in my yard and most of the way down the street and still be alone.

But today Peggy was with me because she was staying with us for a few days. She was standing on the ground, trying to figure out how to get up into the tree. I waited and watched my mother weeding her rock garden, crouching and bending, then standing back to take a look.

"Of course," Peggy said. "I love my mommy. How do you do this?"

I sighed, because climbing a tree was so simple—you just did it—but I knew I would have to show her how, again. I dropped onto the solid ground, the shock of landing vibrating in my feet, traveling up my legs to settle just under my stomach. Landing was almost as good as climbing, a different kind of scary. Landing was solid and hurt my heels just a little. Climbing was fluttery.

"Look, it's easy. One hand here," my left hand wrapped onto the lowest branch, on the spot where it was almost smooth, where there were no hard buds to bite into my skin. "Hold on here and put your foot here," I said, my right foot pressed into the trunk of the tree, steadied by the fist-sized knot that my dad told me had tried to become a branch.

Analysis

From up in a dogwood tree a young girl or boy watches her or his mother weed a garden, while down on the ground below her or his less tree-worthy friend Peggy watches. Like the previous opening scene, with its grudgingly shared awarenesses and insights ("I sighed, because climbing a tree was so simple—you just did it—but I knew I would have to show her how, again.") this one also puts me in mind of Dan Pope's *In the Cherry Tree*—not just because of the tree, but since that book, too, does a superb job of rendering childhood on the verge of adolescence.

Pope's novel opens:

> Summer days began without a plan. You got up. You had a bowl of cereal. You went outside. A lawn mower hummed. Ducks passed overhead in perfect V formation like World War Two bombers. A dog barked, and another dog barked back. Somebody was hammering nails into a roof. Somebody was bouncing a basketball three streets away. You heard the echo, not the sound itself. A cat crept across the grass and disappeared beneath a hedge. It was hot. The sun was strong. The crickets made a seething noise. A sprinkler came on and made a quiet rain sound when the water hit the grass and then a louder rain sound when the water hit the street.

The effectiveness of Pope's rendering is achieved in large part through a style that leans heavily on blunt declarative sentences ("You got up."), sentences that echo the thudding rhythms of a grade school primer ("See Jane run."). By way of such artless sentences Pope's fictional world—one Baby Boomers will recognize immediately—declares itself to us with the stark immediacy of a series of street signs. *Caution: Children at Play.* No time for fancy wordplay or syntactical gymnastics, only what is—or what was: a world experienced almost exclusively through the senses by characters who, because they are still children, are natural sensualists.

The given opening page achieves a similar effect. The writing, though not as stylistically pointed or original, is assured; there are few wasted words, and the sentences offer syntactical variety without self-conscious effort ("Landing was almost as good as climbing, a different kind of scary."). One can quibble that the verb "to be" is overused—not, as Pope uses it, intentionally for its plodding, blunt-instrument rhythms, but simply through oversight. That's a nitpick.

I question beginning with a snatch of disembodied dialogue, a tactic that I seldom find agreeable, since it takes readers by surprise by withholding context and disorienting them. But to what end? I have no idea who is speaking, nor does the following paragraph answer the question. I have to read on to the next paragraph to encounter another character, and beyond that to find out who spoke that first line. Wouldn't it be as good or better to say up front, "From up in the tree I shouted down at Peggy, 'Do you like your mom?'"

The opening question is important. It points to the heart of this opening and probably of the story itself: the relationship of mothers to their children, and specifically of the tree-climbing first-person narrator's relationship with her or his mother. It's no coincidence that the story opens with the protagonist having gained the perspective offered by a vantage point high up in that tree. It reminds me of Nathaniel Hawthorne's brilliant sketch, "Sights from a Steeple." It begins, "So! I have climbed high, and my reward is small." Being high up off the ground gives us perspective, but it also cuts us off, alienates us, turns us into lonesome gods.

The question imbues this well rendered but rudimentary opening scene with the sense that all may not be sunshine and dogwood petals on Covewood Drive: this opening promises a story that unearths those implications. I would keep reading.

Your Turn

Draft a first-person, present-tense opening from a child's (age 12 or under) perspective in which the child-narrator describes her or his "secret place"—a closet, cave, crawlspace, cavern, forest grove, shelter, or landmark of some other kind shared with no one else or only with a very special friend or friends.

31. Mean December Wind

(Retrospective Narrator / Strong Verbs / Appealing to Senses)

They came to us with the mean December wind, three cars in all. We lived on a desolate country road where approaching sounds could be heard before things happened. There was the muffled rumble of their exhaust reverberating off mounds of snow, then the moaning of their engines. I rushed to the front living room window, pulled the drapery back, and pressed my nose to the pane. My breath fogged the glass and I could taste dust on my lips. Soon, boxed shadows appeared from around the bend. They turned into our long drive in a systematic order, each bumper connecting to the next. Their tires crunched the frozen ground in a slow, torturous grind.

Daddy told me they were relatives coming to pay their respects. We, my two brothers and I, didn't need to bathe or put on school clothes. "They're not that kind of company," Daddy said. His voice quivered with anger.

It was the day after Christmas, 1956. I was only twelve years old, and I didn't understand Daddy's coldness towards our visitors. What I did understand was the fact that my mother had died, in the morning hours of Christmas Eve from what was described to me as "woman cancer." The nurses at the hospital whispered it behind the shield of their hands, as though it was a dirty secret and by speaking the words out loud they too would be cursed with the same kind of cancer that claimed Mom.

Watching the cars approach I wondered if that's what they were coming for, to claim Mom, or what she'd left behind. The joke was on them. She didn't have anything left, nothing of value. Just some old, worn dresses, a wedding ring Daddy said he got out of a Crackerjack box, and two fancy hairpins she wore to proper occasions: nothing worth bickering over.

Analysis

The opening sentence of this first page puts us in capable hands: "They came to us with the mean December wind, three cars in all."

The cunning juxtaposition of a personified wind (picture a cartoon character with furrowed brow, puffy ruddy cheeks, quivering jowls) with those three matter-of-fact cars, is unsettling, as it's meant to be. It thrusts us into the psyche of the narrator, a child to whose home on Christmas Eve an uninvited visitor arrives. Not Santa, with his brimming sleigh of gifts, but the Grim Reaper, who has come for her or his mother.

Several things account for the effectiveness of this opening. For one, it appeals immediately and thoroughly to the senses. First, we have that "mean" wind. I've said elsewhere that adjectives aren't descriptions, but opinions. Yet thanks to that "mean" we don't need to be told that the wind is cold, or harsh, that it lashes cheeks and draws tears.

Next, we're treated to the ominous rumblings of those approaching cars, "their exhausts reverberating off mounds of snow, then the moaning of their engines." Note the choice of words: "muffled rumble," "moaning"—sounds that connote the mother's final breaths and moans of agony during her death throes. Drawn by the "moaning" of those engines, the narrator (we're not told her gender; I'll assume she's a girl) rushes into the living room where she "[pulls] the drapery back." I can feel those heavy drapes parting under the influence of small hands as the girl "[presses her] nose to the pane." What the character sees through that icy pane is no longer the benign world so familiar to her the day before, but a world transformed by death.

According to the narrator's father, the cars hold "relatives coming to pay their respects." And though the narrator may not say so, or even know it, we feel that for her those three cars with their ominous rumblings stand for death itself. Is it a stretch to assume that the breath with which the girl fogs the glass is as fleeting as the oval of fog itself? And that the dust she tastes on her lips is the dust from which we're all born, and to which death will eventually return us—and sooner than any of us care to think?

The narrative's retrospective approach is likewise well handled. The story is set in the now fairly distant past—1956—before more than a few of today's readers were born. And yet it opens with a sensual immediacy that brings the past into the present and makes it as real to us as our own breaths and sensations. By the time we learn that "It was the day after Christmas, 1956," we are already there, inhabiting that past as though it were ours.

And that's crucial since, whether or not we admit it, ultimately the only stories that matter are those we inhabit personally, not just with our minds, but through our senses. Remember: the fiction writer's job (or that of any storyteller, whether the stories are imagined or real) isn't to report experience, but to *create* it. And experience is processed in the mind by way of the senses.

Here, the author skillfully tucks exposition into narrative: "Watching the cars approach, I wondered...." Though background information is supplied ("It was the day after Christmas, 1956"), it never carries us out of the scene. Nor are we ever removed—through incongruous diction, extraneous exposition, or anachronistic awareness—from the psyche of the girl whose nose is pressed to the cold pane as she peers out at those arriving cars. Like a sponge, the vividly rendered moment soaks up all background exposition introduced into it.

This is a very strong opening.

Your Turn

Revise the first page you drafted for the previous prompt (30) from the perspective of an adult looking back over time to that period of his or her childhood.

32. Art's Highest Purpose:
To Complicate Our Feelings

(Child Protagonist / Humor and Danger)

Mom told me just yesterday not to ever leave the Lovin' Cup Cafe at nightfall. That even in the tiny city of Pleasantville, nestled up against the Canadian border, strange things can happen as night descends. Note to self: listen to Mom more often.

I watch as Jeff McKinney and Ralph Jones walk into the triangle of light formed by the street lamp next to the road and pause. I walk back into the alcove formed by the handicapped ramp as it rises to meet the cafe's entrance.

"Well, look what we have here," Jeff says, smiling right at me and then at Ralph, who smiles back at Jeff like he always does.

I slip my hands into my jacket pockets so they can't see they're shaking.

"If it isn't Jamie Domedian," Jeff says, pronouncing my last name so it rhymes with comedian. It doesn't, but I won't correct him.

Tonight is a first. I've never been alone with these two. Their harassment always takes place in crowded school hallways or waiting in line for the bus ride home.

As they walk toward me, I take another step back and feel my thigh up against the wheel of my ten-speed. I do a half-turn, insert the key into my bike lock, and yank the lock cord free, stuffing it in my pocket.

"Don't you two have cows to milk back at the farm?" Everyone knows McKinney and Jones live miles from here in cow town with all of their farmer neighbors.

Turn the handlebars toward the parking lot. Run, left foot on the pedal, sit on the saddle, and go!

It's a grand exit until McKinney makes a lunge and grabs the center of the handlebars.

"We're not here to talk farming," Jeff says.

Analysis

Now and then my students and I broach the unavoidable question: What makes a work of art? The question can be stood on its head: What makes art *work*? They're the same question, really, with (to me, anyway) the same answer: a true work of art is something that doesn't merely express our emotions—as any Hallmark card will do. It confronts us with emotions that don't quite fit into any of our ready-made boxes.

A simple but good example of this can be found in Jasper Johns's famous painting of the United States flag. From a distance it looks like any US flag, but step closer and you see the heavy impasto strokes of encaustic (wax) paint. It's *not* a US flag; it's a *painting of the US flag.* A flag is a symbol; it has a utilitarian purpose. It represents a nation. It's no more open to interpretation than (for most drivers, anyway) a stop sign. By converting it through an unusual medium and removing it from ordinary contexts, Johns's painting of the flag opens the flag up to interpretation. It no longer merely denotes. It *connotes.* It suggests feelings beyond its literal meaning.

Complicating our feelings: that, to me, is art's highest purpose.

Which may seem a highfalutin approach to discussing this first page of a young adult novel in which the young narrator (I'm assuming he's a boy) is menaced by two bullies, but the fact is that, in its humble way, this first page does what great art does: it complicates our feelings by confronting us with an unstable blend of danger and humor.

The opening sentence ("Mom told me ...") establishes not only the youthful narrator's voice, but the setting—both time and place—while foreshadowing conflict: something bad has transpired at the Lovin' Cup Café at nightfall. By saying "Mom" rather than "My mother," the narrator instantly establishes intimacy with his or her readers, an intimacy that bonds us to him before we set eyes on his nemeses.

The next sentence of this deft opening nails down the location: not only the size ("tiny") of the small-town setting, but its situation "nestled up against the Canadian border." The last sentence of the paragraph drives home the foreboding hinted at in the first, and does so wittily via a note to the narrator's "self." Dangerous humor; humorous danger.

Having established setting both generally (tiny city near Canada) and specifically (café at nightfall), the author paints an exterior street scene with a few expressionistic strokes, the "triangle of light" from a "street lamp," and the more specific "alcove formed by the handicapped ramp"—a detail that, because it's so specific, adds gritty authenticity. We have all we need now to form a solid picture and inhabit this scene.

The first two paragraphs having engaged our sense of vision, with the third paragraph a snatch of dialogue ("Well, look what we have here") pricks up our ears. However tinged with cliché (and let's face it, bullies *are* clichés), the words offer their own touch of menace, as does the smile that goes with them and that Bully #2 mirrors. (If there's one thing worse than an antagonist, it's a *smiling* antagonist.) The fifth paragraph treats us to yet another authenticating touch: how the protagonist's name *isn't* pronounced. Note how this is delivered not as a piece of inert information, but through a dramatic moment, an *active* description. It's also ironic in ways that are, again, equally funny and dangerous. Though his name may not rhyme with one, Jamie is something of a comedian. His sense of humor puts him at risk.

Lest we wonder if we might be dealing with routine, paragraph six ("Tonight is a first") smashes that. What we have here is an event, an inciting incident: something that breaks with routine ("I've never been alone with these two"). The next sentence contextualizes the routine against which this exceptional event occurs. It gives us a frame of reference for the bullying that, apparently, has been going on for some time.

The next paragraph has the narrator backing into his bike, feeling his "thigh up against the wheel." In the movie version, this is one of those moments when the audience gasps and jerks up in their seats. Without needing to be told, we imagine the narrator's nearly simultaneous responses: first, the shock of being touched by someone or something he didn't know was there; then relief on realizing it is his means of escape.

Next paragraph, first line: "Don't you two have cows to milk back at the farm?" Like all good dialogue, it does double duty: evokes character while carrying information. From this one line we know that a) however dangerous they are, wise-ass Jamie doesn't have much respect for his enemies; and b) our two bullies live in the boonies.

Next: "Turn the handlebars toward the parking lot. Run, left foot on the pedal, sit on the saddle, and go!" Why simply describe a series of actions ("I turned my bike around and pedaled out of the parking lot") when you can describe them so they convey character? Remember: whatever we do that evokes character is probably a keeper. My one quibble here is that I'd eliminate articles and conjunctions: "Turn handlebars toward parking lot. Run. Left foot on pedal, sit on saddle. Go!"

I've said more than enough. Humor and danger on the same page—what more can we ask for? This opening got me. Has it got you?

Your Turn

In drafting or revising a first page—yours or someone else's—see how many
of the following you can accomplish:

- establish setting and atmosphere
- break routine
- foreshadow conflict
- engage multiple senses
- evoke character via description
- combine disparate emotions (e.g., humor and danger).

E. Genres

"[T]he only means I have to stop ignorant snobs from behaving
towards genre fiction with snobbish ignorance is to not reinforce
their ignorance and snobbery by lying and saying that when I write
SF it isn't SF, but to tell them more or less patiently for forty or fifty
years that they are wrong to exclude SF and fantasy from literature,
and proving my arguments by writing well."
URSULA K. LE GUIN, *The Wild Girls*

"I've been as bad an influence on American
literature as anyone I can think of."
DASHIELL HAMMETT

A GENRE IS A TYPE OF SOMETHING, FOR OUR PURPOSES A TYPE OF
narrative. Sci-fi, mystery, detective, western, thriller, fan fiction, YA ... these
are just some of many popular genres of the novel—which, once upon a time,
was itself a literary genre.

A genre implies all the conventions and expectations that adhere to it. As
John Mullen explains in *How Novels Work*, his insightful survey of fictional tech-
niques, "A genre is not just a category for literary critics, it is also a resource for
the writer. [...] Genre offers a challenge by provoking *a free spirit to transcend the*
limitations of previous examples." Genre gives the writer something invaluable:
a set of requirements and constraints to work with or against, rules to obey, or
flout—or both.

Novelists and critics alike haven't always viewed genre in such a positive light.
As G.K. Chesterton (whose own detective novels featured a priestly sleuth named
Father Brown) lamented back in 1901: "Many people do not realize that there is
such a thing as a good detective story; it is to them like speaking of a good devil."[5]

---

5. G.K. Chesterton, "In Defence of Detective Stories" in *The Defendants* (1901).

While some, like George Orwell, admitted to enjoying Sherlock Holmes and Dracula, even they drew the line at taking genre fiction seriously.

Others were even less charitable. "Reading mysteries," Edmund Wilson wrote, "is a kind of vice that, for silliness and minor harmfulness, ranks somewhere between crossword puzzles and smoking."[6] Such appraisals didn't go unchallenged. When Wilson's views went public in 1944, they provoked more letters of protest than anything he'd ever written. Among the dissenters was Raymond Chandler, whose detective novels Wilson judged inferior to anything by Graham Greene. Chandler's response? "Literature is bunk."[7]

More recently, when President Obama awarded horror novelist Stephen King the Medal of Arts in 2015, it caused an uproar among literary critics, including Harold Bloom who sniffed, "King is an immensely inadequate writer ... [of] what used to be called 'penny dreadfuls'"—another genre.

Given the rise in both popularity and sophistication of the young adult novel over the past ten years, it's no longer so easy to look down on genres from the lofty heights of "literary fiction"—itself a genre, but whose conventions are fluid. Far from being frowned upon, genre is seen especially by younger writers as a vital, vitalizing force. More and more literary novelists—David Mitchell, Annie Proulx, Gish Jen, Jhumpa Lahiri, Haruki Murakami, and Kazuo Ishiguro, to name a few—incorporate or pay tribute to genre through their works. For their part, through such things as deep characters and sophisticated language, genre authors challenge the limits of their own conventions. *The Hunger Games* qualifies as romance. So does Cormac McCarthy's *The Road*. While George Orwell's *1984*, Margaret Atwood's *A Handmaid's Tale*, and Emily St. John Mandel's *Station Eleven* certainly qualify as works of science or speculative fiction, they are also works of literary fiction. Literary fiction's subsumption into other genres, and vice versa, has become so pervasive one must wonder what distinction if any can still be claimed by "pure" literary fiction beyond ... um ... pretentiousness.

Tempting though it may be to flout or challenge the conventions of genre, there's also a lot to be said for playing by the rules. In this section, we'll scrutinize the first pages of works in progress that play by the rules of their genres, and some that don't.

---

6   Edmund Wilson, "Why Do People Read Detective Stories?" in the *New Yorker* (October 1944).

7   Letter to Helga Green, September 1957.

33. Zechs's Deal:
A Routine Awakening

*(Sci-Fi or Speculative Fiction / In Medias Res /
Dramatized Routine)*

The deal was set to happen in twenty minutes. Zechs was cutting it close, but his ship was only a short stroll from the loading area. The worst consequence was hearing them complain, if that. If his clients had any sense, they wouldn't talk back to him.

Zechs touched his face, feeling the bristles that had popped up overnight. Shaving every morning was a hassle, but he looked good without facial hair. Zechs hurried and finished his business at the bathroom sink. Then he walked to his closet to get dressed.

Zechs picked out one of his markedly Astrian suits. He buttoned up the mauve shirt, leaving it untucked and the collar crooked. The jacket and the pants were woven from the fleece of an animal on his home planet. A very rare animal, at that. The fabric shimmered from black to dark red under the light as he dressed. Finishing up, Zechs grabbed his omni-com and left the bedroom.

Stepping down the spiral staircase, a custom addition for his starship, Zechs flipped open his omni-com and moved the cursor over to the planet's time program. 8:21. Just looking at the readout made him want to yawn. The wrought iron staircase ended at the bridge. The room was dark, but the controls station was illuminated by the blue glow of churning winds and streaks of lightning. Not a place he'd ever like his ship to be, but it made a good screensaver for the forward-view monitor.

On the opposite side of the bridge, the glass door leading to his laboratory opened. Zechs entered and then veered off to the adjacent room, a makeshift kitchen.

He selected a few pills from the colorful pile of Astrian vitamins he'd left on the counter. After downing them, he started going through the cabinets. He pushed all the test tube racks out of the way and, from memory alone, grabbed a bottle. With a twitch of his nerves, Zechs read the note. Completely out. But it didn't matter. It wasn't like he needed it right now. Or period.

Analysis

To paraphrase Tolstoy, "All good writing is good in pretty much the same way." Whatever the genre, when it comes to telling stories, certain ideals, conventions, and principles apply. The law of economy and efficiency; concreteness over abstraction, experiences over information. Don't state what is or can be implied.

Then there's the previously discussed convention known as *in medias res*, the structural technique whereby, instead of telling stories from the very beginning, authors plunge their readers into conflicts already underway. Especially with respect to the first pages and scenes of our stories, ideally we want to invite readers into worlds populated by characters whose lives are already complicated by situations which, if they haven't set a plot in motion yet, will do so soon.

The genre here is science or speculative fiction. The story opens with Zechs, the hero, twenty minutes from a confrontation with some rivals to whom he is about to make an offer they can't refuse; at least he *hopes* they won't refuse it. In the bedroom (or its equivalent) of his starship, he picks out a suit custom-tailored back in Astria (his home planet) from the fleece of a "very rare animal." He shaves his stubble and—later, in the kitchen adjacent to his starship laboratory—takes his daily vitamins (likewise a product of Astria). And though he wishes to swallow them with something presumably stronger than water, he finds the bottle empty. But then it doesn't matter. Whatever was in the bottle, he doesn't need it anymore.

Take away the sci-fi trappings—the starship, the "omni-com," the mention of other planets and rare creatures thereof turned into suits—and what's left? A man getting up in the morning, doing his toiletries, getting dressed. In a word: banality.

Generally, whether on earth or some other planet, opening with a character getting out of bed is a bad idea. There are of course exceptions (Kafka's "The Metamorphosis," for one).

And no one would call this opening of Mary Renault's *Fire from Heaven* banal:

> The child was wakened by the knotting of the snake's coils about his
> waist. For a moment he was frightened; it had squeezed his breathing
> and given him a bad dream. But as soon as he was awake, he knew what
> it was and pushed his two hands inside the coils. It shifted; the strong
> band under his back bunched tightly, then grew thin. The head slid up
> his shoulder along his neck and he felt close to his ear the flickering
> tongue.

Still, why do so many draft stories start with characters waking up, stretching, brushing their teeth? Maybe because their authors haven't located the true beginnings of their stories, or they're too timid to plunge into situation and conflict. Or maybe they feel they want to "milk" things a bit more before getting into the action.

Where no suspense has been created, there's nothing to "milk." A character getting out of bed is a character getting out of bed—whether the bed is in a suburban tract house in Pine Hill, New Jersey, or on a space station orbiting among Saturn's rings, makes no, or little, difference. Just as looking at the readout on his omni-com makes Zechs want to yawn, so readers are likely to find themselves yawning through this opening scene, despite its author's game effort to frontload it with suspense by telegraphing a future dramatic event in the first paragraph. But that event won't occur for another twenty minutes. Nor do we appreciate its significance, having no idea what's at stake. Meanwhile we're stuck with a character contemplating his razor stubble while we're treated to a nickel tour of his spacecraft.

My suggestion: open *in medias res*, with the promised dramatic deal scene. We can learn about Zechs's suits and razor stubble later.

Your Turn

Draft a speculative or science-fiction story opening wherein a character awakens, and in which his or her awakening is a dramatic, rather than routine, event.

34. To the Core

(Science Fiction / Humor / Tongue in Cheek)

"That's one small step ... for [a] man ... one ...
giant leap for Mankind."
NEIL ARMSTRONG, FIRST PERSON ON THE MOON

"Like Armstrong, and like Columbus before him, we tread today on a
new world. A world truly beyond the gravity and influence of Mother
Earth, in a way that neither the moon nor the 'New World' ever were.
We step here today in the view of all Mankind."
CARY ESTERHAUS, FIRST PERSON ON MARS

"Cary, come on for Pete's sake! Step on it, will you?"
HELLA VERNON, SECOND PERSON ON MARS

"Crap, what did I step in?"
NILS ARMSTREN, FIRST PERSON ON ALPHA CENTAURI 6
(no relation to Neil Armstrong)

A careful remote scan told Armstren and his crew that the site they chose for their historic first landing outside Sol system was suitable for the obligatory ceremony. Solid ground, hard and dry and barren, even devoid of the round-leafed yellow vegetation that covered much of the level ground in the mid latitudes of AC6. But on Armstren's third historic step, on his way to plant the symbolic flag with the blue-white globe of Earth—sufficiently obscured by clouds that the land masses were unidentifiable, ensuring that no nation could charge favoritism in the design—his booted foot sank through some mushy, viscous *something* before coming to a stop shin deep. It was at this point that he uttered the words he would always be remembered for.

* * *

When she first heard the sounds of the new creature, she thought she must be mistaken. They seemed to be coming from the core. But that was impossible.

To a human ear, her name would sound approximately like "Burreler." Among her people, she also had a number of nicknames, which would translate to human concepts like "Explorer," "Reckless One," and "Trouble."

Burreler traveled farther inward than any of the other people, but even she didn't visit the core. The core was death. Everyone knew that. The very world itself acted to keep people from the core. Gravity pushed all things down, outward, away from the deadly center of the world.

Analysis

Whether set in a distant galaxy in the future or in the past or present of our own planet, all fiction is speculative. It creates a hypothetical reality and peoples it with hypothetical characters.

With science fiction, the speculative element is overt, with the emphasis on alien landscapes and life forms allowing authors to engage their knowledge of and passion for the sciences. The genre also invites philosophical explorations on the impacts of science and technology, making it a genre not only of nightmarish fantasies and wish fulfillment, but of serious ideas. It presents authors with the challenge of writing convincingly not only of events and places that don't exist, but that expand our boundaries of perception and possibility.

Jules Verne, a pioneer of the genre, secured his reputation with books like *From the Earth to the Moon* and *20,000 Leagues Under the Sea*, works that treat readers to encyclopedic tours of speculative settings—this from a man who, as a child of twelve after being whipped by his father for trying to stow away on a cargo ship bound for India, famously stated, "I shall from now on only travel in my imagination."[8] The best thing about Verne's stories (and those of H.G. Wells) is that they let us speculate about the future from the past, *retrospectively*, so we experience a curious blend of wonder and nostalgia.

One of Verne's most famous books, *A Journey to the Centre of the Earth* (1864), treats a theme similar to that of the work presented here. It tells the story of German professor von Hardwigg's journey with his nephew down one of a series of volcanic passages leading to Earth's center, where they encounter all kinds of marvels and hazards, from giant mushrooms to prehistoric reptiles. Their journey ends prematurely with the explorers regurgitated up a volcanic chimney and deposited on the Italian island of Stromboli.

---

8   Source unknown.

Professor von Hardwigg's adventure is inspired by an encrypted code in runic script that he and his nephew discover hidden within the text of an Icelandic saga. Translated, the code turns out to be a message left by Icelandic alchemist Arne Saknussemm, who claims to have discovered a secret passage to Earth's core, joining the parade of great Nordic explorers that began with the Vikings.

In this opening of a novella titled "To the Core," the grand tradition continues with one Nils Armstren ("no relation to Neil Armstrong"), the first man to set foot on Alpha Centauri 6.

What, exactly, Nils sets foot on (or in) is the object here not just of speculation but of wit. The novella opens slyly with a quartet of epigraphs, the first quoting Neil Armstrong's first words on the moon, a matter of historical record, the second a sober projection of the proximate future (mankind's first landing on Mars), and the last two quotations parodying the others. Had the author observed the Rule of Threes and left out the fourth quote, it might have been better. Still, it's clever enough, since it gives a wink to everything that follows.

And that's a good thing, since most science fiction takes itself too seriously. Yet despite the tongue-in-cheek epigraphs, what follows in the first scene is convincingly shored up by specific details, down to the "symbolic flag with the blue-white globe of Earth—sufficiently obscured by clouds [so] that the land masses were unidentifiable, ensuring that no nation could charge favoritism in the design." This perpetuates the humor while keeping us firmly grounded in earthly human foibles even as we tread on Alpha Centauri.

Before the opening scene takes us anywhere, it ends, and we're transported to a different realm wherein an alien of female gender who has already "traveled farther inward than any other people" (but has never reached the core) hears the sound of a "new creature" coming from there. We've barely landed in this author's speculative world and already we've encountered, indirectly, strange creatures.

The second scene feels premature; the first feels truncated. Between them lies the "core" of this novella. I'm also troubled by the logic of the last sentence, which has gravity pushing all things down and outward at the same time.

Your Turn

Draft an opening of a story or novel set on another planet in which a description of the landscape sets the stage. Think of E.M. Forster's opening to *A Passage to*

India ("Except for the Marabar Caves—and they are twenty miles off—the city of Chandrapore presents nothing extraordinary.") or the opening of Steinbeck's *East of Eden* ("The Salinas Valley is in northern California."). In other words, describe this landscape as you would a place on earth, with the same matter-of-factness, so it reads with the humble authority of an encyclopedia entry.

35. U'gen Cadets

(Speculative Fantasy / False Suspense / Clarity & Precision)

Rachael dropped from the last step of the bus, grateful to be away from all the thoughts that had intruded upon her mind, and looked out across the park. Her school, a looming remnant of an ancient society stood at the end of the path, its cream-colored stones bright under the hot sun. Inside, Visionary students and U'gen cadets learned everything about military strategy.

Taking the path through the park, she headed toward the inevitable. Her mind drifted along, searching for an open mind to read as it always did, against her will, but no one wandered the street. They were busy working, as she should have been. While she normally skipped her first class, today she had a proper excuse. She had to report a vision. The blood-filled battlefield of her future-sight popped to the forefront of her thoughts with little prodding.

Blood flowed down the street in her mind, leaching from the dying or dead bodies of the U'gen soldiers. Lapping fires licked at crumbling buildings lining the street littered with glass and rubble. Light filtered through the haze of dusk. Rachael could still feel the thrumming of helicopter blades chopping in the distance as it propelled itself toward the smoke-filled landing zone. Gunfire from unseen muzzles blasted down the street, the bullets sending up small puffs of dust as they embedded in the skeletal structures. She heard the splashes of running boots as a soldier fled with some coveted item protected in his arms. Sorrow welled up inside her as he died, sputtering crimson blood....

Rachael froze. Her heart pounded as she looked before her and saw Randall. Sitting on the academy steps, he chewed a toothpick he held, his elbows on his knees. His bloodied visage still occupied her thoughts, particularly the blood-soaked picture he had clung to in his last moments—what she assumed were his loved ones. She closed her eyes and tried to push the image of the soldier's death from her mind.

Analysis

How much do readers need to know, versus how much they should be kept in the dark?

To describe what writers do, Frank Conroy—who before his death in 2005 directed the Iowa Writer's Workshop for over 30 years—used the metaphor of a mountain hike. In writing fiction, we equip readers for a journey up a mountain. When they get to the top, assuming that they get there, they'll be rewarded with an expanded view not only of the fictional world in which they've been immersed, but of human nature—and, assuming the story rises to the level of great literature, life itself.

But to get there readers will need certain things. The trick, Conroy explained, is to give them everything they need for the journey—compass, map, hardtack, water—but nothing they don't need (yoyo, kazoo, kaleidoscope), and nothing sooner than it's needed (telescope, flag, champagne). Supply too much information or supply it too soon, and you kill suspense. Supply too little, and what you generate isn't suspense, but confusion and frustration.

This opening generates a lot of false suspense, the kind that has readers asking not *What's going to happen next?* but *What am I reading, and why am I reading it?* From the profusion of blood-soaked visions experienced by the heroine to the mystifying "U'gen," this first page offers mostly confusion.

Who is Rachael? How old is she? Where is she? What is she doing there? When did those intruding thoughts of hers—the ones she's "grateful to be away from" in the first paragraph—intrude? During the long bus trip? If indeed she has gotten away from those thoughts, why, two paragraphs later, is she seized by a vision that appears to be part and parcel of them? Is this the same vision she's on her way to report? Do these visions pop "into the forefront of her thoughts with little prodding" or against her will? What, if any, is the relationship between Rachael's visions and her mind's autonomous habit of drifting into other "open minds"? Those other minds—are they the source of Rachael's visions?

We don't know, nor can we be sure if Randall is the dying soldier in the vision, and if the "coveted item" he embraced with his dead arms is the family photograph mentioned later. As to the nature of the relationship between Randall and Rachael, there, too, we're left clueless.

What we do know is that, for reasons unclear, Rachael is able to see into the future, and that that future is apocalyptic, with blood "leaching from ... dead bodies" and "streets littered with glass and rubble." Then again, the story itself appears to be set in a none-too-charming future in which U'gen cadets and "Visionary students" (author's capitalization) rehearse military strategy as they gear up for the coming apocalypse.

Lack of contrast via contextualization also works against this opening. Were they cast against a less dismal present, Rachael's "horrifying" visions might indeed horrify. Instead, they spill blood and darkness into a vision already murky. Just as in Rachael's vision "light filter[s] through the haze of dusk," this opening sheds little light. All is hazy, dim, obscure.

Where not obscure, the writing is sentimental, serving up emotion in excess of experience, as in this sentence, "Sorrow welled up inside her as [the soldier] died, sputtering crimson blood," which tells us how Rachael *feels about* the soldier's death and even splatters us with his blood *before* we see or otherwise experience him dying or even falling as he runs.

Between Rachael's vision-muddled mind and the author's lack of clarity and precision (is the school alluded to in the first paragraph a "looming remnant of an ancient society" or active and still in session?), this opening leaves us too much in the dark.

Your Turn

Revise this opening based on my critique and your own observations. Taking imaginative license, fill in missing information to mitigate as much false suspense as possible, while at the same time minimizing sentimentality by making subjective emotional responses subject—if not secondary—to concrete objective experiences.

36. A Dragon's Protection

(Fantasy / Appealing to the Senses / Metaphysical Elements)

6 September 1930

Master Jacks dug his one remaining hand into the pocket of his tweed waistcoat. He brought out a fresh white handkerchief for the eleven-year-old Nick Parter to bleed into. "Here." He offered it to the boy across his wide mahogany desk. "Use this."

Nick took it. "Thanks."

They were in Jacks's oak-paneled study. Artifacts from the man's travels—tribal masks, blunt spears, general knickknacks of wicker and weave—cluttered the walls. The shouts and screams of young rugby players, enthusiastic and terrified, drifted in through the window from the fields below.

Nick spat a pink mixture of saliva and blood into the cloth before pinching it under his nostrils. He tipped his head forward and held the position, waiting for the bleeding to stop. The front of his jersey was soaked with red.

"Do you have an explanation for me?" asked the teacher. He was thin and hard, with iron-grey streaks peppering his dark hair. He had lost his right arm in 1916, at the Somme.

"It was a fight. Fights happen."

"To you, Nick, they happen a lot. Four in the first three days of term, all with older boys. I've never known such behavior. The idea, Custodian, is that you try to fit in."

"It hardly matters." Nick looked up at his teacher, his eyes fierce. "I'm in the wrong time without a dragon's protection. We both know I'm dead if I can't get out."

Analysis

Up to its second-to-last line, this opening page might have been torn out of James Hilton's 1934 bestseller, *Goodbye, Mr. Chips*. Set a generation earlier than the first page in question, Hilton's unabashedly sentimental novella portrayed the life of its eponymous self-effacing hero, Arthur Chipping, a career school-master in an English public school.

In Hilton's story, having retired after decades of teaching Roman history and Latin at Brookfield School, Mr. Chips is called back to service during World War I, which has sent younger teachers off to the trenches. For Hilton, the peace and prosperity following the Great War represented an oasis in civilization—or the mirage of an oasis, soon to be obliterated by Hitler and the smashing of the Versailles Treaty. In another novel written before *Goodbye, Mr. Chips*, Hilton celebrated this oasis metaphorically, through a fictional utopia set high in the mountains of Tibet. That novel was called *Lost Horizon*, and the utopia was "Shangri-La," a term that has become synonymous with the notion of an earthly paradise, often used with a pejorative intent.

I mention this because, up to the last paragraph, there's something dreamily quaint about this opening of a fantasy novel. Here is Master Jacks, the schoolmaster in his tweed waistcoat, comforting and admonishing his eleven-year-old charge, Nick Parker, in his oak-lined study bristling with anthropological artifacts. Through the study's window "shouts and screams" drift in from the rugby fields, where Nick had gotten into a scrap with one or several of his schoolmates. It's not the first time. Indeed, three days into his first term Nick has already earned a reputation for fighting. Nick's teacher, no stranger to combat himself (he lost an arm in the Great War), lends Nick a "fresh white handkerchief" to blow his bloody nose into.

All of this is conveyed deftly in an opening passage that's alive to all the senses: sight (the pink color of Nick's blood mixed with his saliva), sounds (the shouts and screams from the rugby field), textures ("knickknacks of wicker and weave"—note how alliteration and meter create their own texture). A good ear for dialogue ("To you, Nick, they happen a lot.") together with a sharp eye for telling details (the objects cluttering the master's walls) make this a winning opening. In a few paragraphs, I feel I know Master Jacks and his pupil. And though—excepting the last lines—there are no throat-grabbers here, still, there is conflict. I for one would read on to discover why Nick is having such a hard time fitting in with his fellow students.

Then comes the dragon in the last paragraph. Suddenly I've traded the genteel Shangri-La of Mr. Chips and *Dead Poets' Society* for Tolkien's Middle Earth. True, the title warned me, or should have, though once I started reading I fell into the charm of those opening paragraphs and forgot the warning.

Thanks mainly to Harry Potter, these days dragons and boarding schools are as ubiquitous in works of literature as angels, witches, and vampires—a fact that I for one lament. The moment we introduce supernatural phenomena into fiction, we undermine the *human* element, with curses, spells, and potions augmenting—if not replacing entirely—psychological cause and effect.

The fantasy genre to which such phenomena belong doesn't merely allow for impossible events, it *insists on* them. Though traditionally—as with Tolkien—fantasy novels are grounded in medieval settings, thanks to Ann Rice and Harry Potter we may now expect witches, vampires, and dragons to pop up anywhere, anytime, including a boarding school between the world wars.

Starting with the dragon that guards the golden fleece at Rhodes, on through the unnamed dragon in *Beowulf* and Tolkien's Glaurung and Smaug, with each decade the number of dragons in books has multiplied, with the past decade furnishing us with many dozens if not hundreds of novels featuring the mythological serpents, making me wonder why Saint George ever bothered. Why so many readers and writers still share this obsession with our medieval forebears may be explained partly by the wish to return to more innocent and colorful myths, coupled with a dissatisfaction with—or disbelief in—the fruits of science.

Though I share those dissatisfactions, I personally can live without dragons. But then mine is the bias of someone who prefers to stare down real monsters rather than mythological ones.

That said, injected into this otherwise quaint scene, the sudden allusion to dragons in the last paragraph is jarring. The author might better prepare us for it by dropping a hint earlier. A set of dragon etchings on a wall of the teacher's study? Dragon claws in the curio cabinet?

Your Turn

Into a first page that you've already written of any genre, introduce a supernatural element: a mythical creature, a magic potion or power (your protagonist can fly!), something that breaks the laws of our everyday world. Do so in a way that, though surprising, is convincing and feels inevitable, or anyway isn't jarring.

37. Celestia's Last Battle

(Prologues / Fantasy / Adjectives / Suspension of Disbelief / Telling vs. Showing)

Prologue: The Cage

It was the most dangerous fight of them all. Only one person ever left, the winner. That is how you must win. You kill your opponent and, automatically, you are the winner. It was very rare that the loser ever survived. In some cases however, there have been winners so full of grief and regret, they had attempted to revive their opponents. Only once has a person who lost survived, and many say it would be life fulfilling to meet her.

Celestia Monte. How little people actually knew about her. Her past, her present and what came to be her future. She was the strongest, most vigilant fighter, and I knew, because many times I had watched her fight. Each and every round, her opponent fell before her feet. Dead. She showed no mercy, for she was strong. I had many times applauded her and praised her.

It was only then, at her last battle, did I never clap again. It started as any other Cage battle, with her leading her opponent to his doom. However, if you had ever watched her, as I had in those past fights, you could see her lacking in her power. She was neither tired nor injured. Her weakness was her opponent: Brutus Monte. He was her love, her student and her life. She knew that if she killed him that would be her ending anyways.

So, on they fought. Both avoided hurting each other, and the crowd was growing aggravated. They wanted blood; they wanted a real fight. Celestia was concerned but threw a more vicious blow with her sword, but she made a mistake. Brutus saw that she no longer guarded her side and took his chances.

Analysis

Prologues let us dip into our stories out of sequence. They may reach back to some event in the past, giving readers a prequel to what follows. Or they can dip into some dramatic moment in the future—the heroine being escorted to the gallows—with the tale that starts with Chapter 1 telling us how, exactly, she got there.

This prologue presents us with the spectacle of gladiatorial combat, or something like it: a sport where people (in this case women) entertain audiences through deadly hand-to-hand combat. Historically, gladiatorial games took place during the Roman Empire. Many gladiators were soldier-prisoners who volunteered for gladiatorial combat training as a way to regain the honor lost through their having surrendered or been captured. It's a colorful if gruesome sidebar of history, one exploited often by novelists and filmmakers, and therefore rife with clichés.

Whether the author of the given prologue is describing Roman or some other form of gladiatorial combat isn't clear. No dates or place names are given; the one specific detail provided by the prologue is the professional combatant's name: Celestia Monte—an odd choice, Monte being short for either Montague (French in origin; not commonly used until the nineteenth century) or Montgomery, which dates back to the Gauls (the Romans began overtaking Celtic Gaul in 121 BCE). "Celestia," on the other hand, is strictly New Age. It sounds like the name of a Tom Robbins protagonist, or a popular brand of herbal tea infusions.

Maybe the prologue is set in some distant future wherein gladiatorial combat has been revived. For all we know, it may be set on another planet, in another universe (as suggested by the main character's cosmic name). In any case, this material demands much suspension of disbelief from readers, meaning great confidence in the author—a confidence not inspired by this first page.

One reason: the author's clumsy handling of grammar and syntax ("It was only then, at her last battle, did I never clap again."), owing to carelessness. Or maybe English isn't the author's first language. If so, I have to admire his or her audacity. Editors, publishers, and agents will take a much dimmer view.

Apart from grammatical challenges, there are other problems with this prologue. For one thing, it doesn't do what prologues do best: claim the reader's attention by way of a dramatic scene that provides a context for the main story to follow.

Though the raw materials are dramatic and even sensational, what's on the page here isn't that exciting. A fiction writer's first job is to create experience; here, no experience is offered, at least not directly. Instead of "seeing" Celestia Monte in action through the eyes of a narrator, an eyewitness, we're *told things* about her. "She was the strongest, most vigilant fighter." So says the narrator, who piles on more adjectives ("she was strong," "she showed no mercy," "she was neither tired nor injured"). Adjectives are opinions, not descriptions or facts, to be treated as we treat most opinions, with some measure of skepticism if not outright distrust. The advantage of showing versus telling is that it lets readers form their own opinions based on concrete evidence. Here, though, instead of being offered the sensory evidence supplied by the narrator's eyes, ears, and other organs, we get only his conclusions and opinions.

Since nothing is shown and everything is told, nothing is terribly convincing. Given the sensational nature of the material, unless the author manages somehow to suspend our disbelief through amassing authentic details, our skepticism will grow greater and greater, burgeoning into a complete rejection of the author's fictional universe, until we either close the book or fling it across the room.

There *is* a place for exposition in fiction—for telling rather than showing. There are times when our narrators should summarize actions and events and even editorialize or reflect on them. The best place to do those things probably is *not* in the midst of a spectacle, especially one served up as an attention-grabbing prologue. The crowd wants blood, sweat, gore, gristle, and grit. So do readers of stories about gladiatorial combat.

Instead of talking about it, I'd plunge readers into Celestia's last battle. Isn't that what prologues are best at—plunging us into dramatic events?

Your Turn

Draft a prologue for a novel that doesn't have one. Any novel will do. For instance: a prologue to *Moby Dick* that dips us into a dramatic scene with Ahab confronting the white whale *before* losing his leg.

38. A Psycho in the Making

*(Horror-Thriller Genre / Psychopathic
Characters / Muffled Implications)*

The moment he awoke he knew something was wrong. The clock on
the wall read nine; nothing moved in the rest of the house. The sky
through his window was overcast, the air like a wet flannel on his face.
He stumbled down the hall, bleary-eyed, and found her in her bed.
At first he thought she was sleeping, but when she did not respond
to his question, he peeled back the blanket to discover what he had
always feared.

The cat padded into the room mewing for its breakfast, its tail
a plume of blackness. Ordinarily he would have booted it away: he
hated its piteous pleading. But today he lifted it gently, and in the
kitchen put milk into its bowl and set it down to drink. It was too late
to go into work and her hens needed feeding. He scattered their seed,
retrieved the newspaper from the front lawn, and trudged back inside.
For a while he sat in the front room, slumped in an armchair—her
chair—staring ahead, his mind vacant of thought.

Again the cat appeared, mewing. It weaved its body between his
legs, rubbing against him and when he did not respond, leapt onto
his lap. It was then that he came to from his reverie, then that he
put his hands around its scrawny neck and squeezed until it slumped
limply, dead.

For most of the day he moved in a trance, unable to comprehend
her death. He knew that it would come one day, of course, and he knew
that the hacking cough of late was leaving her breathless and clutching at her chest, wincing with pain. But he did not know that today she
would die. And he did not know what he ought to do with her now.

He returned to her room and did what he had not done since he
was a small boy—he lay beside her and slept. When he awoke and
found that no, it was not a bad dream—she was still there and motion-
less—he brushed back a strand of grey hair that covered one eye. He
traced the contours of her face with his fingertips, explored the landscape that was her wrinkled brow, her sunken cheek, her withered lips,
her chin dinted and spiked with hairs. He did not weep. He had forgotten—if he had ever known—how to grieve. What he felt most was the
sense of being, for the first time in his life, utterly alone in the world.

Analysis

A man (or boy) of indeterminate age wakens to find his mother dead in the other room. This monumental occasion in his life has not come unexpected; we are told (improbably) that it is something "he had always feared." Having given his mother's cat a bowl of milk and fed her chickens, the protagonist assumes a catatonic state in his mother's armchair "staring ahead, his mind vacant of thought." When the cat makes its next appearance, the protagonist emerges from his stupor just long enough to strangle the creature to death with his bare hands, after which he curls up in bed with his mother's corpse. The passage ends with his realization that "for the first time in his life" he is "utterly alone in the world."

If in reading this passage you sense a Norman Bates in the making, you're not alone. Bates, for those who've never seen Alfred Hitchcock's *Psycho*, is the title character, rendered to a fare-thee-well by Anthony Perkins. He operates a small motel at the bottom of the hill where he and his mother share a forbidding Victorian house—his dead mother, that is. Mrs. Bates has been dead for six years; Norman has kept her mummified body and propped it in her rocking chair.

I imagine a similar future in store for this protagonist, minus the motel. The protagonist does not need to travel great psychic distances from strangling cats with his bare hands to stabbing people to death in shower stalls. Whatever his fate, what we're dealing with here is at best a creep, at worst a serial killer in embryo.

Which makes this an effective opening, provided that the story that follows it lives up to its creepy nature, as I suspect it will. After all, any story whose first page dishes up two deaths (one a murder) isn't likely to turn into a romance—or, for that matter, a nuanced work of psychological or social realism. Especially not with passages like this

> It was then that he came to from his reverie, then that he put his hands around its scrawny neck and squeezed until it slumped limply, dead.

that call to mind Vincent Price's voiceover sessions for Michael Jackson's hit song "Thriller." Here and at other points the style feels downright gothic, the author having dipped his nib into Poe's inkwell. Nothing wrong with that, except that it plants us firmly in genre/horror/thriller territory. If the story that follows doesn't measure up, disappointment is sure to follow.

There are grammatical issues. The handling of tense is less than masterful. One example is in the second to last paragraph, when, after his mother's death we read that the protagonist "knew that it would come someday" (the tense should be past perfect "had known"). In the same paragraph, we get, "But he did not know that today she would die." Though writers do it all the time, it seems to me that in a past-tense narrative, unless it truly refers to a present day from which the narrator is looking back, the word "today" has little meaning and less place. "But he hadn't known that she would die that day," conveys the same meaning grammatically.

The last line spells out what should be more than implied by the time we read it: that the protagonist feels "utterly alone." End with the line before, and the scene's implications resonate. State what's implied, and you muffle those implications.

Your Turn

Evoke a psychopathic character through dialogue, action, or a combination of those things. Catch him or her in a relatively undramatic moment, doing something mundane, or not overly violent or psychotic. Yet still somehow convey the character's pathology.

39. Death on the Freeway

(Detective Fiction / Clairvoyant Dreams)

The girl was wearing a red robe when she fell from the overpass. Detective John Hsiao had spent the past hour interviewing people on the shoulder of the freeway, and that was about the only thing any of them remembered.

"Did you see anybody else on the overpass?"

"No."

"Did you see what she was doing before it happened?"

"No."

"Did you see anything at all?"

"She was wearing a red robe...."

Detective Calhoun was on the overpass itself. There had been a serious, but relatively smaller, accident there around the time of the girl's very messy death. Calhoun was interviewing the survivors and watching a few lab techs search the overpass guardrail for trace evidence.

John noticed the older detective motioning him up, so he thanked the last of the witnesses and jotted a few more notes in his blotter, then started towards the grassy slope off the shoulder. Amidst the empty cars on the freeway, the DA's criminologists were still scraping the girl's remains off the hot tarmac.

As he walked, John tried to shake the feeling that he'd been through this before.

Every three days for the past six months, John had had the same dream.

It started high in the mountains of Guangdong province. John had never been there, but had heard his grandfather speak many times of the way the peaks rose from the mists, rounded islands of green and brown in a sea of roiling white.

In the dream, a young girl with glossy black hair and a vibrant red gown walked on one of the islands. Two shadowy figures followed close behind her. Every few steps, the girl spun around to look at them, her hair a whirlwind of movement. Each time, she turned again after a moment of stillness and continued walking. Sometimes her steps were slow and faltering; other times she moved quickly, as though traveling to a destination far away.

After several of these ... confrontations? Pleas? John was not sure what they were, but there came a point in the dream when the girl did not turn back around. Instead, she strode towards the couple—quick and purposeful.

Analysis

A detective at the scene of a possible murder. A girl has fallen from an overpass. Or was she pushed? Eyewitnesses say the girl wore a red robe.

A corpse, a private (or public) investigator, a suspicion of foul play: all standard ingredients of a subset of the mystery genre known as crime or *detective fiction*, a genre dating back to *One Thousand and One Nights*. Among the tales Scheherazade spins to keep from losing her head, "The Three Apples" (aka "The Tale of the Murdered Young Woman") unravels the mystery of a young woman's body discovered hacked to pieces inside a locked chest. The Abbasid Caliph Harun al-Rashid, who bought the sealed chest from a fisherman who found it on the banks of the Tigris river, gives his vizier Ja'far ibn Yahya three days to solve the crime, or else. From there "The Three Apples" piles on suspense, intrigue, and a whiplash-inducing series of plot twists. It laid the foundation for countless subsequent dramas and thrillers, from Shakespeare's *Othello* to Hitchcock's *North by Northwest*.

The Chinese have their own tradition of folk detective stories, going all the way back to Bao Gong stories of the Ming Dynasty and later exemplified by the eighteenth-century Judge Dee Mysteries (translated into English by the Dutch Sinologist Robert van Gulik). In these mysteries the detective role is performed by a judge or local magistrate, and the criminal and his crime are revealed early in the story, so that suspense owes more to how the crime is solved than to its solution. Based on real murder cases, the stories are laden with historical and philosophical digressions. They often even include official documents.

Meanwhile here in the West, in "The Murders in the Rue Morgue," Edgar Allan Poe established a plot formula for detective stories that's been in use ever since. Unlike the Judge Dee cases, Poe's stories center around the slow unraveling of the truth, or what Poe himself called "ratiocination"—a process wherein the hero detective applies a combination of observation, intuition, forensic analysis, inference, and persistence. Poe's stories lead to Arthur Conan Doyle and Sherlock Holmes, the world's most famous sleuth, and the progenitor of every fictional private eye thereafter, from Sam Spade to Lieutenant Columbo.

In this opening of a detective novel, we are presented with two scenes— one grounded in reality, the other in dream. Though competently written, each leaves something to be desired. In the first scene, we are offered one tantalizing detail: that of the red robe. This is first stated as a fact in the opening line, then reiterated through dialogue too schematic to earn its keep. In any case, since the robe must still be on the corpse, the testimony amounts to naught.

Which leaves us with the detective (or two detectives; their relationship is unclear) at the scene of a potential crime and no truly tantalizing detail to seduce us deep into the story—only the vague reference to the detective's sense of déjà vu. Then the scene ends.

Reduced to its essence, it might read:

When she fell from the overpass she wore a red robe.

The rest is redundant, irrelevant, implied, and/or obvious. To get pulled into this mystery, most readers will want more—and dreams won't do. As a scene unto itself, the dream sequence fails for the same reason the opening fails. It gives us too little cause for suspense.

Supposing the dream were worked into the opening scene; supposing, as he examines the corpse, Detective Hsiao has his moment of déjà vu, thrusting him back into his recurrent dream of a girl being pursued by shadowy figures. But in the dream the girl wore a red gown; this murder victim is naked. True, the only eyewitness (can there be more than one?) swears that the girl wore red. She must be confused. As the detective covers the corpse a shout comes from the nearby slope. They've found something. A cop holds it up on a stick: a scarlet robe.

It will fall on the author (or her narrator) to explain this clairvoyant dream.

Your Turn

Revise this opening as suggested per the penultimate paragraph of my analysis.

40. Bases Loaded (a Crime Thriller)

*(Crime Thriller / McGuffins / Dramatized
Routine as Harbinger of Violence)*

Shoulder resting gently against shoulder, they nestled on a supple leather sofa, Barry absorbed in the sixth game of the World Series, Sheena enjoying the only baseball she watched all year. At each highlight, a key pitch, hit or catch, he offered commentary, she smiled and sipped a white wine.

"Play ball!" the umpire signaled the start of the fifth inning and Barry crossed fingers for his Orioles. Facing them on a 75-inch flat panel, the Braves pitcher gripped a ball hidden in his glove, peered out at the couple and nodded.

The view from the centerfield camera jumped onto the screen and now Sheena and Barry were behind the pitcher, looking past his red "37" at the nervous hitter flexing his bat while the umpire crouched and the catcher raised his mitt to the inside of the plate. The pitcher wound up and fired a fastball and flinched at the crack of the bat blasting a blur over his head through the top of the TV. The image reversed again to capture the shortstop's skyward grimace and bring into focus the ball sailing far above the left fielder before arching down to clip the foul pole and carom fair into the fourth row of dismayed fans.

"Hell yeah, it's gone," Barry cheered, "Turner nailed that fastball."

The picture switched back to the hitter almost to first base, slowing to a trot and thrusting up his fist in joy, then cut to a close up of the pitcher's face, bent down to study the cloud of dust he had just kicked up on the mound.

"Looks like we'll be tasting victory champagne, Sheena." He tilted his face to hers, his styled gray hair grazing honey blonde tresses a generation younger. "We're going to win this. The Braves are cooling down and the O's are getting hot."

"Hope you're right." Sheer pink fingernails brushed a tuft of golden bangs away from an eye.

Analysis

Reading this first page, without the help of a tersely lurid title (*Dead Cold, Sweet Death, Blood Secrets, Dark Waters*) and one of those covers, you know the kind, with raised metallic 200-point gothic type superimposed over silhouetted figures casting ponderous shadows, you might never guess that it's the opening of a legal or crime thriller, but according to the author's note it is. So we can be fairly sure if not absolutely certain that something extremely unpleasant and of a criminal nature will befall this romantic pair of baseball watchers.

Still, this opening generates too little interest in its romantically involved characters, who, though of different ages, with her "honey blonde tresses ... a generation younger [than his gray hair]," are otherwise not developed. As for the baseball game, World Series or not, and however deeply invested these lovers may be in it, in itself the game holds no interest for this reader.

Though he didn't invent it, for the role played by baseball in this opening scene, Hitchcock, the aforementioned director of *Psycho* and *North by Northwest*, popularized the term "MacGuffin" or "McGuffin," meaning an otherwise irrelevant object or device that triggers a plot—or, as the Master of Suspense put it less charitably, "The thing that the characters ... care deeply about ... and for which the audience does not give a damn."

Though rendered in great detail, the baseball game here exists mainly to establish this couple's interest in the game along with (possibly) Barry's betting habit, the routine against which an extraordinary event will soon play itself out with presumably deadly results, launching the criminal or legal proceedings that will drive this novel's plot through several hundred pages.

As I've said elsewhere, routine is important. Without routine the extraordinary events that make for a plot have nothing to work against or to set them into relief. I'm reminded of that passage at the opening of the most famous of crime thrillers, Truman Capote's *In Cold Blood*, in which he establishes the story's setting: Holcomb, Kansas, the small Midwestern town where Herb Clutter lived with his family, and where their grisly murders occurred:

> Until one morning in mid-November of 1959, few Americans—in fact, few Kansans—had ever heard of Holcomb. Like the waters of the river, like the motorists on the highway, and like the yellow trains streaking down the Santa Fe tracks, drama, in the shape of exceptional happenings, had never stopped there.

The trouble with routine is that it can't be dramatized, nor should we bother trying. When we do, the best we can hope for is *dramatized routine*—a contradiction in terms, routine and drama having about the same relationship as water and oil. However much action, dialogue, or loving description we pump into the corpse of routine, however heroically we try to resuscitate it with artful similes, hyperventilating adjectives and adverbs, and other linguistic life-support systems, the result will most likely still be dead on arrival.

Most likely, that is, unless while establishing routine we're also doing something else: *evoking character*. As I've also said before: if something we write evokes character, we should probably keep it. If it doesn't, we do well to question it.

In the given opening, though it establishes Barry's gambling habit (which may or may not play a role in what's forthcoming), watching him and Sheena watch a baseball game tells us little if anything about them. But it could if the perspective were altered. Were the scene written from a close third-person subjective viewpoint, one that immersed us—however briefly—into one or both of the characters' sensibilities, through their individual perceptions of and responses to the game we'd know them as individuals, as people. Do Barry's bigwin dreams feature palm trees and infinity pools? Does Sheena wonder if he's getting himself in over his head? We would therefore care about them, and therefore care that something (we intuit) bad is going to happen to them, and therefore feel not boredom, but suspense.

Instead, the author uses a point-of-view strategy that curiously puts us and the watching couple *into* the baseball game—or rather into the television screen in which the baseball game is taking place. It's a compelling strategy, but one that gives us no access into the characters' interiors, and that makes the ball game—the McGuffin, the very thing we *don't* care about—its subject.

Something else that wouldn't hurt this opening: a topic sentence that makes clear what we're getting ourselves into: a story not about baseball or a pair of baseball-loving lovebirds, but of crime and punishment. How differently we'd read the same opening if it started thus:

They died in the third inning with bases loaded. That's the opening strategy Stephen Booth uses in his crime thriller, *Scared to Live*:

Even on the night she died, Rose Shepherd couldn't sleep. By the early hours of the morning, her bed was like a battleground—hot, violent, chaotic. Beneath her, the sheet was twisted into painful knots, the pillow hard and unyielding. Lack of sleep made her head ache, and her body had grown stiff with discomfort.

In her short story "Home, Sweet Home," Hannah Tinti takes a similar approach:

> Pat and Clyde were murdered on pot roast night. The doorbell rang just as Pat was setting the butter and margarine (Clyde was watching his cholesterol) on the table. She was thinking about James Dean. Pat had loved him desperately as a teenager, seen his movies dozens of times, written his name across her notebooks, carefully taped pictures of him to the inside of her locker so that she would have the pleasure of seeing his tortured, sullen face from *East of Eden* as she exchanged her French and English textbooks for science and math.

In both cases from the throat-grabbing opening sentence each author goes on—not to establish routine—but to evoke character. The author of our first page has a chance to do both.

Your Turn

Draft an opening in which a tragedy or violence of some kind interrupts a banal routine. Example: a retired librarian shot dead by a stray bullet while mowing his lawn. Without telegraphing what's going to happen, somehow imply the coming tragedy. Hint: avoid anything overtly ominous. Do *not* make it a cloudy or fog-swept day. On the contrary, the brighter the circumstances, the more we expect something to go wrong.

41. Hit and Run

(Detective Fiction / Noir / Hardboiled Prose)

Death had come airborne and metallic. Not in the streamlined shape of a bullet, but in the blunt square shape of the front of a car. A car going so fast it had become airborne at the top of the hill, just before slamming into its victim.

Matt Selden shivered, and pulled his coat closer around him. He wished he'd put a beanie on. When he got Liz's phone call, he'd just leaped out of bed, yanked on a coat and shoes, jumped into the car, and raced his way here as quick as he could. Under the coat, he was still wearing his pyjamas.

Dawn was just breaking. The first rays of the sun sparkled on the spire of the stately old church building behind him—the church that had been the only witness of the hit and run which happened a couple of hours ago, in the lonely pre-dawn darkness.

The police had cordoned off the northeast corner of the crossroads. They'd drawn chalk circles around little bits of glass on the pavement and road. Shattered headlight? Matt mused. Maybe even a cracked windscreen? His eyes narrowed as he saw a change in the colour of the bitumen. There was a large oval patch of darkness on the road. Tendrils drifted downhill from it like a jellyfish, snaking their way to the edge of the road, and into the gutter. Matt's stomach turned. It was blood.

Inside the police cordon were two officers. The short, burly sergeant was facing away from Matt, his hands on his hips, muttering to the other policeman, a constable. The constable caught Matt's eye, and his brow wrinkled in a frown. The sergeant turned around. The moment he saw Matt, his eyes narrowed, and his lip lifted in a sneer, exposing nicotine-stained teeth. "Ah, Jesus," he snapped.

"No, just one of his faithful ministers," Matt replied with a pained smile.

"What the hell are you doing here, Selden?"

"At the moment, Sergeant Parker, I'm standing on a public pavement, talking to you. That's not breaking the law, I trust?"

193

Analysis

Here we have a private investigator arriving at a crime scene. The murder weapon: neither a bullet nor the gun that fired it, but "the blunt square shape of the front of a car" traveling fast enough to have "become airborne ... before slamming into its victim."

Though not stated as such, these observations clearly belong to Matt Selden, private-eye, as he takes in the scene, "pull[ing] his coat closer around him." We don't have to wonder what sort of coat he wears. As befitting the grand tradition of hardboiled crime fiction into which this snugly fits, it has to be a trench coat, one with the lapels flipped raffishly up and that has no doubt seen better days, as has its haggard, cynical owner.

Without even having read beyond the second paragraph, already I feel I know Matt, or know his type. I've met him many times before in books and movies. He is Sam Spade in Hammett's *The Maltese Falcon*, Marlowe in Raymond Chandler's *The Big Sleep*. No stranger to violent crime or danger, he has engaged in a little of both himself, now and then, for the sake of his clients. He's cocky, tough, a bit on the flip side—but not without principles, or a heart. He may not always get his man (or woman: the hardboiled school doesn't discriminate on the basis of sex), but his batting average is better than that of the cops with whom he shares a common goal, and with whom he nonetheless always finds himself working, usually at cross purposes.

Pioneered in the 1920s by Carroll John Day and popularized in the 1930s and 1940s by Chandler and Hammett, the hardboiled genre—referred to less than charitably by some as "pulp fiction"—remains hugely popular to this day. Part of that ongoing success may be owed to the genre's timelessness and versatility. After all, as long as there are criminals and crimes, someone will need to solve them—or try. That may explain why the genre has attracted writers as otherwise unlike each other as John D. MacDonald, Robert B. Parker, Sue Grafton, Walter Mosley, and others whose titles dominate bestseller lists, each of them giving the hardboiled theme a different twist.

Here, the "twist" seems to be that Matt Selden, private-eye, is also a man of the cloth. "No," Matt replies when a burly police sergeant who is also at the scene sneers "Ah, Jesus" at him, "just one of his faithful ministers."

It's not the first time that a fictional man of the cloth has slummed as a detective. In the early part of the last century, English novelist G.K. Chesterton published 52 short stories starring Father Brown, a priest who moonlights as a Sherlock Holmes-like detective. Unlike his hardboiled successors, Father Brown exemplified the quiet humility of his *other* calling, and seldom spoke except to utter something profound. More recently, Fr. Brad Reynolds and Andrew Greeley (himself a priest) have given us mystery-solving clergymen.

Though Hammett was an exquisite stylist (his dialogue was so strong, for the screenplay of *The Maltese Falcon* director John Huston supposedly had his secretary strip everything else out of the book), and beautifully crafted hard-boiled novels exist, to succeed at the genre gorgeous prose is by no means a prerequisite. "Adequate" sums up the style of most such novels.

Here the prose is better than adequate. "Death had come airborne and metallic" draws me right in. There's a wisecracking, street-slangy-poetic edge to it that, I soon learn, is a product of the protagonist's steely cynicism. However hardboiled, the prose still makes room for atmosphere ("The first rays of the sun sparkled on the spire of the stately old church") and convincing detail ("His eyes narrowed as he saw a change in the colour of the bitumen"). The trails of blood drifting away from the corpse are likened to the tendrils of a jellyfish. Though I regret the lack of faith in the reader that has the author assuring us that the tendrils are of blood, still, the description works.

With equal efficiency via a brief exchange of dialogue the author effectively renders the strained relationship between his protagonist and the beat sergeant.

Mean, lean, and clean—almost (but not quite) slick: befitting a genre of which we've come to expect no more or less.

Your Turn

Draft the first page of a detective novel in the hardboiled tradition of Hammett and Chandler. Use first person. In addition to the requisite cynicism, endow your detective protagonist with a unique perspective, condition, or attitude: make him or her OCD or Tourettic (like the detective hero of Jonathan Lethem's *Motherless Brooklyn*) or deeply depressed (see Martin Beck's *The Laughing Policeman*) or deadpan (*Dragnet*'s Sergeant Joe Friday). Start with a dead body; any dead body will do. What matters here is the quality of character as conveyed by your detective narrator.

42. Detective in a Department Store

(First Sentences / Information vs. Evidence / Dramatized Routine)

Maybe you've been inside Drake's department store in upper Manhattan. It's got the same brand names and glitzy merchandizing that department stores across the country have. I pay attention to these details in my line of work, especially the brand names.

I entered Drake's at 10:30 in the morning a few weeks ago and was greeted by the rhythmic beat of rock music, while elegantly dressed salespeople swarmed around me like locusts and beckoned with atomizers of Chanel perfume and Polo by Ralph Lauren cologne. I brushed by the salespeople and the morning shoppers and walked through the cosmetics department, where I noticed a young woman, possibly a student from nearby Columbia University, who was seated and receiving a complimentary facial from an Estée Lauder sales associate in a white smock. Off to the right, a strobe light flickered on-off, on-off beside a rack of designer *Guess?* jeans.

I passed the escalator that led to the second floor, where the counterfeit Paul Sterling & Company cashmere sweaters were on sale....

Analysis

First sentences are so important. They tell us what a writer considers his "best foot forward." If that "best foot" turns out to be lame, it doesn't raise great expectations for what follows.

Here, the first sentence ("Maybe you've been inside Drake's department store in upper Manhattan") raises doubts. First, there's that tentative "maybe." As the first word of what is presumably to be a novel of two to three hundred pages—a detective novel no less—the writer may want to ask herself, "Do I really want to start off on such a wishy-washy note?"

A wishy-washy opener can serve a purpose. The best example I can think of is the opening to John Barth's early novel, *The End of the Road*:

In a sense, I am Jacob Horner.

Barth's novel is essentially about a man who cannot make up his mind about anything. Compare Barth's opening shrug with the sledgehammer blow that launches *Moby Dick*:

Call me Ishmael.

I'm far from convinced, however, that the wishy-washiness that attends the opening page in question was intended. My confidence is further undermined by the questionable authenticity of a department store named Drake's and located in "upper" Manhattan. As a former Manhattanite I can tell you that there is no singular "upper Manhattan." There are the Upper West Side and the Upper East Side (and never the twain shall meet). I know, too, that there isn't and has never been a department store named Drake's; in fact there are no department stores anywhere above 59th Street, where, if it hasn't gone out of business by now, Bloomingdale's is located. Why not choose a real department store in an authentic Manhattan, and not a generic—and less than credible—substitute?

The third sentence, too, can be strengthened. Rather than details already mentioned (and that, as discussed, aren't very convincing), the author might share her character's solid, specific, and authentic observations, rendering his point ("I pay attention") explicit and vivid, rather than making us accept this as a matter of faith.

In the same vein, in the next paragraph, instead of telling us the salespeople are "elegantly dressed," why not let us see, from the narrator's perspective, what they are wearing, providing us with specifics—down to brand names, if appropriate and necessary. Mere epithets won't do.

Remember:

Adjectives = Opinions
Opinions ≠ Descriptions

Lack of authenticity with respect to specific details can cost us readers. But there are other kinds of inauthenticity we should guard against. Look at the first sentence of the third paragraph, in which the detective describes what's on the second floor before taking us up the escalator:

I passed the escalator that led to the second floor, where the counterfeit Paul Sterling & Company cashmere sweaters were on sale.

For one thing, department stores don't sell fakes. And though we may assume that the detective has been to the store before, still, he must have been there very recently to know those cashmere sweaters are still there. Yet nowhere on this first page is a prior visit alluded to, so the snarky remark about those sweaters feels at best like an authorial intrusion, information known to the author but that's beyond the character's experience. Then again, once the narrator does go up that escalator (not before), he might authentically describe not only those cashmere sweaters, but the department store's glass-floored mezzanine, and the candy store where the counter clerk wears a conical paper hat, and the men's dressing room, with its varnished wooden stalls smelling faintly of ear wax and vinegar.

Finally, this opening could be enhanced by starting with a dramatic scene in progress rather than inert information, with the detective already in the store, watching the young woman getting a facial. Whenever a first-person narrator describes things to us, he or she is also potentially describing his or her character. Opportunities to do so are missed here; the "girl getting facial" scene is brushed aside, as are those swarming salespeople.

How much stronger this opening would be if, through this carefully rendered scene of a woman getting a facial in a department store, we experience the protagonist's eye for details—which, after all, is what the scene is ultimately about.

Such an opening scene might also go a long way toward establishing the detective's remoteness and his detachment. He sees the pretty young woman; his trained eye captures every detail, but he responds to her clinically, rather than sympathetically, passionately, or poetically. Not only do we get the scene, we get the character of the man experiencing it. Two birds with one stone.

Your Turn

Write five alternative first sentences for this novel opening.

43. Mommy Get Your Gun

(Satire / Spoof / Importance of Grammar)

I crouched, unmoving and stifled; the garbage bins masking my position. I was unsure as to whether my threat still remained. I desperately wanted to sneak a peek, but having been shot at once today was already one time too many for me.

I figured I could safely stay cramped here for a while longer. The stench of the garbage-filled bins was already losing its pungency through familiarity, and the kids' school bell wasn't due for at least another hour and a half.

"You're a big fat fraidycat!" I silently admonished myself. Well perhaps I was! I'm sure I used to be braver, but I heard age can soften you up. And hadn't I just unceremoniously celebrated my 39th birthday. One more year till I'm old!

Suddenly the silence of the alley was disturbed by the chirping of an annoying ring tone. I was right, my shooter was still out there, and so close; in fact he was directly at the bins. His phone went unanswered and I had the discomfort of listening to the dreadful default Nokia ring tone—just like mine!

"Oh heck!" I cursed, it was my phone. "Bloody bugger, shit shit shit!" I was as good as dead anyway since I had just given away my hiding spot. I took a look at who was using Murphy's law to call me now, and help prepare me for my executioner.

The school's number was blinking on the screen. Rising slightly so my eyes followed the top of my head, I looked across the bin lids. Empty, the alley was empty! "Hello," I stage whispered into the phone.

"Ms. Brandez, Jamie has fallen up the steps and given himself a scraped cheek and bloody nose."

I sighed, "How could this happen when there are only two stairs in the entire school?"

"He had his hands in his pockets and they got stuck in there."

I rolled my eyes. *Why me?* I wondered.

I put my gun away, tidied my hair, and headed toward my car so I could pick up one of my clumsy fatherless kids. This is my life!

Analysis

Behind trash bins in a garbage-strewn alley a woman seeks cover from a gun-toting assailant. Of the assailant's identity—or the cause underlying his or her murderous pursuit of the protagonist—we learn nothing, at least not by the end of this first page. We know only that the protagonist is the single mother of a boy named Jamie, who, in the midst of his mother's back-alley struggle for survival, has taken an accidental fall at school and bloodied his nose.

The juxtaposition of two incongruous fictional worlds, of *noir* detective and struggling single mom—Raymond Chandler meets Murphy Brown—is tantalizing but also perplexing. Assuming this woman is ducking *real* bullets, how did she get herself into such a fix? Equally impressive—and no less perplexing—is the nonchalance ("I rolled my eyes") with which she shrugs off what a few moments before had been or seemed to be a serious threat to life and limb in order to rush to the aid of her slightly injured child.

Was the threat serious? Are we being played with? What, exactly, is going on here?

Whatever is going on, one thing is clear enough: that somewhere a tongue has been lodged firmly in a cheek. The world of this novel isn't my everyday world, or yours, but one that exists in a parallel universe, where gun-toting mothers interrupt back alley shoot-outs to kiss their offspring's skinned knees: The world of satire or *spoof.*

The word "spoof" derives from the name of a card game invented around the turn of the nineteenth century by British comedian Arthur Roberts. Since the game involved hoaxing, trickery, and nonsense, in time the word itself came to stand for tomfoolery. As applied to literature, it denotes a light, playful parody—which, presumably, is what we have here: a parody of a detective novel in which the detective is a struggling single mother.

On this first page, however satirical, the world is created with considerable authority, an authority earned in part by the author's unwillingness to explain, apologize, or make excuses for her far-fetched premise. No sooner do we read, "I crouched, unmoving and stifled; the garbage bins masking my position," then we're ensconced in that ironic world. By plunging us directly into the action, the author avoids exposition and explanation.

In a similar way, by way of a single sentence, Franz Kafka convinces us that overnight a man has turned into a giant beetle. Exactly how and why this transformation has occurred, Kafka (wisely) abandons to the reader's imagination. It is a *fait accompli.* The reader has a choice: accept it, or stop reading.

But there are other, smaller ways in which this author undermines that same authority, including poor punctuation (that imprudent semi-colon in the first sentence), subject-verb disagreements (see sentence 3), tense shifts (sentence 4: strictly speaking, it should be "I could have stayed cramped there"), and a beginner's loving embrace of adverbs ("desperately," "suddenly," "directly," "slightly").

Given this far-fetched premise that asks much of readers by way of suspending disbelief, the author has no wiggle-room for such confidence-shaking errors: she had better get everything just right. And there's no way she can get away with telling readers that her heroine's eyes "[follow] the top of [her] head." Even in a world where single moms shoot it out in blind alleys, we still expect eyes to tag along with the skulls that hold them.

Your Turn

Draft the opening of a story or novel with an outrageous premise. Example A: A world in which men are half the size of women (literally, not figuratively). Example B: A world where life and death have switched places, so life begins with death and ends with birth. Example C: A bank heist undertaken by: a) pubescent children; b) pregnant women; c) escapees from a retirement home. Whatever your far-fetched premise, whether satirical, tongue-in-cheek, or dead serious, your mission is to suspend the reader's disbelief enough so they buy into it.

44. Lady Pamela's Surgeon

(Romance / Bodice Ripper / Where to Begin?)

"*Really*, darling—I can't believe you're marrying a girl you haven't even met," Lady Pamela Whittington drawled. Her slim taut shoulders shuddered delicately under her red silk blouse. "It's not like you have to look far to find a woman to share your life." Reaching up, she ran the tips of her red painted fingernails down Alfie's cheek.

Damn her and her kind, thought Alfie, smiling slowly; a smile that started at the corners of his sculpted lips and slowly dimpled his cheeks before moving to his heavy-lidded black eyes. He looked deep into her baby-blue eyes, framed by wrinkle-free eyelids and thick lashes. "You bloody charmer," Lady Pamela murmured. Her fingers moved down his cheek and caressed his neck, lingering on the top button of his cream raw silk shirt before she stepped back.

"Well, I should let you get on with your surgery, doctor. You have a flight to catch tonight." She eased her petite body into the surgical chair at the center of the room with practiced ease. "Roger and I were discussing last night how hard it must be for you to go back there. All that smell and dirt! And the flies and beggars. Really, *dah*-ling—I can't imagine why you would *want* to go back. You could have flown your family over here. We would have been happy to open our country house for the wedding."

Alfie switched on the overhead lights and angled them to light up her face. Pamela squinted and then gave him a beguiling smile. Alfie turned away as he put on his gown and gloves and loaded the syringe. "Botox injections to your brow and cheek are hardly surgery, Pamela," he said, working hard to keep his voice calm. "And my family and my fiancée's family are in Colombo. It's an arranged marriage, Pamela. The parents of the bride organize the wedding ceremony."

As he turned back to her, he noticed with a thrill of pride that the lip reshaping done eight months ago still looked great.

Analysis

Though women stopped wearing bodices by the end of the eighteenth century, the term "bodice-ripper" is of fairly recent coinage. The phrase debuted in print in the 28th December 1980 issue of the *New York Times*: "Women too have their pornography: Harlequin romances, novels of sweet savagery, bodice-rippers." A second article written in 1980 by Stephen Grover and published in the *Wall Street Journal* characterized bodice-rippers as a strain of romance novels featuring, on their paperback covers, scantily clad women being manhandled by alpha males, and went on to call them "juicy, cheap, predictable, and devoured in stupefying quantities by legions of loyal fans." No wonder authors of romance fiction haven't embraced the expression. They consider it an insult.

If there's a line between bodice-rippers and more "serious" Gothic novels and novels of manners, it's blurry, but then so too is the line between romantic fiction and such darlings of the literary canon as *Jane Eyre*, *Wuthering Heights*, and *Pride & Prejudice*, the latter of which, despite having been published in 1813 when the genre per se didn't exist, has been called "the best romance novel ever written." Actually, if we define romance novels as novels of courtship told from the perspective of the heroine and that end happily, the prototype may be Samuel Richardson's *Pamela, or Virtue Rewarded*. Published in 1740, Richardson's novel was one of the few of its time to supply a happy ending. It was also one of the first blockbusters. Written in the epistolary mode (in the form of letters), it opens:

> Dear Mother and Father,
>   I have great trouble, and some comfort, to acquaint you with. The trouble is, that my good lady died of the illness I mentioned to you, and left us all much grieved for the loss of her; for she was a dear good lady, and kind to all us her servants. Much I feared, that as I was taken by her ladyship to wait upon her person, I should be quite destitute again, and forced to return to you and my poor mother, who have enough to do to maintain yourselves; and, as my lady's goodness had put me to write and cast accounts, and made me a little expert at my needle, and otherwise qualified above my degree, it was not every family that could have found a place that your poor Pamela was fit for: but God, whose graciousness to us we have so often experienced at a pinch, put it into my good lady's heart, on her death-bed, just an hour before she expired, to recommend to my young master all her servants, one by one; and when it came to my turn to be recommended, (for I was sobbing and crying at her pillow) she could only say, My dear son!—and so broke off a little; and then recovering—Remember my poor Pamela—And these were some of her last words! O how my eyes run—Don't wonder to see the paper so blotted.

However purely expository owing to its rhetorical strategy, Richardson's opening plunges us headlong into his protagonist's grief at the loss of her "dear good lady." Of course we want to know who she was and why she died. Through this parted veil of tears we enter that story.

However much (or little) prestige we assign to the romance genre, with its shuddering shoulders and lingering caresses the first page under scrutiny here fits the bill. Even the main character's Christian name, by design or not, blows a kiss to Richardson's 1740 prototype.

Whatever else may be said of the genre, its entertainment value can't be denied. Fast-paced, suspenseful (inasmuch as any story whose conclusion is foregone can hold suspense), studded with mildly pornographic scenes, with little tolerance for subtlety and ambiguity, and as hospitable to cliché and stereotype as a mosquito-ridden Ugandan swamp to malaria.... In few words, the literary equivalent of a soap opera.

Which isn't to suggest that the romance genre lacks sophistication. In its own way, it's quite sophisticated. There are first of all many more rules that must be followed than with mainstream or literary fiction. The protagonists must meet early, adultery must be avoided, and ultimately, emotional commitment must be rewarded.

For sure, many romance novels have been written that deviate from these rules. The given example, with its male protagonist and Botox-enhanced antagonist, certainly does. But even when deviating from them, it takes skill to negotiate all the rules and restrictions and still evoke breathing characters seemingly capable of exercising their own free will.

And this author demonstrates considerable skill. From Lady Pamela's first drawled words ("Really, darling—I can't believe you're marrying a girl you haven't even met"), I get a strong sense of her less than exemplary character: a spoiled rich woman with (perhaps) her own designs on Alfie, a man committed to his marriage—not out of convenience or greed, but out of, if not love, duty.

However entertaining, what's presented here feels less like the opening scene of this novel than one from much deeper into it, after the relationship between Alfie and his Sri Lankan bride-to-be has been established, along with Lady Pamela's stake in all of this, such that when we arrive at this scene we'll appreciate the dynamics that underlie it.

Though I've painted Pamela as antagonist, for all we know this could be *her* novel, and we're meant to cheer her on in her quest to rescue Alfie from a potentially doomed, loveless marriage.

Whether that turns out to be the case or not, from what we're given here we aren't sure who we should care for, or why we should care for them.

Your Turn

Read this first page again. While doing so, on a sheet of paper divided into three columns by lines drawn down the page, and labeled "A," "B," and "C" make three lists as follows:

1. List A: things you know and learn about the characters and their situation
2. List B: things you don't know but are willing to learn in due time
3. List C: things you want to know immediately.

45. The Pleasures of Genre

(Regency Romance / Strong Verbs / Close Third Person / Feelings)

January 1, 1806
Stanford On Avon, Northamptonshire

"A burial is not the way to start a day, let alone a year." Cranny—Lucien Charles Sedgewick, 12th Duke of Cranleigh—took no comfort from his friends' grunts of agreement. The corpse-grey morning seemed surly, as if it knew 1806 had arrived with Death as its companion.

And a close friend—Edward Melton, heir to the Earl of Highgate—was Death's first prize.

Faust squeezed Cranny's shoulder. "Come on, Cranny. It's time."

Cranny trudged over the snowy ground and under the earl's stricken gaze, joined his friends around the funeral wagon. For the first time in two years their close-knit group of ten were together, though not as they'd imagined. Not with Edward in the casket. Even Chipper had left his sick bed and made the arduous journey north, though ill health rendered him too weak to do more than walk behind the casket.

They carried Edward's casket into the Melton family graveyard where gravestones huddled together like hardened conspirators, forever guarding their grim spoils, even as time and the elements erased the epitaphs they bore. Solemn funerary attendants stepped forward. The urge to scream at them to be gone clawed at Cranny's throat, but dear, departed Father's edict—whipped into his flesh and burned by pain into his memory—prevailed.

Do nothing to bring shame on the family name.

They surrendered the casket to the attendants and soon the drone of the clergyman's voice joined the low moan of the wind. Eyes narrowed against the whirling snow, Cranny braced himself. As the casket descended into the grave a great knot formed in his throat, every creak of the straining ropes hitting his brain with all the power of a blacksmith's hammer striking the anvil. Edward did not belong in the waiting maw in the cold earth. Not at twenty-six.

Guilt crunched Cranny's heart, and his blood hammered in his ears while his muscles bunched and quivered with an odd need to do ... violence. Some unspeakable cur had attacked Edward and his men and left them dead or dying while the snow bloomed scarlet with their blood. And it is all my bloody fault. His chest hollowed and the ache behind his ribs sharpened, snatching his breath. His vision blurred. God's teeth. I will not cry like a whelp. Spine rigid, he thrust his hands into the pockets of his greatcoat and pulled in a lungful of frigid air. He would see the murderer hang. Dammed if he wouldn't.

Another gust of wind whipped about him, its icy claws slapping at his greatcoat. What lay beyond the grave? The image of a small, white-haired ghost flashed through his head on a stumbling heart-beat. What in Hades? Perhaps the memory was a reminder that life was fragile. Transient. Perhaps it was a reminder he had yet to fulfill his obligations to his dukedom, lest he fall victim to the family curse and end up in an early grave too.

God. Death was a damned sight more appealing....

Analysis

No one had more lovers,
No one needed love more
Than PLEASURE'S DAUGHTER.
She had seven lovers
But only one love and he was ...
The King of England.

The genre of this first page is the "regency romance," a subgenre of the romance novel, the conventions of which Margot Livesey outlines for us in *The Hidden Machinery*, her delightful book of essays on the novelist's craft:

1. The lovers are unlikely in some obvious way.
2. They meet early and are then separated—either physically or emotionally—for most of the narrative.
3. There must be significant obstacles—"dragons and demons"—to be overcome.
4. Changes of setting, even from drawing room to street, are vital for revealing the characters and moving the narrative forward.

5. Many minor characters will assist the lovers on their journey.
6. A subplot, or two, is required to keep the lovers apart, to allow time to pass, to act as a foil to the main plot, and to entertain the readers.

Set in the time of the British Regency (1811–20), regency romances evolved from the "novel of manners" as practiced by Sir Walter Scott and Jane Austen, who dramatized the domestic affairs of the English gentry. The modern regency—written long after but set in the same period—was first popularized by Georgette Heyer, who penned several dozen between 1935 and her death in 1974.

With its provocative opening ("A burial is not the way to start a day, let alone a year") our first page holds out a model of the form. Though starting right off with dialogue has its risks (namely the confusion attendant with confronting readers with an ungrounded, disembodied conversation-in-progress), it also gets right down to business—namely the business of evoking character, as this opening dialogue does very well. We haven't met Cranny; we don't even know his name, yet already this dialogue nails him to the page. It does more: it nails down the point of view. Until further notice—to the bottom of this first page, anyway—everything will be filtered through Cranny's gloomy sensibilities.

That filtering avails itself of free indirect discourse, by which the narrator's voice is colored by the point-of-view character. Note, in the fourth paragraph, the choice of modifiers and verbs ("trudged," "stricken," "arduous"), and how they convey Cranny's grim outlook.

Fifth paragraph: the gravestones "huddled like hardened conspirators"— more Cranny. All is filtered through his perspective, his personality. Though the "free" in "free indirect" means that the simile could be attributed to an objective narrator, nothing on this first page is purely neutral or objective; everything is flavored by our protagonist's bleak disposition. It's the salt in this stew.

Rather than attempt to describe characters' abstract feelings (hard if not impossible), wise writers evoke them as concretely as possible. With "Guilt crunched Cranny's heart, and his blood hammered in his ears while his muscles bunched and quivered" this author does just that, balancing abstractions (guilt) with active, solid nouns (blood/muscles) and verbs (hammered/quivered). This is but one of many approaches the author uses to render Cranny's emotional state, from dipping into his thoughts ("I will not cry like a whelp") to precisely rendering his visible gestures ("he thrust his hands into the pockets of his greatcoat and pulled in a lungful of frigid air.").

Whatever else good writing does, it evokes character. If it evokes character, keep it.

Through a wisely chosen, thoroughly engaged close third-person narration, this author injects us richly, vividly, clearly, and precisely into this opening scene, one we inhabit thoroughly. The weather (the wind, the whirling snow), sounds, temperature, thoughts, memories, opinions, and attitudes—all are there, as are actions, gestures, etc.

Genre or no genre, "literary" or not, this is good writing.

Your Turn

Rewrite an opening that you or someone else has written, published or in-progress, switching it from first person to close third person, so it reads just as (or even more) intimately than in the first-person version.

F. Memoir

"Memoir isn't the summary of a life; it's a window into a life, very much like a photograph in its selective composition. It may look like a casual and even random calling up of bygone events. It's not; it's a deliberate construction."

WILLIAM ZINSSER, IN *On Writing Well*

ASK FOUR PEOPLE THE DIFFERENCE BETWEEN A MEMOIR AND AN autobiography and odds are you'll get four different answers. For Gore Vidal a memoir is "how one remembers one's own life, while an autobiography is history."[9] Will Rogers put it this way in his *The Autobiography of Will Rogers*, "When you put down the good things you ought to have done, and leave out the bad ones you did do—well, that's Memoirs." Ian Jack, writing in the *Guardian*, boils the difference down to that between telling (autobiography) and showing (memoir). Orson Welles found the term memoir "pompous."

Nor do dictionaries shed much light on the matter. According to the Oxford English Dictionary, an autobiography is "the writing of one's own history; the story of one's life written by himself," while a memoir is "a person's written account of incidents in his own life, the persons whom he has known, and the transactions or movements in which he has been concerned; an autobiographical record."

For me, the difference is mainly one of audience and intention. Autobiographies are penned by the famous or infamous for an audience interested to hear their life stories. Memoirs are written by the relatively obscure or by those who have merely brushed up against fame, with the intent of treating a specific, broader theme or issue with which the author is intimately and by personal experience acquainted, but that is not purely personal.

---

9   *Palimpsest*, 1996.

Which is a long way of saying that a memoir is about something other than the life of its author. If you're Dolly Parton or Bono, you write your autobiography. If you're somebody like me, and feel so inclined, pompous or not, you write a memoir.

Memoirist Nora Gallagher sums up more succinctly still the secret to good memoirs. "It's not about *you*."[10] When, in her 1994 memoir *Autobiography of a Face*, Lucy Grealy writes about losing half her jaw to cancer and the ramifications of being permanently disfigured, she's not merely talking of her own personal ordeal; she speaks to any and all of us who have ever been self-conscious of our looks or suffered rejection, or endured physical torment and pain, or who've been torn between who we are, and what we wish to be—in her case, someone with a whole face and not one torn in two by cancer. Singularly horrible though her experience may have been, still, there's much in it that we can all relate to. The *relatable* part is her book's true and worthy subject.

Something of the sort is true of all good stories. Yes, they are about people (characters); and yes, they are about very specific characters shaped by unique circumstances and events. But they are never strictly or purely personal: they are about something bigger than the characters' (or, in the case of memoir, our) circumstances. They have themes, and those themes extend into areas beyond the merely anecdotal or personal.

---

10   In conversation with the author.

46. Tanks & Miracles

(Memoir / War / Memoir vs. Autobiography / Theme)

Magic, it is said, is all around us. Prayers are heard. Unattractive girls find husbands, barren women conceive, young heels get promotions, cranky old men see their tumors disappear overnight.

My miracle was not a splashy kind. If you are inclined to, you find miracles easily enough. My best friend when I was ten drowned in the Danube and I did not. Perhaps a miracle. When the tanks rolled through the streets of Bratislava, some young men were killed but I was not. Perhaps another miracle. My parents were divorced in a gaudy public spectacle yet I escaped, relatively unharmed. Was that one? The plane which carried us from Vienna to a new life in Toronto did not crash. That might have been one, too. But I have always felt, having in the past forty years been a part of the miracle of a wedding, and the miracles of the births of two healthy children, that the finger of God was most obviously inter-vening in my life on that third day we were in Canada, the day we wandered through the streets to find food.

Back in Bratislava my brother and I spent about eight months getting used to a new household from which our father had been sent packing and a new man, the Doctor Professor, had been installed in his place. Our father had been laughter, but mainly absence. The stepfather was rules and rigidity. The new regime together was marked by clenched teeth on all our parts. My mother was, I think, happier than she had been, but not when all four of us were together; then she was tears and apologies. The tanks of August 1968 transformed all our lives. Soon after we were on a plane and the promise of yet another new life. I could hardly wait.

Analysis

Displaced by the Soviet Union's invasion of 1968, a young man and his Slovakian family relocate to Canada to fulfill "the promise of yet another new life" there. That's one way to sum up the material in this first page of what I assume is a memoir.

Slipping out from under the treads of tanks is only one of many "miracles" that the narrator has either witnessed or benefited from directly in his life. I put "miracles" in quotation marks, since here they are conflated with other things, with magic and with prayers, hence the term's meaning is broadened to include everything from surviving an invasion by some 2000 Warsaw-Pact tanks, to the "miracles" of marriage, childbirth, and "cranky old men seeing their tumors disappear overnight."

For sure, this expansive definition of miracles makes for a good attitude toward life—though the cynic in me can't help wondering whose prayers were answered by the existence of tanks and tumors in the first place.

As to whether it makes for a good memoir opening, that's another matter.

Clearly the narrator has a story to tell. Indeed, he has a grab bag of stories, surviving Brezhnev's tanks being one of many. He has also survived another displacement, that of his father—whom his mother "sent packing"—by her "new man, the Doctor Professor." This domestic restructuring happened eight months before those Soviet tanks rumbled into town, causing the already unstable ground under the narrator's feet to tremble that much harder. From Bratislava he and his family escaped first to Vienna, and from there to Toronto (on a plane which, we're told, "did not crash")—in itself, according to the narrator, another miracle.

In selecting miracles as his theme, and then defining them so loosely, the author casts such a wide net over his material that it's hard to say what, precisely, this memoir is about, other than the narrator's very eventful life in general— which, however eventful, isn't a fit subject for a memoir. Rather it launches this project into the territory of autobiography. Not a good thing.

While an autobiography is essentially a first-person account of someone's life, a memoir has a thematic focus to which the memoirist's life story has been subordinated. The key to a good memoir, as someone once told me, is that it's not about the memoirist, but about something that the memoirist has experienced firsthand—an ordeal or challenge (Primo Levi's *Survival in Auschwitz*; *Swimming to Antarctica*, by Lynn Cox), or a relationship (Tobias Wolff's *This Boy's Life*; Jeanette Walls's *The Glass Castle*), or life in a particular time and place (*Cross Creek*, by Marjorie Kinnan Rawlings; *This House of Sky*, by Ivan Doig), or a revolution (*Red Scarf Girl*, by Ji-Li Jiang), or a spiritual crisis or journey (*Practicing Resurrection*, by Nora Gallagher; Dan Barker's *Godless*).

Unless you're already a public figure, or known for some other reason, it's questionable whether anyone will want to read your life story; anyway, they would need a reason for doing so. The memoir form supplies that reason by treating the author's biography as the well from which a particular story is drawn, with its specific theme or themes, and doesn't ask readers to drink the whole well dry.

With this first page, the author suggests many intriguing tales, but unless he draws his thematic net tighter and narrows his focus, he will drown himself—and his readers—in autobiography. Which would be a shame, since not only does this author obviously have a story to tell, he has estimable gifts of language, perceptiveness, and wit with which to tell it:

> Our father had been laughter, but mainly absence. The stepfather was rules and rigidity. The new regime together was marked by clenched teeth on all our parts. My mother was, I think, happier than she had been, but not when all four of us were together; then she was tears and apologies.

This is good writing. It only needs to serve an equally good purpose, and that purpose should be not to illuminate a whole life but a particular experience—in this case, I think, how the "miracle" of survival, while it holds out the promise of "yet another life," also subjects its benefactors to further, often even greater, perils.

As for what part of his eventful life best illuminates that theme, the author must decide, and, having decided, cast the rest of his life into the background where it belongs.

Your Turn

Your life is an autobiography with different themes. It holds many potential memoirs. List some of the main episodes/events of your life, things that have happened to you, situations that you've found yourself in, between five and ten events. From the items on that list see if you can extract some *themes*. For instance: Event 1: A week after your twelfth birthday, your parents move to a different part of the country. Event 2: During your first year of college, your mother dies; your father remarries. Event 3: You come home for Christmas break to find your childhood bedroom taken over by one of your stepmother's children. Extracted theme: *Displacement*. Note: it's best to express the theme in one word or a short phrase.

47. A Pilot's Probation

(Memoir / Vocation / Memoir vs. Autobiography)

"You made it, you made it," Rick shouted as he lifted me over his head—not an easy feat, as I was 6'4" tall and liked to eat and work-out, even back then. My roommate was more excited for me than I could show while my head was pinned against the ceiling of our *crash pad* after TWA called to offer me a job, and I was ecstatic. No more turboprops for me. I was on my way to a new life in the world of jets and a seat was waiting for me in the next Boeing 727 class.

The hardest part of any job is getting it in the first place—unless you're a brand new major airline pilot, which I was at TWA in 1988. Then, keeping my job became a full-time commitment for the first year. This period is called *probation* and the company can fire any pilot without even giving a reason. "You're fired," hadn't been dreamed up by Donald Trump and reality TV yet, yet it wasn't far from any new airline pilot's mind. The union doesn't offer any protection until probation is over, either. We're on our own. It was a time to keep my eyes open and my mouth shut, which of course, has never been my strong suit.

Well, a year didn't sound so long to keep my nose clean, but it gets better. At most airlines, this probationary year didn't even start until new-hire training was completed. Three months of basic indoctrination, systems classes with quizzes, and simulator sessions led to a 4-hour checkride ripe with non-stop abnormalities and emergencies.

Analysis

The first page here is from a pilot's memoir. The most famous example of the genre—assuming there is such a creature—is *Wind, Sand, and Stars*, by Antoine de Saint-Exupéry. His memoir opens:

In 1926 I was enrolled as a student airline pilot by the Latécoère Company, the predecessors of Aéropostale (now Air France) in the operation of the line between Toulouse, in southwestern France, and Dakar, in French West Africa. I was learning the craft, undergoing an apprenticeship served by all young pilots before they were allowed to carry the mails. We took ships up on trial spins, made meek little hops between Toulouse and Perpignan, and had dreary lessons in meteorology in the freezing hangar. We lived in fear of the mountains of Spain, over which we had yet to fly, and in awe of our elders.

Note how quickly the focus here switches from the narrator to his fellow pilots in the aggregate ("It's not about *you*."). From this opening paragraph we go on to learn that Saint-Exupéry's book will of course be about him, but on a broader level it will be about pilots, flying, the mail service, and the poetry of land as seen from the air.

By contrast, judging by its opening paragraph, the memoir being considered here, though well written, is strictly personal. And that's the problem. The author has put his best foot forward, so he thinks, and it's an autobiographical foot. It begs the question: *what's in it for the reader?* Why should a perfect stranger care that so-and-so was offered a job at TWA—a company that doesn't even exist anymore? How relatable is that?

From there the narrator treats us to the intricacies of the probationary period. But this too is treated, not historically, or even nostalgically (by way of saying how things were different back then), but *personally*: this is what happened in my case, to me, at my airline. Fascinating? Yes, but only if the reader has some personal stake in the matter, if she knows the author, for instance, or has been a commercial pilot. Otherwise despite the good prose this won't fly.

Solutions may be at hand. One might be to follow Saint-Exupéry's example and switch the focus to the aggregate over the individual, to make this a memoir about flying for the airlines back then, when flying still held glamour—not one person's story, but the story of an industry in its relatively innocent days viewed through the lens of an individual—yet exemplary—experience.

Your Turn

Draft two versions of an opening describing a job where you worked with other people (for instance: waitperson at a restaurant; a player on a team; a performer in a theatrical production). In the first version, use the first person "I" and describe only your own personal experience. In the second version, use the second-person pronoun "we" and describe things from the viewpoint of the collective: all the waiters at the restaurant; every player on the team; all the actors in the play. Which version seems strongest to you? Why?

48. From "Loss ... But Not Lost": A Deathbed Scene

(Memoir / Death / Show, Don't Tell / Inhabiting Scenes)

I don't recall the day my mother died. I wasn't there. I do remember what happened shortly before she died.

We live in Brooklyn. A small apartment on the third floor of a brick building. I just turned six; my brother, three.

My mother is in bed. A white canopy hangs partially down from the top. It is difficult to see her. I feel like a peeping tom. "Mommy, are you feeling better?" She touches my cheek and smiles. She doesn't talk much. I cuddle into her right arm. Smell her warmth. It is a scent of lilac I still experience when I think of her.

Dad's face is haggard. His eyes sad. He hovers by the bed, concerned that I might upset her. Her birth name is Evelyn. Family call her Eva. Dad calls her Honey. I call her mommy.

A week before she dies I hear my parents quietly disagreeing, not realizing their curious daughter hears them. Dad wants her to go into the hospital. She doesn't want to. She has incurable cancer.

"They can manage the pain. I don't know what I can do to help you feel better. You'll be well taken care of there."

Her voice is soft, "I don't want to go back. They can't cure me."

She no longer sounds like the mother who danced with me in the living room; the mother who rubbed me dry after a bath; the mother who tickled my ears and tummy.

She does go to the hospital. I never see her again.

Analysis

"Show, don't tell." So goes the creative writing chestnut. And, like most conventional wisdom, it has something to recommend it. Dramatic writing ("showing") does more than merely tell us *about* an experience; it puts us right there inside the experience with a character or characters, so that we share the experience along with them. And sharing experiences—putting us into a character's shoes, so to speak, having us see what they see and feel what they feel through their nerves and sensory organs—is what fiction, and any form of narrative writing, does best.

Which isn't to say there's no place for telling in good narrative writing. On the contrary, telling is no less important than showing. If showing is more dramatic, more cinematic, telling is more *expedient*. Telling cuts to the heart; it sums up, reflects, adds perspective, and contextualizes. It bridges the gaps between scenes. If scenes are the bricks of good storytelling, exposition ("telling") is the mortar that binds the bricks together. To build a good story, fiction or nonfiction, you need bricks *and* mortar.

One reason behind the supremacy of "show, don't tell" is that telling is, frankly, harder. To gain and hold a reader's attention through action and dialogue is one thing. To do so through exposition is another. Intrinsically, there's nothing sexy about cement. It's the difference between showing someone a movie and asking them to read the screenplay. Good telling—telling that in its way is as entertaining as a dramatic scene—makes far greater demands on our rhetorical strengths, on the quality of insights and ideas and the language by which they are conveyed. With showing, on the other hand, our characters entertain our readers for us. We merely have to report what they do.

In this opening, in which the narrator recalls the days leading up to her mother's death, we get a murky mixture of showing and telling, of experience and information, so that, while we're not clearly lodged inside the mind of a narrator looking back and reflecting on certain events in his or her past, neither are we ensconced in the events themselves. We're presented with dramatic scenes, but we never inhabit them—or we do, but not vividly or deeply.

Before discussing why this is so, I want to digress for a moment and talk about the title of this memoir (*Loss ... But Not Lost*) and titles in general. Whatever stage they're in in their drafting process, I encourage my students to at least have a working title for their stories; in fact I insist on it. The search for a good title helps them learn about their own stories, what lies at their hearts, what they are ultimately about. Is there a strong central metaphor or image, something concrete that, symbolically, may stand for the story as a whole?

One good test for a working title: if it can be applied to many if not most or all stories, then it's probably too general, too "one size fits all." Unless it has something to do with a song by the Beatles, "A Day in the Life" is probably an example of a too-generic title. So is "When Things Go Wrong." And so, alas, is "Loss ... But Not Lost," the title of the work in question. It casts its thematic net too wide. Isn't every story, to some extent, in one way or another, a story of loss turned into gain, and/or vice versa? Aren't "life" and "loss" synonymous? If an author's best effort to arrive at a good title for her or his work results in something generic, it's a safe if not a sure bet that the work itself suffers from a lack of thematic focus.

Now let's go on with this first page, starting with the first two sentences: "I don't recall the day my mother died. I wasn't there." As openings go, in more than one sense this is a non-starter, since it merely conveys in negative terms what will be obvious by the end of the page. For those who will argue that Camus's most famous novel begins similarly ("Mother died today. Or maybe yesterday; I can't be sure"), in that instance the justification for this approach lies in *the fact that the narrator doesn't remember*; that is the point of the opening, one that not only foreshadows the narrator's death, but will cause it.

The second sentence of the first paragraph of this first page will also be obviated by what follows, making it dispensable. As for paragraph 2 ("We live in Brooklyn. A small apartment on the third floor of a brick building. I just turned six; my brother, three."), it's purely informational, providing us with answers to questions yet to be raised by the material—which, so far, has offered us nothing in the way of an experience.

Only with paragraph 3 do we arrive at and enter an actual experience, the scene that each of the two previous paragraphs has been pointing toward: the moment when, as a child, the narrator visits her mother in her sickbed. I would be tempted to begin here, with an experience ("My mother is in bed"), rather than with information ("We live in Brooklyn"). In due time we may learn that the bedroom is in a brick apartment building in Brooklyn, but not before having any reason to care.

But even in putting us into an experience, this opening could be stronger. Take the first experiential sentence: "My mother is in bed." Nothing wrong with it, at first glance. Yet it misses the mark in several ways. Instead of giving us a definitive action through use of a strong verb ("My mother *lies* in bed"), we get a conjugation of the verb "to be," the least active of all verbs—the existential verb: the Camus verb. Our sense of experience is weakened accordingly. But a larger problem here is the sentence's failure to engage point of view. That this mother is lying in bed isn't the point; the point is that the child *sees* her lying there. That's the action of this scene, what's really happening.

That the narrator doesn't position herself (or us) in the scene doesn't help. Is she standing, watching from the doorway, or seated by her mother's bed? As we read on, we learn not only that she is close to her mother (close enough to cuddle with her and smell her lilac scent), but that the father is there in the bedroom with her, something we didn't realize at first because we weren't told— or rather because we weren't *shown* the father standing (sitting?) there through the eyes of the little girl who sees him for us. When dying mother and child cuddle, as we smell the mother's warmth and traces of her lilac perfume, we may wonder why, apart from its intrinsic warmth and sweetness, this moment comforts us so. I say it's because it invests us deeply, sensuously, and for the first time properly in this scene. Then the author destroys the effect by adding, "[that] I still experience when I think of her," wrenching us out of the moment.

As I read on, other things interfere with my ability to fully inhabit this opening scene. In the fourth paragraph, I am told that the mother's "birth name is Evelyn." Yet it's not at all clear whether this knowledge belongs to the child whose perspective we share in the moment or to the older narrator looking back through memory. That the scene is written in the present tense suggests the former. But what is the likelihood that a six-year-old knows this about her mother's birth name?

From there things move to "a week before [the mother] dies," yet it isn't clear whether this week follows or precedes the previous scene, nor do we know where the present scene of the parents "quietly disagreeing" occurs, in what part of the home, at what time of day. Is the mother still in bed? And where is the narrator who "hears them" disagree? The scene isn't properly grounded; it isn't grounded at all. Because it's not grounded, it exists in an unstable zone between experience and information. When, at the bottom of the same paragraph, we read that the mother "has incurable cancer," there again we are forced to wonder whose experience those words convey. True, some sentences later the child overhears her mother say, "They can't cure me." Yet the words "incurable cancer" are better suited to an awareness on the part of the grown narrator looking back than to a child's awareness *then*.

For our readers to fully inhabit and invest deeply in our scenes, we must first, whether through a created fictional narrator or through our own memories, inhabit them thoroughly ourselves, as Charlotte Brontë does in *Jane Eyre*:

> Close by Miss Temple's bed, and half covered with its white curtains, there stood a little crib. I saw the outline of a form under the clothes, but the face was hid by the hangings: the nurse I had spoken to in the garden sat in an easychair asleep; an unsnuffed candle burnt dimly on the table. Miss Temple was not to be seen: I knew afterwards that she had been called to a delirious patient in the fever-room. I advanced; then paused by the crib side: my hand was on the curtain, but I preferred speaking before I withdrew it. I still recoiled at the dread of seeing a corpse.
>
> "Helen!" I whispered softly, "are you awake?"
>
> She stirred herself, put back the curtain, and I saw her face, pale, wasted, but quite composed: she looked so little changed that my fear was instantly dissipated.

"Can it be you, Jane?" she asked, in her own gentle voice.

"Oh!" I thought, "she is not going to die; they are mistaken: she could not speak and look so calmly if she were."

I got on to her crib and kissed her: her forehead was cold, and her cheek both cold and thin, and so were her hand and wrist; but she smiled as of old.

"Why are you come here, Jane? It is past eleven o'clock: I heard it strike some minutes since."

"I came to see you, Helen: I heard you were very ill, and I could not sleep till I had spoken to you."

"You came to bid me goodbye, then: you are just in time probably."

"Are you going somewhere, Helen? Are you going home?" "Yes; to my long home—my last home."

Your Turn

Revise the first page based on any issues you may have with it as well as those I've touched on in my critique, with an emphasis on locating the narrator within events at all times. Have us see things clearly, without confusion, from her vantage point.

49. A Surprise Phone Call

(Memoir / Scene vs. Summary / Clutter / "Glance" / Verbs)

The call came at 12:36 pm on April 22nd.

I wondered who would be calling me in the middle of the day. I glanced casually at the caller ID. It was my dad. What in the world was he doing calling me?

"Hello?" I said.

"Hi honey," Dad said as I picked up the phone. "Have you been keeping up with Allen's Facebook posts?"

Allen was my brother-in-law and my sister Leah's husband. "No," I said. "But I saw Ashley's."

I had just logged in a few minutes ago and she had said something about becoming an aunt. Since she and my brother Tyler had only recently been married and I didn't know much about her family, I thought at first that it might be a birth on her other side. My sister Leah wasn't due to have Clara Elizabeth for another month.

Or so I thought.

"Well, you're an aunt," he said. "Clara Beth came early. She and Leah are both fine. Your mom is doing everything she can to find a sub so she can go out there." My mother was a kindergarten teacher. Finding substitutes was a necessary part of the job when one had to be absent.

"That's wonderful!" I was thrilled that the long wait for the little one was over and that Clara had arrived safe and sound.

"Well, Allen's beeping in," my dad said. "Better take this. We'll talk later. Bye hon."

I hung up and posted my joyous news on Facebook and on my LiveJournal account. I was so excited to be an aunt! My sister had had her baby and everything had come out fine. What more could I want?

I settled back at my laptop, content to read responses to my wonderful news.

Within ten minutes of my niece's birth, though, another feeling overtook me, one I'd been battling furiously through the whole of Leah's pregnancy.

Jealousy.

An intense wave of emotion slammed into me like a tidal wave dragging me under the undertow.

Analysis

When should we dramatize things? And when is it better to summarize, or state, them? That's one question raised by this opening.

On learning that her sister has given birth, a woman is overcome with envy. That's the gist of this first page. Unlike so many openings whose authors err on the side of abstractions, here the effort that has gone into dramatizing this moment in the narrator's life feels misguided. A direct statement could do the trick more efficiently and effectively:

> When I learned that my sister had given birth, at first I was happy. It took about ten minutes for my happiness to turn to envy.

Beyond what's accomplished by the sentence above, what does the rest of the first page achieve?

It doesn't help that we don't know where the phone call is being received. At home? At a place of business? In a car? The moment isn't properly grounded. What follows is cluttered and confusing. We slog through a procession of proper names and relationships—father, siblings, in-laws, adding up to a grand total of seven characters (including the narrator) for us readers to process within half a page: a headcount to make fans of Tolstoy dizzy. Most of these characters have little if any bearing on the present scene; nor does it matter much that the news has been posted on Facebook, since the narrator learns it by phone from her father. That the narrator's mother is a schoolteacher is beside the point. Even if it weren't, do we really need to be told here that finding substitutes is "a necessary part of [her] job"? Is it relevant to the moment?

"Show, don't tell," we're told. But there are times when telling may be just as good or better. The point of fleshing out a dramatic scene or moment (as opposed to summarizing it in a sentence or a paragraph) should be not merely to convey *what* happened, but the particulars of *how* it happened in a way that's visceral and active, in a word: *dramatic*. Those experiential particulars—actions, atmosphere, setting, gestures, body language and facial expressions, a character's thoughts and perceptions as he or she undergoes an event ... put us inside that experience in a way mere summary can't, allowing us to not only *experience* an event, but to interpret it for ourselves.

As dramatic scenes go, telephone conversations offer little in the way of action and few sensory particulars. Though the dramatized scene here makes clear *what* happened, in terms of telling details it doesn't get us very far. The result feels predictable, perfunctory, even. It gives us a detailed outline of the experience as information carried by dialogue.

Which may explain why, with that very last sentence, the author has felt compelled to state the character's emotional response by way of a bold, if some-what forced, metaphor. Had the scene been properly dramatized, we would know—anyway we would have a strong sense of—how the character feels without being so clumsily told.

A nitpicky side note: Why I'm not sure, but for some reason authors, expe-rienced and beginners alike, can't seem resist using the word "glance" in place of "look," though the words have different meanings. To "glance" at something is to look at it fleetingly, out of impatience or carelessness, or to avoid embar-rassment. Here the word is used redundantly and inadvertently: redundantly thanks to that "carelessly," and inadvertently since it must have taken a moment or two for the fact that the number on her caller ID was her father's to register with the narrator. What's suggested then isn't a "glance," casual or otherwise, but something closer to staring in perplexity or astonishment. "Looked" is more accurate. Or "gazed."

Why do so many authors favor "glance" to "look"? Could it be the mistaken notion that a humble verb like "to look" lacks the literary panache of "to glance" or "to gaze"? But the right word to use when writing is always exactly the right word, whether it's humble or not. "Glance" is notoriously overused by writers. So is "placed." "Spied" and "spotted" (as a verb) are also overused. (I'm not sure "spotted" should ever be used except to describe Dalmatians or chicken pox.)

Your Turn

Take a first page that you or a colleague has written and boil it down to a single paragraph or sentence. Do the same for two more first pages. Is the result an improvement on the original?

50. A Rude Awakening

(Memoir / Relationship / Judgments / Righteous Indignation)

When I broke up with Roy he didn't take it well, but I was too preoccupied with myself to notice. All I knew was I could finally breathe. Being in a committed romantic relationship with him had been, to put it plainly, suffocating. I wasted no time celebrating, drinking with my other friends seven days a week.

Though we broke up, Roy and I kept living together. The lease on our New York apartment didn't expire until September, and neither of us could afford to surrender the deposit or, for that matter, live on our own. Our deal was that I covered all of the utilities and groceries and Roy paid the rent. But in June he quit his job—or he got fired, I'm not entirely sure. The next thing I knew, four hundred dollars were missing from my checking account. When questioned about it Roy admitted he'd forged my signature on a check to pay the rent. He assured me that I'd given him my permission to do so. I *had*? Pressed for details he couldn't supply any. Maybe I'd been half-asleep? he speculated. "I mean, your mind does tend to wander," he said. I wanted to believe him. I really did.

When summer ended we both concluded we'd had enough of New York City, and decided to head west to LA. We'd share a rental car. It was one of the dumbest decisions I'd ever made. Nine days of just Roy. The excitement of the road trip faded by Day 2. The ubiquitous cornfields. The decaying farms. The déjà vu of the desert landscape.

Roy's absentmindedness at the wheel didn't help.

"We *missed* the exit," I announced miles after the fact. Before drifting off I'd told him exactly when the exit was and how far we were from it. He *should* have paid attention. Was he that incapable? We had just driven two hundred miles of desert highway. The next exit wasn't for another twenty miles. We'd probably get stranded on a side road searching for gas and be murdered by a psychopath who liked wearing other people's faces. We were going to die and it was all Roy's fault.

Analysis

I've spoken of the risk of autobiographical clutter in memoir, and also of the memoirist's need to restrict thematic focus to prevent memoir from becoming autobiography.

The other great risk faced by memoirists is that of being—or appearing to be—self-serving or judgmental, or worse: bent on retaliation. Though incidentally they may occasionally serve that function, memoirs are not the place to settle scores or exercise grudges. Any sense that an author is out to do so is at best likely to arouse humor, as in the example above; at worst, it will backfire, implicating its author as much or more than it implicates its object.

In fiction or nonfiction (no less so than the novelist, the memoirist creates his or her characters), we can't assume that, simply because their counterparts happen to exist in real life, we don't have to work at creating our characters, that they will emerge full-blown, magically, on the page. When creating them, it's best not to judge them, or worse, to condemn them. The best attitude for an author to take toward her characters, fictional or otherwise, is one of curiosity and open-mindedness. In the case of a character whose actions are unquestionably evil, perverse, or incomprehensible, then the attitude will probably be closer to curiosity.

This is no less so even in those cases where, ultimately, we want our readers to hate or condemn a character. There's a world of difference between letting our readers detest a character and doing it for them. If we do it for them, or try to, we prevent them from forming their own judgments. The better approach is to at the very least appear to be open-minded and non-judgmental while supplying damning evidence.

Another example: A memoirist writes about her abusive father. The man was a religious hypocrite and a drunken womanizer. Fine. Let her tell us all about him, not with an obvious intent to pillory or judge him, but with an intent to see and understand things as clearly as possible.

Show behavior; provide evidence. But do not judge or rant or rage or pillory or preach.

Or do any or all of those things, but realize you're doing so, and that, while they're forming opinions about your characters, your readers will also judge your narrator. In the case of a memoir, that narrator occupies a space perilously close to the author's.

The lens of self-righteous indignation isn't always the best instrument through which to view the world clearly. Whether or not it is fair, a self-righteously judgmental narrator is likely to be seen as ... self-righteously judgmental.

Your Turn

Revise this first page removing all traces of judgment and condemnation, replacing them, when possible, with an effort on behalf of the narrator to understand, or simple curiosity. How is the result different? How has your view of both characters shifted, if at all?

51. The Year of 14 Jobs

(Memoir / Implication vs. Statement / Abstract vs. Concrete)

> *"The purpose of poetry is to remind us how*
> *difficult it is to remain just one person."*
> CZESŁAW MIŁOSZ

When I was 16 years old, no one told me I was supposed to desire only one thing. I had multiple desires, like most girls my age, mostly about what it might mean to put childish things away and start a process to find out what life was all about. This memoir, about my life and the lives of my friends in 1969, doesn't travel down one path, but goes down many, 14 to be exact, that helped me begin to discover what made the world tick and where my place in it might be.

Some wild women may have 14 lovers in a year. More intro-spective types may read 14 books or see 14 movies annually. Some fun-loving women might purchase 14 swimming suits (my friend Dottie owned 18), swim in 14 different swimming pools, or scream through 14 roller coaster rides. In 1969, I held a total of 14 different part-time jobs over the course of the year.

I was a high school student on the far northwest side of Chicago, had a social life, somehow got my homework done, but seemingly also liked to sample and be a part of Chicago's renowned identity: The City That Works. If you asked me, at least when I was 16, I'd say I was neither necessarily a wild, introspective nor crazily fun-loving type of woman. I'd probably claim to be all of the above. But one thing's for sure: I was a Chicago-type of woman. And because I liked having some cash in my pocket that meant I liked being on the job, even if I didn't keep jobs for long.

My part-time jobs, like my romantic relationships at the time, lasted anywhere from one day (and I don't mean a one-night stand) to a few months. I wasn't like some of the other girls I knew at school, who worked at the local drug store part time until they graduated, then married their high school sweetheart. I, like many other teen-agers, didn't know what I wanted, but was interested in finding out.

It was a year of extremely low unemployment. The econ-omy was good and jobs were ubiquitous. At times, it seems I went through them like tissue paper. The year 1969 was dedicated to, among other things, "the dawning of the age of Aquarius." At least that's what the song said. According to a Chicago radio station, more than 40 years later, 1969 was the "Feel-Good Year of the Century." Of course, they meant the twentieth century. I'm not sure if the twenty-first century has a feel-good year yet.

Analysis

One of the hallmarks of good writing is its power to suggest. This is true not only for poetry and fiction, but for works of nonfiction, too, for essays and memoirs, even sometimes for journalism. Conclusive statements may or may not always convince us. But when authors provide readers with the raw, visceral evidence from which such conclusions can be drawn, allowing us to reach them on our own, then the conclusions are much harder to argue with. In that case, the only person we have to argue with is ourselves.

In this opening passage from a memoir in progress about a year in a woman's life, everything is stated, and little if anything is implied. We are told, among other things, that during the course of that year she held fourteen jobs:

> Some wild women may have 14 lovers in a year. More introspective types may read 14 books or see 14 movies annually. Some fun-loving women might purchase 14 swimming suits (my friend Dottie owned 18), swim in 14 different swimming pools, or scream through 14 roller coaster rides. In 1969, I held a total of 14 different part-time jobs....

The last sentence here ("In 1969, I held a total of 14 different part-time jobs") states the memoir's central subject, one that the passage as a whole puts into perspective, or tries to, with its series of variously obsessed women. At the same time the passage highlights the uniqueness of its subject: *how many people do you know, male or female, who in the course of one year have held fourteen different jobs?* On the whole, the paragraph is well written. It has the cumulative power of many parallel constructions ("It was the best of times, it was the worst of times."). And it offers us something irresistible: an eccentric, struggling heroine.

Yet somehow the passage, and the opening as a whole, fails to engage. The author seems less intent on dramatizing her material than on arguing for it, telling us not just what she has to offer, but *why* we should care. *Because in a year other people may have fourteen lovers or fourteen books or fourteen bathing suits. But other people don't have fourteen jobs.* This claim may or may not be true. Even if true, do jobs compare with lovers—or books, or bathing suits? Even accepting the logic of the claim, whether that claim justifies a memoir remains to be seen.

Analogies aren't the point. The point is, or should be, that *in a given year a young woman held fourteen jobs.*

That point, or something like it, provided Charles Bukowski with the subject of *Factotum*, his second novel one that certainly reads as autobiographical. It follows Bukowski's alter-ego, Henry Chinaski, from one dreary, degrading, menial job to the next after he has been rated 4-F by the armed services and thereby exempted from serving in World War II. The novel consists of 87 brief passages or chapters, each devoted to one such crappy job. The first passage begins:

> I arrived in New Orleans in the rain at 5 o'clock in the morning. I sat around in the station for a while but the people depressed me so I took my suitcase and went out in the rain and began walking. I didn't know where the rooming houses were, where the poor section was.
>
> I had a cardboard suitcase that was falling apart. It had once been black but the black coating had peeled off and yellow cardboard was exposed. I had tried to solve that by putting black shoepolish over the exposed cardboard. As I walked along in the rain the shoepolish on the suitcase ran and unwittingly I rubbed black streaks on both legs of my pants as I switched the suitcase from hand to hand.

So begins Bukowski/Chinaski's descent into the underworld of unemployment, with him cast to the very lowest circle, that of the *unemployable*. Note how in opening his novel Bukowski states nothing. He doesn't announce his intended theme, let alone make a case for it. Nor is there any intent to force perspective on us before we've been presented with any matter (scenes, events, experiences) to put into perspective. Instead, what we get is the matter itself: a down-at-the-heels guy in search of a rooming house in the rain, whose search will soon turn to one for gainful employment. Meanwhile his luck, like the black shoe polish on his suitcase, drains into the gutter.

My suggestion to the author of this memoir is that she begin similarly, with concrete matter rather than with abstract statements. In time we will learn that her fourteen jobs "lasted anywhere from one day … to a few months," as we will learn that the memoirist "wasn't like some of the other girls [she] knew at school who worked at the local drugstore." Such facts are best learned through experience. And the proper goal of the memoirist, no less than that of the novelist, isn't to present information, but to render experience.

Your Turn

Draft a first page of a memoir or personal essay about a work experience in which you describe your first day on a job.

52. The Road Train

(Memoir / Travel / Flashback / False Suspense vs. Generosity)

The road train floated towards us above a hot blue lake across the road—a dead straight road away to the horizon. The monster was wavering across the water and I couldn't decide whether it was really swaying or just the mirage trembling. It looked exactly like a boat with a cresting bow wave ahead of it.

We'd left early that morning, and perhaps by then I was a bit mesmerized by the road because I had a delusion that we were sitting still while a tunnel of bush streamed past us.

It was looming—closer and closer—its second trailer swinging over the double white line. There was a small white shape in front of it. The truck was frustrated, trying to find a clear section long enough to pass a caravan lolling along well below the speed limit. It had its overtaking indicators on. It couldn't pass—surely it'd seen us. I braced myself for the collision—the smashing, shrieking, grinding impact of a sideswipe. Its shock wave buffeted me, and then it pulled out to pass behind.

The fright jolted elusive memories. Tormenting images from a film out of focus. The smell of burning oil. Someone screaming: *get us out, get us out.* Hot metal ticking. Simon's face, greying, blood oozing from his ear. Rhythmic blue lights and sirens bouncing off buildings through the towns. And the next day, when Langston told me Simon had died, my disbelief that I had no memory of the last twenty-four hours and how the crash had happened.

A year later—and I was traveling east on the same road. Setting my mind to the four-thousand-kilometer drive across Australia. I'd heard people say they could do it in forty hours or so, but this wasn't a speed trial—I just had to complete the crossing. I'd made the decision to leave Perth, move to Sydney. The removalist's doors had closed on our things, I'd packed Alice, our bags and the last bits into the car and now I felt that I had finally reached a point of no return.

Analysis

Though the term is more familiar in Australia, a road train (or "land train") is a truck pulling two or more trailers in tandem. In this effective opening, the road train becomes a source of anxiety and terror looming on the wavering horizon, "float[ing] towards us above a hot blue lake across the road"—like one of those B-movie monsters from the 1950s, *The Blob* or *Empire of the Ants*. No longer simply a conveyance transporting innocent merchandise from point A to point B, here the road train becomes Yeats's vast image "arising out of the desert sand ... moving its slow thighs ... slouch[ing] toward Bethlehem to be born." The narrator finds it scary and so do we.

In fact, the truck is only a truck—but still a source of fear and anxiety as it bears down on the protagonist in her car "like a boat with a cresting bow wave ahead of it." We are in Australia, somewhere in the Outback, presumably. As one of the road train's trailers swings over the double white line, the narrator braces herself for the inevitable collision, for "the smashing, shrieking, grinding impact of a sideswipe"—which, of course, doesn't come.

Instead of being smashed to death, the narrator is jolted into the past, into a memory of another violent disaster. Evocations of fire, screaming, hot metal ticking, "blood oozing," of sirens wailing and emergency lights flashing off of buildings. The memory is vague yet vivid. We learn that someone very close to the narrator—Simon, possibly the narrator's husband—died in "the crash."

Then the flashback ends and we return to that wavering stretch of highway—the same road, apparently, where Simon met his fate a year earlier. She is traveling from Perth to Sydney, a distance of over 4,000 kilometers, or over forty hours, traveling "with Alice [her daughter?], [her] bags, and the last bits [of her life] in her car." The rest of her belongings are in the hands of "the removalist," the Australian term for a moving contractor.

A successful opening depends almost entirely on the ratio of information provided versus questions raised. Provide too much information, and you mitigate suspense; provide too little, and you cross the line from suspense to confusion and frustration.

Beginning authors tend to err on the side of confusion/frustration. They withhold too much information, making it hard or impossible for readers to follow—let alone to appreciate—what's happening. They trade in *false suspense*: suspense that asks not "What's going to happen?" but "What am I reading?"

More experienced and confident writers tend toward generosity rather than stinginess. They aren't afraid to make things clear, to give us all or most of the information we need to understand what's happening in any moment or scene, making it easier for us to wonder—based on what we already know—where things are going, what's going to happen next.

Generosity takes confidence: you have to believe that you have a good story to tell, and that the more you give, the more readers will want. If beginning writers often play hard to get, it's because they aren't so sure.

With this opening the writer achieves a good balance of information vs. suspense. Though little is spelled out, much is conveyed. A mother whose life has been shattered by tragedy, hoping to leave that tragedy behind and begin a new life, travels along a desolate stretch of desert highway. Will she make it? The road itself becomes a hazard, a portent, a metaphor for the journey that has just begun—and which, with its wavering mirages and hazards, is bound to be treacherous. This is a strong opening.

Your Turn

Draft or revise a first-person opening (fiction or nonfiction) scene in which, while traveling from Point A to Point B, the narrator recalls some event or moment from the past. The memory should be motivated by something in the present scene. Note: the purpose of the present journey, and/or its destination, should be indicated. Try to write the scene such that we are grounded in both the present journey and in event(s) of the past.

53. The Substance Abuser's Wife

(Memoir / War / Drug Addiction / Cliché at the Root of Conception)

Once I lived in a war zone. In Sarajevo, I met a man and married him. He should still be here to share memories, reveling in how precious peace is, but that is not what happened. I am in a pretty Connecticut suburb without him. Years have passed. I continue to search for answers, remembering the beginning and the end. I write.

Sometimes I wished Ian were a drunk instead of a coke addict. Unbearable as that would still be, at least I might smell the substance destroying us and have bottles to brandish accusingly. Evidence is elusive with cocaine, but I looked anyway, hoping and dreading I'd find proof. While he slept leaden in bed, I went through the house and his clothes foraging for drugs.

One night, grabbing his jeans from the floor, I took them into the bathroom. The pockets were empty but for bits of brown tobacco from the stubs of cigarettes he smoked all day. Opening his slim brown wallet, I flipped through the contents—a collection of business cards, his driver's license and a few dollars. Nothing else. No credit or debit cards since both the banks and I cut him off over a year ago. Lightly licking the edges of the hard paper and plastic in search of the bitter taste of coke, I sat on the edge of the bathtub, Ian's jeans in front of me.

The bathroom door slowly opened. Frozen, expecting to see Ian's angry face, instead, there was only space. Looking down, I saw the mass of grey fur of our Cairn terrier and let out a sigh of relief. Tetley toddled over and flipped onto his back, tail wagging. Ashamed, I shoved the cards back in Ian's wallet and care-fully returned it to the same pocket. "Good boy," I whispered, scratched his belly then crept back to the bedroom and dropped the jeans where I'd found them before crawling into bed, shivering. The dog jumped up after me and I pulled him close for warmth and comfort. An acrid taste lingered on my tongue, probably just from the plastic lamination. But then why did the bed quake from the force of Ian's leg tremors?

Analysis

In choosing her subject, it's not a bad idea for the memoirist to imagine that many others in her audience have undergone the same or a similar experience, and write with that in mind. Any assumption to the contrary may prove disastrous.

Here, the subject is living with a substance abuser. The substance is cocaine. Assuming no shortage of coke addicts in the world, one may also assume as many abused significant others to go with them. There are even organizations (Al-Anon, Cocaine Anonymous) devoted to helping them. And though not all spouses, lovers, and other co-victims of substance abuse have written or intend to write memoirs, more than a few have already done so.

There've been very good books about drug addiction, both from the point of view of the abuser and from that of someone emotionally attached to him or her. Alexander Trocchi's *Cain's Book* plunges us into the mind—and the philosophy—of a heroin junkie living on a gravel scow in New York harbor. Presented to us as a novel in the form of a journal, it begins:

> My scow is tied up in the canal at Flushing, NY, alongside the landing stage of the Mac Asphalt and Construction Corporation. It is now just after five in the afternoon. Today at this time it is still afternoon, and the sun, striking the cinderblocks of the main building of the works, has turned them pink. The motor cranes and the decks of the other scows tied up round about are deserted.
>
> Half an hour ago I gave myself a fix.

There have been drug-centric novels and memoirs going all the way back to Thomas De Quincy, whose *Confessions of an English Opium-Eater* (1821) is the first and most famous. *Novel with Cocaine* (1934) by M. Ageyev, set in Moscow on the eve of the Russian revolution, does for that time and place roughly what Jay McInerney's *Bright Lights, Big City* (1984) did for Manhattan and cocaine in the late 1980s. As for narratives about or by people living with abusive family members, there've been no shortage of those, either. Jeanette Walls's earlier-mentioned *The Glass Castle*, her chronicle of growing up with an eccentric mother and alcoholic father, is a recent example. So is Nick Flynn's *Bullshit Night in Suck City*.

Right from the start, each of the books I've mentioned offers to us something above and beyond substance abuse or its direct or collateral consequences. Trocchi gives us the atmosphere of the New York waterfront, with its deserted motor cranes and sun-spackled cinderblocks, while Walls juxtaposes, to heartbreaking effect, party-going yuppie daughter with dumpster-diving Mom and Flynn's fragmentary style effectively renders the workings of a drunkard's mind.

Which leads to the next good question for the memoirist to ask herself: *What can I bring to my familiar subject that no one has brought to it before? How will it be different not only in its particulars, but essentially, so readers won't have read anything quite like it?*

The first page under discussion here calls no attention to its style, nor does it break any formal ground. And yet by means of her italicized opening paragraph the author does answer, or tries to, the question: *what can I bring to my familiar subject that no one has brought to it before?* She does so by front-loading her story with a nod to the recent Bosnian war, where, one reading suggests, she met her future, coke-snorting husband. Like many an italicized opening, this one is meant to grab our attention, and does. But it's the war in Sarajevo that grabs it, not the husband or cocaine abuse, and the scene in Roman type that follows (and that is itself a teaser—the author plunging us *in media res* into the ostensible heart of her story) comes as a letdown. We start with a Balkan war, and end up—or rather begin again—sitting on a stateside toilet rifling a man's wallet, one that, incidentally, has nothing special in or about it.

By trying to do too many things at once, this opening loses—or never achieves—focus. It lacks an organizing principle to unite its disparate themes (civil war, spousal addiction). The word "survival" might hold the key, might be the hinge holding these parts together.

> I survived a war in Sarajevo only to face another disaster in Connecticut.

That sentence, or one like it, that juxtaposes and unites the memoir's two primary themes without getting into too much nitty-gritty (Sarajevo, cocaine addiction), could serve as the portal through which we enter the story. From there, in a separate paragraph, we might accompany the narrator as she sneaks into the bathroom and combs frantically through the contents of her snoring husband's jeans. What is she searching for? Ah—evidence of cocaine snorting! But what of that "war" mentioned in the first sentence? We'll find out in due time.

For now, my focus is on a wife who suspects her husband of drug abuse.

Your Turn

Revise this opening based on my suggestions and/or your own.

54. An Addict's Perspective on Addiction

(Memoir / Addiction / Reflection / Unreliable Narrator)

CHAPTER 1: XANAX 2011

"KEVIN!"

My husband, Kevin had never denied me anything. And Sunday October 9th, 2011 was no different. Six months earlier, he had given me his kidney. That morning, all I needed were my pills.

All 97 pounds of me quivered in bed with one objective. Kevin has to pick up my Xanax. I could hear him walking in and out of the house, packing up our one car with his tripod, lights, and zipping up the pockets of his camera bag. He had to be in Orange County by noon to work a wedding. Plenty of time to get my pills, come home, and go to work. Dragging my shaking hands through my hair, I glanced at the alarm clock. 10:07 am. Why was he dawdling? Why was he not at Rite Aid by 9:59 am as the pharmacy's steel door rolled up offering its medicinal charms to the world? He was such an ass.

I was not sick, but dopesick. A bag of bones wracked no longer with the nausea associated with renal failure, but straight up addiction. My legs twitched under the sheets, knowing my prescription was ready and waiting. I rubbed at my eyes with agitated fingers, aimless fingers that had no purpose unless they were plucking pills from the bottom of their plastic home.

Kevin and I had gone to the pharmacy the day before. I had been told it was "too soon" to pick up my prescription—the dreaded phrase sinks the hungry heart of every pharmaceutical whore. I had thrown myself across the counter angling my scrawny frame towards the pharmacist. Trying to explain why it would be just fine to give. me. my. pills.

Analysis

Writing about addiction is tricky. While most stories have a single protagonist, addiction narratives are usually about two people: the addict deep in the throes of their addiction, and the recovered narrator looking back objectively on the experience. In that sense, addiction narratives have split personalities, offering two perspectives—one reliable, one unreliable—opposing and informing each other. How those two perspectives are apportioned determines the nature of the result.

From its capitalized one-word opener ("KEVIN!"), this first page of a memoir about a woman's addiction to Xanax put us firmly in the mind of an addict so obsessed with her next fix ("my pills") she can think of nothing else. Owing strictly to his failure to drive to the local Rite Aid "by 9:59 am, as the pharmacy's steel door roll[s] up offering its medicinal charms," the same husband she shouts for—the one who, six months earlier, "gave [her] his kidney"—is now "an ass."

Does the narrator see the irony and injustice in this? If so, she doesn't let on, not to us readers. She is—at best—unreliable.

Though this opening puts us in unreliable territory, it does so retrospectively, in the past tense, with its narrator looking back across so many years. Hindsight usually gives us *some* perspective on events. For this reason we expect a past-tense narrator to not merely tell us a story, but to shed some light on it.

If, on the other hand, the author's purpose is to describe addiction subjectively, from within the experience, the present tense would be more fitting. With the present tense, we're locked with the narrator into the moment, able to see only as far and as clearly as she sees, with as little objectivity, and no reflection. That's the technique James Frey uses to launch his controversial (published as nonfiction but subsequently exposed as largely fictional) addiction memoir *A Million Little Pieces* (2003):

> I wake to the drone of an airplane engine and the feeling of something warm dripping down my chin. I lift my hand to feel my face. My front four teeth are gone, I have a hole in my cheek, my nose is broken and my eyes are swollen nearly shut. I open them and I look around and I'm in the back of a plane and there's no one near me. I look at my clothes and my clothes are covered with a colorful mixture of spit, snot, urine, vomit and blood. I reach for the call button and I find it and I push it and I wait and thirty seconds later an attendant arrives.

How far we've come from the diffident opening of Thomas De Quincey's *Confessions of an English Opium-Eater*:

> I here present you, courteous reader, with the record of a remarkable period in my life: according to my application of it, I trust that it will

prove not merely an interesting record, but in a considerable degree useful and instructive. In *that* hope it is that I have drawn it up; and *that* must be my apology for breaking through that delicate and honourable reserve which, for the most part, restrains us from the public exposure of our own errors and infirmities.

Which isn't to say that the past tense can't convey an addicted psyche. In *Pill Head*, his 2009 memoir of addiction to prescription painkillers, Joshua Lyon uses it to superb effect:

> *I was feeling no pain.*
> I cared about nothing but this.
> It wasn't just an absence of pain. It was warm waves pulsating through my muscle and skin. Breathing was hard, my chest felt weighted down by my own ribcage but I didn't panic because it's impossible to feel anxiety about anything when every inch of your body is having a constant low-grade orgasm.
> I don't know how long I lay there on my bed, watching the blades of my ceiling fan slowly turn, lazily spinning tufts of dust before they floated down through the air around me like so much gray snow. Through half-lidded eyes I watched Ollie, my cat, go ape-shit chasing the dust puffs, and it took every ounce of strength to turn my head toward the other side of the bed....

While it painstakingly recreates his experience ("warm waves pulsating through my muscles and skin"), this opening also objectively *reflects on* the narrator's experience ("I cared about nothing but this"). We're aware of his wish to describe that experience as precisely as possible—down to admitting when he can't be precise ("I don't know how long I lay there ..."). Here the presence of what Phillip Lopate calls "the intelligent narrator"—the narrator who has not only lived to tell his tale, but to tell it accurately—is everywhere in evidence.[11]

With the first page in question, on the other hand, we wonder how much we should trust the narrator, or if we can trust her at all. She doesn't lie. But though she is looking back at her experiences over time, she offers no perspective, no reflection, nothing to suggest a survivor's hard-won grasp of her experiences. Unless leavened by the sort of insights that only come with reflection,

---

11   Phillip Lopate, "Reflection and Retrospection: A Pedagogic Mystery Story" in *The Fourth Genre* (2005).

memories and memoirs boil down to anecdote. We get experiences vividly rendered—but, with no perspective to go with them, aside from the vicarious thrills, why should we care? A memoir with no reflection is sex without love, wine without the glass.

Maybe the reflections come later, on the next page. But why not have the intelligent narrator there from the start?—that or lock us into her addictive psyche in a present tense prologue, one that raises the two most pertinent questions: 1) *How did the narrator get here?* and 2) *How will she get out?* Then, switching to the reflective past tense, answer them. Either strategy beats having the narrator looking back on the past without perspective.

This well-written first page also suffers from impatience, with the author trying to do too much at once. It can be whittled down.

Here, whittled, as present tense prologue (minus the hectoring ALL-CAPS):

"Kevin!"

Six months ago my husband gave me his left kidney. This morning all I want are my pills.

"Kevin!" all ninety-seven pounds of me shouts from my bed.

Footsteps pad across the kitchen, a screen door slams. I hear the Honda trunk open, zippers zipping, picture Kevin packing his camera, tripod and lights. My bones twitch under the sheets. My hands shake. My aimless fingers quiver as they pluck absent pills from the bottom of an empty plastic vial. I look at my dresser clock. 10:07. My Xanax is ready and waiting at Rite Aid. Why the hell is he dawdling?

"Kevin!"

More foot treads, more zippers, more doors slamming....

I think: *you are such an ass.*

Your Turn

Introduce some reflection into a first-person, nonfiction opening you have written, a moment or moments in which your narrator comments retrospectively, from their present vantage point, on the event or events of the past that are being related. Such reflections might begin with the words *Though I didn't know it then* or *Looking back, I wonder....* The great advantage of reflections is that they allow your narrator to understand and describe events more clearly and objectively than they could possibly have seen them while in the midst of them.

55. Clinic Caper

(Memoir / Humor / Story vs. Anecdote)

The nurse ushered Jim and me into the treatment room at the far end of the clinic's hallway. Not often are a husband and wife seen by a doctor in the same room, but the few skin issues we have, and at the age of sixty-six and forty-one years of marital bliss, gave us no reason to occupy separate rooms.

Fifteen minutes overdue, and with the room turning stuffy, Jim opened the door for a little air circulation. He sat in one of the upholstered chairs against the wall, while I occupied the one in the center of the room—the one that resembles a dental chair, feet up, lean back.

Jim noticed a button that could raise and lower the chair electronically, and, just like a man, wondered what would happen if he pushed it.

He pushed it. The chair dropped with a jolt—me with it.

I said, "Leave it alone. We'll have it all screwed up and the doctor'll walk in wondering what in the heck we're messin' with her equipment for."

Jim sat down in his upholstered chair with that squelched look all over his face, like—"Ah, c'mon, let me just have a little fun here."

That was all it took. I started giggling then laughing and there was no stopping it. I looked over at Jim, who shrugged and gave me the "no clue" look. This made me laugh harder, one of those uncontrollable belly laughs. An entire cartoon streamed through my imagination. Between gasps, I managed to share my visuals with him: "I can just picture you pressing some button and the chair starts spinning round, faster and faster. At least we have air circulation now. 'Woo-hoo!' So you try the button next to it. The chair shoots up. Another button and the chair thuds down, my chin hitting my chest. The last button launches the chair horizontally, blasting me through the stucco wall, leaving a hole the exact shape of me grasping the chair armrests. I imagine hearing the doctor's voice from somewhere around the corner. What will she say when she sees me in the middle of the hallway, covered with plaster and sheetrock? I say as if nothing is out of the ordinary, 'Good morning, Dr. Rashid. Just trying to get a little air.'"

Analysis

This scene of marital bliss set in the confines of a dermatologist's examination room feels more like something complete in and of itself than the opening of a longer work. If there's any doubt, the title seals it.

Not that there's anything wrong with telling a story in a page or two. In fact, anyone who can do so earns my admiration. The trick, though, is to tell a story and not just an anecdote.

Anecdote: a short narrative constructed around a unique, curious, often provocative incident, one that typically reveals character through extreme circumstances and almost always with humor as its end. The term comes from the Greek word *anekdota*, meaning "unpublished"—and indeed, most anecdotes are relayed orally and not intended for nor worthy of the printed page except as illustrations serving some larger purpose: evoking, for instance, some facet of a character or characters. Served *à la carte*, anecdotes tend to be as ephemeral as they are amusing. They are garnishes, or appetizers, not the main course.

Though nicely written, the opening scene here feels more anecdotal than it might were the emphasis less on the singular, curious, and provocative event in the clinic, and more on the two principal characters, Jim and his narrating wife. As it stands, I can imagine such a tale being told at a dinner party (a popular venue for anecdotes). The guests, who know this couple well—and who've also had their share of cocktails—are extremely amused, weeping with laughter. Their host is on a roll. When she gets to the part about the dermatologist's fiendish chair launching her through the stucco wall, I see them all doing spit takes with their wine into their Roquefort pear salads.

But literature isn't a dinner party, and the "dinner guests" (unfamiliar readers) need something more than cocktails to satisfy their appetites. They need context, some sense of who these people are when *not* goofing around at the dermatological clinic. That sense, the little of it that we get, is tucked into one sentence in the opening paragraph ("at the age of sixty-six and forty-one years of marital bliss, we saw no reason to occupy separate rooms"). We're told that they're an older, happily married couple, a statement the rest of the scene goes on to confirm. It does so charmingly, and with considerable skill. It meets our expectations, but nothing more. It neither suggests nor reveals anything more or less about who these people are or why we should care about them enough to keep on reading.

And since the scene merely confirms what we've already been told—without a hint of irony or paradox or a shadow of doubt—I'm left unsatisfied. Again, at a dinner party I would be content to know that my hostess and her husband are lovely, happily married people. Sure, it's not the whole story; in fact it may well be a total illusion. And yet what are dinner parties for, if not to parade ourselves in front of our guests in our favorite masks?

If literature serves any purpose at all, it's to tear those masks off or let us peek through or behind them and glimpse the genuine lives underneath. Here, with this opening, I'm shown only the mask: a bright, smiling, charming mask.

Supposing the shenanigans in the examination room were underscored by something serious? Supposing this routine visit to the dermatologist turned out to be anything but routine? Supposing "everything" was not "all right," that the small blotchy growth on his shoulder turned out to be a stage-three melanoma. Then this opening of a memoir would be revelatory of a devoted wife's courageous humor in the face of tragedy, and not a mere anecdote. Perhaps a revelation like that is coming. In that case, I think it should be telegraphed, possibly in the first sentence.

Does the underlying event or matter need to be as grim as cancer? No, but it should carry us beyond the anecdotal.

Your Turn

To the top of this lighthearted opening add a sentence that points to something serious. How does that addition change everything that follows?

56. Leaving Jumana

(Memoir / Framing Questions Effectively)

I left the island of Jumana under a cloud, deported for an undisclosed crime. As my daughter and I boarded the plane, I turned for a last glimpse of palm trees backlit by the setting sun and a pale horizon of sand framed by a turquoise sea. My hand trembled as I gripped the railing to steady myself.

"Go ahead, Sunny," I said with a gentle nudge. She stepped into the plane.

I followed, bumping my wheelie suitcase up the last metal tread. Arab and Asian families and businessmen with attaché cases blocked the aisle, but moved ahead all at once. I put our bags in the overhead compartment. We took our seats, and Sunny huddled against me.

As we buckled our seatbelts, a voice in my head kept repeating why? why? I shifted in my cramped economy class seat that was ill-suited for a six-foot-tall woman with long legs.

At least the flight to Dubai would be brief, since Jumana was only thirty kilometers off the south coast of the Arabian Gulf. It was a flight we had taken many times on excursions to Dubai, but this trip was different. My thoughts kept circling around the same obsessive orbit. Caught in the whirl of my mind, details and fragments of things churned like a sand devil spinning across the desert. I leaned over to squeeze Sunny's hand. "Don't worry. It's going to work out."

"I know, Mom." She peered at the photo she was clutching of our dog. A friend was taking care of him. Her face clenched up, but she didn't cry. "When can he come to Dubai?"

"Once we find a place to live, someone will bring him here on the ferry. I promise."

Sunny nodded, but anguish flickered in her eyes. She was being brave for my sake. What could I say to my ten-year-old daughter, who'd had to pull up stakes abruptly, leaving her friends, her school, and her beloved dog?

I had been given forty-eight hours' notice to leave the country. No reason why. No explanation why the Women's College of Jumana University fired me after seven years of teaching. It was a mistake. It had to be. What could I have done to warrant being branded persona non grata and thrown out of the country like a piece of trash?

Analysis

*"The writer's task isn't to answer the question,
but to frame the question correctly."*
CHEKHOV

Sometimes everything we need for our openings is there, more than we need, in fact. It's just a matter of cutting and rearranging.

This opening is of a memoir about the experiences of an expatriate professor at a fictional woman's college located on the island of "Jumana" (a feminine Arabian name meaning "silver pearl") in the Persian Gulf thirty kilometers from the city of Dubai.

The first page finds the narrator/protagonist boarding a passenger plane with her ten-year-old daughter, having been fired from her job and deported without explanation, raising in readers the same questions the protagonist asks herself, namely, *Why are we being deported? What did I do?* From here the novel is bound to go back in time to tell us this woman's story.

The strategy being used here is called a *framing device* or a *framed narrative*. What it "frames" or sets up is a long flashback—in this case presumably the length of a novel—one that will answer, or at least partly answer, the question(s) it raises.

The author launches her first page not with an experience, but with information: "I left the island of Jumana under a cloud, deported for an undisclosed crime." The drawback to this approach is that the information provided answers a question that hasn't yet been raised in the reader. We read this first sentence with no awareness that the protagonist is boarding a plane, let alone where she's going, or that she's been forced to leave against her will. Only halfway down the first page, when the narrator tells her daughter, "Don't worry. It's going to work out," are we given cause to wonder what circumstances have prompted this involuntary voyage.

By answering up front the very question that the scene exists to arouse in us, the author subverts her own purpose. This is not the same as *withholding information* or creating what I call *false suspense*. It's simply a matter of giving readers the experiences *before* supplying information that explains or categorizes them, rather than afterward.

Otherwise the scene makes too much ado of boarding the plane, of rolling and stowing luggage—mundane actions with which most readers are familiar and that don't require dramatization. The sooner we get to "Don't worry, it's going to work out," the better.

Here's my edit, with the crucial dialogue engaged within a few lines. What's been cut is implied or can wait (we needn't know, yet, that the narrator has lost her job at the Women's College of Jumana). In the original opening, the beloved dog's name is withheld, why I don't know. I have included it, since withholding it from us seems artificial and adds a note of *false suspense*.

Revised opening:

> "Go ahead, Sunny," I said, nudging my daughter past Arab and Asian families and businessmen with briefcases. We took our economy-class seats (mine ill-suited for a six-foot-tall woman) and fastened our seatbelts. Sunny huddled close. I squeezed her hand.
>
> "Don't worry," I said. "It's going to work out."
>
> "What about Fido?" she asked.
>
> We had left under a cloud, deported for reasons undisclosed. Through the puddle jumper's window I caught a glimpse of palm trees backlit by the setting sun and a horizon of pale sand framed by a turquoise sea. My hand trembled. At least the flight would be brief, Jumana being only about thirty kilometers from the coast. It was a flight we'd taken many times.
>
> "When can he come to Dubai with us?"
>
> We'd been given forty-eight hours to leave. No explanation. After seven years. It was a mistake. It had to be. What could I have done? And what could I tell my ten-year-old daughter, who'd had to pull up stakes abruptly, leaving her friends, her school, even her beloved dog?
>
> "Once we find a place to live, Dolores will bring him to us. I promise."
>
> Sunny's face clenched. Anguish flickered in her eyes, but she didn't cry.

This version raises and answers the same pertinent questions, in that order.

Your Turn

How would you revise this opening? Improve on both the original and my version.

57. I'm Not Chinese

(Memoir / Precision, Authenticity, Humility)

The first thing you need to know is I'm not Chinese. My name is Raymond Wong, and I stopped being Chinese at the age of five.

Twenty-eight years ago, my mother left my father in Hong Kong to come to America in search of a better life. Don't ask about my trip to the US. I don't remember. I was just a little boy.

What I do know is I'm American. In school, children are cruel to those who are different. Speaking Chinese made me different. I don't speak Chinese anymore.

It's not a big deal. I live in San Diego. My stepfather is named Roger, and he's from Minnesota. My friends speak English.

Speaking Chinese would only make me an outsider, and that's something I've struggled against my whole life. In school, kids used to always ask me what I was. What they really wanted to know was where I came from and if I ate with chopsticks.

My answer—British. True. The British government ruled Hong Kong for over 150 years. My response never failed to bring a puzzled frown, and this gave me great satisfaction.

Still, no matter how hard I tried, I couldn't fit in—even in my own family. Though I refused to speak Chinese, it didn't bring me closer to the man my mom married when I was six. Roger called me his son, but the words were empty, like a birthday spent alone.

Analysis

Precision, authenticity, clarity, and humility: those are the four qualities that a memoirist—or any writer, for that matter—brings to bear on his or her subject, and this last first page of this memoir opening has all four in great abundance. Look for a trace of pretension: you won't find it. Nor will you find anything obviously or self-consciously "literary," no clever metaphors or similes, no perfunctory adverbs or grandstanding adjectives or somersaulting sentences. Nothing showy.

Not that writers can or should never show off. But when they put pyrotechnical displays ahead of other concerns—ahead of *precision, authenticity, clarity,* and *humility*—usually something crucial is lost. That something crucial is the reader's trust.

Writers should serve their stories, not the other way around. We must be their humble servants.

Everything for the story; nothing for the writer.

When I say "for the story," of course I mean for the reader, too.

Your Turn

Revise an opening page, your own or someone else's, making the writing as simple, humble, authentic, and precise as possible. Keep sentences short and vocabulary limited.

G. Style

STYLE IS SUBSTANCE. WHEN STYLE AND SUBSTANCE ARE DIVIDED, if one isn't integrated with the other, both suffer or fail. Style can't be added to our writing like salt or pepper to a stew. Ideally, it comes *with* the writing, is part and parcel to that other foundational element of narrative prose: point of view, informing not only how ideas are expressed, but *what* is expressed.

Who we choose to narrate our stories makes all the difference regarding their style; in fact, it determines and guides it. Choose the right narrator, and—assuming that you are equipped with sufficient vocabulary and grammatical skills—style should pretty much take care of itself. What is style, after all, if not a sensibility coupled with diction and syntax?

That said, now and then we authors need to intervene to exercise some restraint on our narrators or help them make certain decisions. For instance, should an event be summarized or rendered fully as a scene? When should we slow a passage down with description—or do the opposite, trim a description that slows things down too much?

When it comes to style, what we mainly bring to bear are our *editorial* skills. The narrator tells the story; we edit. This is especially obvious when it comes to dialogue—which, ideally, is *recorded* rather than written, with our narrators reporting what they hear or have heard. Our job, then, as editors, is to see to it that what's reported is *worth* reporting: that what stays on the page is the filet mignon of the dialogue, not gristle and fat.

Something of the sort pertains to editing in general, only instead of a dialogue between two or more characters, what we're editing is our narrator's *monologue*, trimming and tightening it, strengthening, supervising syntax, diction, and grammar. Editing, in other words, for *style*.

In this section, we'll focus on such things as sentimentality and the distinction between writing *experientially* and *informationally*. We'll also look at the role of modifiers—adjectives and adverbs—and at verbs and figurative language (similes and metaphors). We'll look at how writing engages the senses, and highlight the importance of precision and clarity. We'll look at genericism and cliché and other qualities that add (or subtract) authenticity to writing.

Perhaps most important at all, we'll look at how a piece of writing is enhanced through cutting, by implying things rather than stating them, through saying more with less.

58. A Stormy Opening

(Writing Up a Storm / Poetry vs. Histrionics / Inadvertent Comedy)

On a peninsula of a peninsula in the month of hurricanes, a tropical storm bore a tempest named Michael and a girl named Emma. Pregnant clouds, swollen with sea and rain and fury, dilated with every electrical contraction. Thunder cracked in suffering echoes. Heaven pushed and moaned and cried out in grunting spasms. The tempest's breath labored in panted exertion. In its uncontrollable thrashing, it flung itself wide open, dilating from horizon to horizon. Tender linings of cloud bellies ripped in the delivery of itself into the rough hands of the Atlantic seaboard.

"The first miracle is birth."

The coast locked its doors, boarded its windows, collected drinking water and sought refuge. Bridges tumbled under the fury of the sea's salt licks. Roads drowned in the high-rise waters. Colored with mucous and blood, the storm's water broke in a torrential gushing and splattered the inhabitants' lives with uncertainty. There was no sun in the Sunshine State. For the moment, its perpetual promise of paradise was eclipsed by the fury of cloud dragons. They fed off of the fear and the chaos emitted into the atmosphere through the most basic acts of Darwinism—survival of the fittest. Survival leveled the hierarchy of all the peninsula's living creatures to their most primordial state.

The closer the storm got to the peninsula's most southern tip of shoreline, the greater it swelled in velocity and strength. Just as the winds reached 12 on the Beaufort Scale an unborn infant stopped her downward motion toward the birth canal. She sensed her mother's fear. She clung to the security of her mother's womb. A synapse fired in her brain and she remembered her original nature ... bliss ... wholeness ... belonging ... purpose.... She sensed her mother's fear again. Another synapse fired ... expectancy ... performance ... anticipation ... combustion ... pain ... falling ... separation ... survival ... loss ... fear ... another synapse fired ... safety ... the umbilical cord. So, the infant turned and hid her face. The contractions stopped. But the womb was as elusive as a sandbar in an open sea; one wave shifts the illusion of safety.

The woman's body took the brunt of the child's indecision. The woman screamed out in an agonizing, guttural bark to release the pain of her next contraction. The pain peaked. Relief. When she realized the contractions had stopped, she spread her legs even wider—beckoning the child in a desperate plea to *come forth!* The infant ebbed into refuge, and the woman's fluids dried up like a receding, low tide. The woman s-c-r-e-a-m-e-d obscenities at the naked hospital walls. She pleaded for relief. She confessed her sins into the empty room, and the walls wept tears. She begged for forgiveness. She cried out in an exhausted whimper, "You must come, my child, or you shall kill us both!"

Analysis

Wordsworth defined poetry as "the spontaneous overflow of powerful feelings: it takes its origin from emotion recollected *in tranquility*."[12] If we broaden that definition of poetry to include poetic prose, then expand it further to include all writing that successfully evokes a subjective experience, then—assuming Wordsworth is right—the best condition for good writing isn't feverish intensity, but calm equilibrium.

This flies in the face of the popular cliché: the masterpiece produced in a "white heat," with the author foaming at the mouth while spilling his blood and guts on the page (the visual artist equivalent: Van Gogh as played by Kirk Douglas, gripping his straw hat and licking his brushes in the grip of insanity and the mistral).

For every successful work created under such conditions, there must be thousands of failures. Van Gogh painted despite his madness, not thanks to it. It may not sound very romantic, but most successful art is produced by sane, calm, rational people.

On the first page in question a woman gives birth during a violent storm. The opening itself is a tempest of frenzied, feverish diction. Among adjectives we get swollen, dilated, labored, grunting, uncontrollable, torrential, desperate, exhausted, agonizing, guttural. Verb choices are no less turbulent: cracked, pushed, ripped, moaned, cried, clung, fired, pleaded, begged. Whether this opening was produced in a state of fervor or one of serenity I'm in no position to say, but here an emotional experience is recollected not tranquilly or objectively. It's whipped into a squall.

---

12   Preface to *Lyrical Ballads*, 1798. Italics mine.

Not that the writing isn't effective; it is. The prose is so intent on jolting us, reading it is like sticking your finger repeatedly into a live socket, or being pummeled by a boxer. By the fourth paragraph, I found myself gasping on the ropes. So did the writer, apparently, as evidenced by all those sentences spluttering and coughing up ellipses like bullets from a tommy gun.

This sort of breathless prose stuffs the pages of many a bestseller, especially thriller and horror novels (I'm thinking *The Da Vinci Code*). No denying it, heavy breathing sells books. But does it make for good writing?

Am I saying all descriptions—especially those of violent events and emotions—ought to be calm? Heavens, no! Imagine Poe's "The Tell-Tale Heart" relayed by a calm narrator, or Dostoyevsky's Underground Man[13] minus his bile. Calmed down, what would be left of King Lear's famous storm speech in Act III of his play:

Blow, winds, and crack your cheeks! rage! blow!
You cataracts and hurricanes spout
Till you have drench'd our steeples, drown'd the
      cocks!
You sulphurous and thought-executing fires
Vaunt couriers of oak-cleaving thunderbolts,
Singe my white head! And thou, all-shaking thunder,
Strike flat the thick rotundity o' the world!
Crack nature's moulds, all germens spill at once,
That make ingrateful man!

Notice, though, the absence of abstract modifiers in this most histrionic of speeches. In place of pat adjectives like "torrential" we get "oak-cleaving thunderbolts" and "thought-executing fires"—compound modifiers formed of solid nouns and kinetic verbs. Rather than imbue his storm with feelings ("Thunder cracked in suffering echoes. Heaven pushed and moaned and cried out in grunting spasms"), Lear puts us right in the thick of his storm; he drenches and drowns and singes us.

Shakespeare and Lear notwithstanding, in works of prose the union of frantic subject with frantic description is often an unhappy one. Rather than complement the thing being described, a frenetic style adds up to overkill—like putting ketchup on gravy. The sensational experience can no longer speak for itself (as does "I was born in the belly of a white elephant during a 30-day dry

---

13   *Notes from the Underground* (1864).

Northeaster," the opening line of Christopher Cook Gilmore's *Atlantic City Proof*). Instead, the author seethes and shouts.

Another danger posed by pumping up already dramatic events with breathless prose: inadvertent comedy. Benjamin Cheever once explained comedy to me this way: "You take a very tragic event, make it more tragic, then make it even more tragic. Then it's funny." He offered the example of a woman in labor driving herself to the hospital at two in the morning. On the way her car gets a flat tire. It's raining. Still in her nightgown, with her contractions mounting, she jacks up the car only to open her trunk and find the spare tire flat or missing. As she stands by the roadside weeping, a trailer truck roars through a puddle, spattering her with mud. When I relate this scenario to students, before I even get to that truck or the puddle they're already tittering. My students aren't sadists. It's just that the situation is so over the top. They could laugh or cry. They laugh.

Reading *The Da Vinci Code*, I had a similar experience. By the end of the prologue, when the museum director scrawls an encrypted code on his chest with his own dying blood, I laughed—not what Dan Brown intended (though I imagine him laughing, too, all the way to the bank).

Personally, I'd rather have dramatic actions speak for themselves than have an author or his narrator shout them in my face.

Your Turn

Render a violently dramatic event—a car accident, a house fire, a flood, a physical fight, a hurricane, a mugging, a murder—as coolly and clinically as possible. Let the event's intrinsic drama speak entirely for itself. Then rewrite the same scene, this time injecting as much emotion through language as possible.

59. A Letter from Tehran

*(Sentimentality / Grounding Scene in
Setting / Implication via Action)*

I tear at the envelope, the Farsi script sprawls dotted and curlicued, the edges tattooed with red airmail chevrons. And the four stamps frighten me all over again, images of a woman shrouded in black with large round eyes staring at me, eyebrows arched and sweeping up like a vulture's wings. I feel the helpless anger, the fearful submission imprisoning my brain as if I'd never left Iran.

My dog Skipper nudges my leg as if to say, "Come on. Time to go back." But my worn sneakers sink into the gravel berm and I stare down the highway, a black tar seam cutting through the virgin pine and cedar forests of Wintun Mountain. The spring wind loosens the strands of my grey hair and I pull my checked wool shirt closer around my shoulders. Heart pounding, hands unsteady, I lean against the mailbox and the metal flag falls. How dare they write to me after all these years when nothing in that world can matter to me again, when I have found peace far away from them? I reach inside and remove the sheet of lined copybook paper. My eyes read the Farsi words:

"Dear Madame Gael,

"I pray for your health and God's blessing upon you. This is Sakineh, you remember. I write because Madame the mother of Omid cannot sleep. Saint Reza has come to her many times and told her what she must do before she dies. She is afraid of Allah's hell fires and she must return to you the share of the land that is yours."

I crumple the paper in my fist. Wasn't the old lady dead and buried yet—she must be ninety, but she lives on. Everyone around her is dead. And now she has to pull me into one last game, her cruelty alive after all this time. But I had never been strong against her, and just holding the letter has already ruined my simple life, my weekly drive down to Wintun Mills to cash my pension check, to buy groceries and flowers for the cemetery.

Skipper and I walk down the driveway, back to the old frame house. My father's junkyard is now gone, the old porch rebuilt. I sit outside in the April sun and smooth the letter on my jeans.

"She must have your forgiveness. An agency is sending the ticket so you can come to Iran and sign the papers and give your forgiveness. When you are coming, write or call. It will be good to see you Madame Gael. You were always good to us.

"Your loyal dear friend, Sakineh."

Analysis

When analyzing a piece of writing, I find it helpful to try and summarize the action in as few words as possible. Here, accompanied by her dog, a woman (thanks to that "checked wool shirt" for a while I thought she was a man) receives a letter informing her that she must come to Iran to claim her share of a parcel of property that she is to inherit from the soon-do-die mother of a man (Omid) with whom she—the letter's recipient—had a relationship of some sort years ago.

That's quite a bit of plot squeezed into one sentence, and even more gets stuffed into the rest of this opening page. It's an enticing opening, one that promises two stories: one about the events that have led up to this moment (including the mysterious relationship with the mysterious Omid), and one about what will happen from this moment forward, when and if the letter's recipient makes the journey to Iran.

However well written and enticing, this opening does raise a few concerns, foremost among them being sentimentality: emotions in excess of experience.

We've established that the fiction writer's primary purpose isn't to convey information, but to create experiences. By way of those experiences, we arouse feelings in our readers. The problem of sentimentality occurs in one of two ways: 1) when the actions of characters are themselves out of proportion with events (e.g., a character vomiting, bursting into tears, or punching the boss in the nose on learning she's been fired from a job); or 2) when the emotional weight carried by the narrator's language or tone surpasses our experiences, such that our own emotions lag behind the narrator's.

This opening confronts us with sentimentality of the second sort. In the first six lines alone we get the following words: tear, sprawls, frighten, shrouded, black, staring, arched, sweeping, vulture's, helpless, anger, fearful, submission, imprisoning—words that, if not overtly laden with emotional import, are certainly not emotionally neutral. Such language doesn't merely invite emotions; it demands them by forcing emotions on us, and does so before we have begun to know who this narrator is and what situation she finds herself in.

It asks us to feel more than we can possibly feel given our own experience of the character's circumstances.

The opening continues in this vein, with emotionally laden descriptions ("sneakers sink into the gravel berm" "a black tar seem cutting through the virgin pine") that color, shape, and quantify our responses to a story we've barely dipped a toe into. Add to that the narrator's overt emotional responses to her situation ("How dare they write to me" … "I crumple the paper in my fist" … "Just holding the letter has already ruined my simple life"), and you have an opening passage that, if not manifestly or blatantly sentimental, risks being so.

Though sentimentality is the main concern raised by the first paragraph, it's not the only concern. There's also again the question of how effectively the opening grounds us in the moment at hand. With no clues to the setting, no suggestion of where, when, or under what circumstances the tearing open of that envelope occurs, we are left with at best a vague image of someone (woman? man? young? old?) reading a letter somewhere (indoors? outdoors? city? country? night? day? sunny? rainy?). We must read on to discover that the letter recipient is a woman old enough to have gray hair, and that she is outdoors with her dog, Skipper. True, within a sentence or two of her novel the author can't be expected to supply us with all the necessary information to shape a crystal-clear image. But imagine how much more effective—and less sentimental—this moment would be if we had just a few more pieces of the puzzle:

> The letter arrived on a rainy Friday morning. I'd stepped out to the mailbox as usual with my collie, Skipper, and found it there among the usual bills and supermarket circulars, in a tattered envelope tattooed with red airmail chevrons.

By setting the scene in the first sentence, the author would avoid the disorientation that occurs in the second paragraph, where suddenly we find ourselves standing outdoors in the middle of a road, forcing us to retrofit our experience of the first paragraph.

Rather than state emotional responses ("How dare they write to me"), it's better to let actions speak for themselves. For them to do so, we have to provide some context for those actions: somehow we need to establish, or at least give some sense of, a character's routine ("I'd stepped out to the mailbox as usual") in order for our readers to appreciate the events that depart from that routine (a letter from Iran). Without proper contextualization, it's hard if not impossible for us to share a character's emotional responses, which is why this author feels compelled to lay those emotions on us with a trowel. The essence of drama lies in events that shatter routine. But unless it has been established, a routine can't be shattered.

Finally, the deeper I read into this opening, the more I suspect that this letter reading scene will serve as a prologue or a framing device for a story set in the past, one that will involve us in the letter-reader's love affair with a man named Omid, and that will circle back to this moment. Given that suspicion, it seems to me that in and of itself the letter serves perfectly as a prologue, that what matters is what the letter says, its contents, not the recipient's overt (or implied) emotional response to it, or the scene that carries it.

So—why not just present the letter? That it has been received, opened, read, and reacted to, is, after all, implied. Not only is the letter the heart of this scene; it *is* the scene. The rest can be cut. From there the author might go on and tell the story of the events behind this letter, or that it precipitates. Or both.

Your Turn

Draft three different versions of an opening in which a character receives a letter of some import. In the first version, have us read the entire letter. In Version II, share only a portion of it. In the final version, share none of the letter, but suggest or imply its overall tenor if not its contents.

60. A Lion in the Room

(Defamiliarization / Throat-Grabber Openings / Metaphor)

I froze in the chair. There was a lion right there. In the room, on the other side of the table.

Just what I'd been warned about, but hadn't believed. I tried not to move. Maybe he'd ignore me.

No such luck. His shoulder muscles bunched and his eyes blazed red as he looked at me. Avoid eye contact, Gran'd told me. Don't challenge them. I looked down at my beer.

Must be an acid flashback, I thought. Johnny going on about Gran's old stories must've brought it on—lion spirits possessing people and all that San Bushman stuff.

"I'm in charge at the loony bin, Pete. My cabbagepatch. Like when the loonies get the shits I take care of things. Fix 'em up. They're always so friggin' grateful."

I looked up and saw just plain old Big Sid hunched forward over the table, pint in paw, with the light from the 'DEPARTURES' sign outside the bar reflected on his bottle-bottom thick specs.

He chugged beer, burped, and carried on. "The doctors think they know it all. Nobody else could do their job. Bloody power freaks don't want us to do medical stuff, even simple things. They keep it all complicated. Keep it all scientific and that. I mean, look at how they treat someone who's dehydrated. Simple, all they need is fluids in them."

I looked down at my mug and tried to keep my face expressionless, but couldn't help thinking, 'Power-freak yourself. Bloody predator. Everyone's just prey, ego-food on the hoof to you.' I wanted to say that, but I knew there was no way a guy like Sid, five years older and a foot taller, could let me score any points.

So I played along. "Go on then. Tell us, Sid. What's wrong with how they treat that, then?"

Analysis

Defamiliarization (or *ostranenie* in the original Russian) is a technique whereby artists force their audiences to look at familiar things and ideas in new, unfamiliar ways. The term was coined by Russian author and critic Victor Shklovsky in his 1917 essay "Art as Technique." Shklovsky distinguishes between poetic and practical language: language used to describe or explain, as opposed to language used to impart perceptions or heighten existing ones.

An excellent example of defamiliarization is found in Tolstoy's "Kholstomer: The Story of a Horse," in which we experience the horse from a novel perspective: its own. A passage:

> The words 'my horse' referred to me, a living horse, and seemed as strange to me as the words 'my land,' 'my air,' 'my water.' But the words made a strong impression on me....

Poets and poetic artists typically use defamiliarization to breathe fresh life into things ordinary and banal. Similes and metaphors work this way. When Lorrie Moore compares a mother's face to "a big white dumpling of worry" or Richard Brautigan compares a dish of ice cream to "Kafka's hat," they force us to look at something familiar in an unfamiliar way. We're momentarily disoriented—shocked, even—but then we say to ourselves, "Oh, yes: I see it now."

Here, defamiliarization is used exclusively for shock value: not to impart a fresh way of looking at things, but to catch the reader off-guard and keep him that way. It's not the first time that literature has furnished us with examples of men and jungle cats confronting each other at close quarters. The most notorious recent example is Yann Martel's *Life of Pi*, where the cat is a tiger, and the confrontation happens across an ocean in a lifeboat. But the man sitting across the table from the narrator in this first page isn't a lion; he's Big Sid, a hospital orderly with a taste for lager who stands (sits?) a foot taller than his companion. Otherwise, unless we count bunched shoulder muscles and blazing eyes, there's nothing all that lion-like about him.

Which is all right, assuming that the comparison isn't meant to be symbolic or even poetic, but is a literal description of a hallucination—a possibility that the narrator himself raises in the fourth paragraph. If so, it's not the first time that literature has given us a hallucinating mental hospital denizen, either. The most famous of those is Chief Bromden, the narrator of Ken Kesey's *One Flew Over the Cuckoo's Nest*, who bears witness to events through a hallucinatory, psychotropic drug-induced fog. However, the hallucinatory explanation here is quickly cast aside; indeed, the rest of the passage shrugs off the whole lion analogy, which at the bottom of the page gives a little roar with the words "bloody predator" but otherwise makes itself scarce.

Two solutions suggest themselves: either throw out the analogy completely, or weave it more thoroughly into Sid's description, emphasizing his leonine features. This way readers will see him as his narrator does, rather than having the comparison force-fed to them.

But what brings Big Sid to life in this opening page isn't the narrator's shock-tactic metaphor. It's Sid's strong dialogue ("I'm in charge of the loony bin, Pete. My cabbagepatch.") as well as his actions ("He chugged beer, burped, and carried on.").

Big Sid speaks for himself. He doesn't need his author to roar for him.

Your Turn

Describe someone or something in a way that renders it freshly using defamiliarization. Choose an unexpected metaphor (a human equated with a household appliance or piece of furniture) or a unique perspective (a piano or a bicycle as experienced by a cat or a dog).

61. Back to School Night

(Scene vs. Summary / Description vs. Exposition / Show, Don't Tell)

The second Wednesday in September is Back to School Night, and as Stephan goes over his World History syllabus, he avoids the eyes of Mona McCullough and feels choked by the collar of his French-cuffed shirt. The summer is behind him, but its heat endures, heavy as ever, and as he presses on about the weight of the past, sweat streaks his ponytail and soaks cold ovals at his armpits. The fluorescent lights remind him of an interrogation.

This is Stephan's second year at Alamo Heights, and though he's used to the glazed looks of seventeen-year-olds, parents still make him squirm. Crammed into desks, they put on tense grins while Stephan hashes over the first six-week grading period—the Roman Empire, an essay on a major historical figure. Stephan knows they are wary of him, these mothers and fathers, troubled by his long hair and stud earrings, the same quirks that, along with his founding of the school's cycling club, have made him so popular among students. Unlike his colleagues—frock-clad women in orthopedic shoes, or paunchy men in plaid shirts—Stephan sports slim-fit jeans and never wears a tie. He is boyish and fun and well put-together, with green eyes and a complexion soft as whipped cream. But what separates him from his fellow teachers is greater than looks and age; Stephan understands his students. He gets them. In times of teenage strife, when one of the girls is sure she's too fat to find a date for senior party, when a boy doesn't know if it's okay to wear socks with topsiders, Stephan is an able listener and adviser, a new member of the adult tribe, seasoned by age yet unspoiled by its coming strain. He could easily pass as one of their older brothers—could almost pass as one of them.

Analysis

There are two principle ways in which characters are evoked: descriptively, through summary or exposition, or dramatically, through action.

In this opening of a short story about a popular young high school teacher who is discomfited by his charges' parents and by one mother in particular, the summary method is used with great skill. "Show, don't tell," we're told.

But there's nothing wrong with telling; it just has to be done well. Here, except for that overstuffed first sentence, it's done well. Note how much better that sentence reads when broken in two:

> The second Wednesday in September is Back to School Night.
> As Stephan goes over his World History syllabus, he avoids Mona McCullough's eyes and feels choked by the collar of his French-cuffed shirt.

For the same reason that a single-pronged spear penetrates better than a trident, a longer, complex sentence with several clauses isn't always or even often better than two shorter sentences. Let the conjunction—the relationship between the two sentences—be implied. I've also changed "the eyes of Mona McCullough" to "Mona McCullough's eyes." See what you think.

The next long paragraph of this first page is packed with summary exposition about the protagonist, Stephan, information that serves not only to orient us to his status as a high school teacher, but to lend authenticity through telling details (he founded the school's cycling club; his male colleagues wear plaid shirts). By the time I get to the bottom of the page, there's no doubt in my mind as to the existence of this earnest, long-haired, tieless, earringed teacher "seasoned by age yet unspoiled by its coming strain." I feel I know him, more than that: I feel I know something of what it's like to be him.

The advantage of summary exposition is that through it authors can convey a lot of information in a little space, as here. Summary description is expedient: it does the job quickly and efficiently. The disadvantage is that, unlike dramatization, which conveys characters through actions and dialogue, exposition renders it exclusively as information: rather than form our own conclusions based on material evidence, we're forced to take the narrator's word for things. Assuming the narrator is reliable (as most are), exposition supplies strong, if not damning, evidence. For damning evidence, nothing beats actions.

In this opening, unless we count the sweat breaking out under Stephan's armpits, the only solid action is the negative one of him avoiding Mona McCullough's eyes. From there we plunge into the long expository passage concerning Stephan's relationship with his students. As written, the page reads quite well. Still, supposing the ratio of action to exposition were more balanced, if the author had lavished as much time and detail on the first paragraph as on the second?

Were he to return Mona McCullough's gaze, what would Stephan see in her eyes? Disgust? Pity? Contempt? Curiosity? What does this mother look like, by the way? How is she dressed? Formerly Fashionably? In a frumpy housecoat? Might her appearance or her posture offer more clues to her character and how she feels about her child's teacher? Of all the parental eyes in that classroom, why is our protagonist so intent on avoiding Mona McCullough's? Is it merely because she happens to be seated front and center and so her gaze is the hardest to avoid? Might there be other reasons why he dreads her eyes in particular? Perhaps Stephan's closeness to his students extends beyond the pedagogic? Might Stephan have a thing for this mother's daughter (to whom she bears an unsettlingly uncanny resemblance)—or her son? Or is it just the way that she's looking at him? While Stephan avoids Mona McCullough's eyes and pretends to look at something on his desk, what thoughts, ideas, images, or fantasies flit through or flood his mind?

None of these things need to be broached on this first page; they may not need to be broached at all. The story that follows may have nothing to do with Ms. McCullough, who is merely representative of the parents in that classroom. And Stephan's discomfort may just be that of a young and insecure teacher. Still, for me at least these are questions that the material raises.

Exposition is most effective when linked directly to an action, as in the following passage from *Lolita*, in which Humbert Humbert's gaze falls both upon its titular object and on a distant memory:

> It was the same child—the same frail, honey-hued shoulders, the same silky supple bare back, the same chestnut head of hair. A polka-dotted black kerchief tied around her chest hid from my aging ape eyes, but not from the gaze of young memory, the juvenile breasts I had fondled one immortal day. And, as if I were the fairy-tale nurse of some little princess (lost, kidnapped, discovered in gypsy rags through which her nakedness smiled at the king and his hounds), I recognized the tiny dark-brown mole on her side. With awe and delight (the king crying for joy, the trumpets blaring, the nurse drunk) I saw again her lovely indrawn abdomen where my southbound mouth had briefly paused; and those puerile hips on which I had kissed the crenulated imprint left by the band of her shorts—that last mad immortal day behind the "Roches Roses." The twenty-five years I had lived since then, tapered to a palpitating point, and vanished.[14]

---

14   *Lolita* (1955).

I'm not suggesting that the author of this first page write like—or in any way compete with—Nabokov: who can? Still, these kinds of specific, concrete observations and reflections could form part of the action of the opening scene, rendering Stephan as well as the mother who is the object of his discomfiture vivid before—or as—we drift into summary background.

Your Turn

Write or revise a description of a setting, room, or some object as seen very specifically from that character's perspective. Third-person or first-person. The description should tell us as much about the character as it does about the setting, room, or object.

62. The First Day of the War

(War / Tense / Authenticating Details)

The war started today. Although some might call it merely an escalation of hostilities—if indeed the word *merely* were at all applicable. Dawn is clouding as I look through the window in my study. The weather is gray with mist as thick as these cheesecloth curtains, an ignominious beginning. I had always imagined a war to commence with the fanfare of trumpets and coronets, and banners flying in the wind. But it only rains as the news again comes over the radio.

I shake my head. It is time. I put on the collar, run my finger between it and my neck to relieve the chafing, cross myself and pray for those first victims along the banks of the Tigris so far away. By now the congregation is assembling, poor souls. In a time of peace how warm and safe might they imagine themselves, huddling in the pews and gossiping with their neighbors. They have seen the bombardment on their television screens. What are they thinking? That soon we will greet spring as though nothing has changed? If only that were true. I wish. I wish.

I wrap the amice about my shoulders. Now the alb; I pull it over my head, push my arms into the sleeves. This vestment always makes me feel uncomfortably feminine, but I dismiss the thought and thank our Lord for the strength He provides. I am obedient to His will and repress the old memories of childhood, the taunts of boys who called me sissy and girlish, and pushed me to tears because I exhibited a grade school timorousness—and let them push. They taunt no more; instead, should I return to the old Chicago neighborhood, the men would greet me with respect, and their children would look up to me. I knot the cincture around my waist; it is too loose, and I retie it. Over my shoulders I drape the stole, its fringes swishing. I pin the maniple to my sleeve, then finally put on the chasuble.

Analysis

At the onset of war a pastor prepares to address his congregation. Though many novels end with the outbreak of war (*War and Peace*, *From Here to Eternity*), and many more deal with the time leading up to war and then go on to treat the effects of that war on the characters, at the moment I can think of no novels that actually begin on the *first day* of war.

Two reasons why this may be so occur to me. The first is that, since wars are cataclysmic, climactic events, it makes more sense for a novel to end with the outbreak of war than to start with it. The second is that, while the ends of wars tend to be clearly demarcated by treaty signings, unless prompted by singular events like the attacks on Pearl Harbor or the World Trade Center, their precise starting points can be difficult to pinpoint, and are often only made clear to the general public historically, in retrospect.

Still, it's an intriguing conceit, and well handled here, with the description of the priest/narrator putting on his vestments closely observed ("I run my finger between [my collar] and my neck to relieve the chafing.") and well-integrated with his internal ruminations ("What are [the members of my congregation] thinking? That soon we will greet spring as though nothing has changed?"). Some of these musings are too obvious ("If only that were true. I wish. I wish."), while others (his dwelling on the taunts he endured as a shy child, his concern that his priestly garments make him feel less than masculine) feel incongruous. That a man of the cloth would routinely harbor such thoughts is unlikely; that he'd do so on this of all mornings seems bizarre. At the very least such reflections should be provoked by specific stimuli and not come unbidden.

That said, owing largely to the attention given to his clerical garments and other pastoral accouterments—*authenticating details*—the portrait of a pastor that emerges from this opening is convincing. Unfortunately, the portrait is marred by less-than-perfect handling of tense. The first sentence is problematic. If the war started "today," when—relative to that starting point—does the present-tense monologue occur? If "dawn is clouding," the day itself has just begun, in which case when did the priest and his congregants get the news? Were they watching the 2 am news on TV? If so, something might be said to that effect. Anyway, the war started before dawn, so it would be more accurate to say, "The war started early this morning." It's not as brisk and brazen a sentence, but it's also less confusing. A few sentences later, the author shifts from the present to the past tense ("I had always imagined ...").

Despite these technical errors, I'm curious to hear what this preacher will say to his flock, and to learn if and how his faith will hold up under the assaults and insults of war.

Your Turn

Authenticating details are so important to our writing. Think of a place, person, or profession with which you are closely familiar. Make a list of authenticating details: very specific, telling details that lend authenticity to that subject. If you care to go a step further, take a page or a scene you've already written and add an authenticating detail or two (or three).

63. Gramma's Death Bed

(Framing Device / Perfunctory Adverbs / Death)

"Holly," Mom said, appearing at my door, "Gramma wants to talk with you."

I immediately dropped my book and ran downstairs, painfully stubbing my toe on the raised kitchen tile in my hurry, and finally slowing down a few feet from her bedroom door. Gramma Cathie, my favorite and only grandparent, was dying. She refused to talk with anyone for days, and I was afraid I might never talk to her again. Then I was nervous. What was she going to say? Goodbye?

I slowly opened the door and stepped into her dark room. It took a moment for my eyes to adjust.

"Holly, dear, how are you?" she asked in a weak voice. By now I could make out her pale, wrinkled face surrounded by wispy, once golden hair sprawled across the pillows of her deathbed. I couldn't help wondering if behind her thin, tired smile, she was scared.

Her eyes gleamed like they did before she told me an old memory, or family secret. I expected her to say something inter-esting, dramatic, something you might expect a dying person in a movie to say. She was still. Then I realized she was waiting for my answer.

"Oh, umm, my toe kinda hurts," I said. "What did you want to talk to me about?"

"Don't be nervous around me, dear. I'm just your old Gramma Cathie."

"But aren't you scared?" As soon as I had said the words, I wished I hadn't. Her face became solemn. Not angry, or fearful, I noted with relief, but thoughtful.

"No," she replied softly, "I am not. I am thankful, Holly, that the Lord chose to let me die peacefully. It could have been worse. It almost was. You know, I think part of me did die that summer."

I had no idea what she meant. "What summer?" I asked. "What part of you died?"

She decided to ignore my question. Instead, she asked her own. "You tripped over the tile again, didn't you?"

Analysis

A dying woman shares a secret memory with her grandson or granddaughter. A classic opening strategy: the deathbed scene that will—I assume—serve as a portal to Grandma's confession about "that summer" when "part of" her died.

We enter this story through an extended flashback or framing device, namely the grandmother's deathbed scene through which we'll experience all or part of her life as told to her granddaughter.

Good stories have been told this way. Lord Byron's nameless Giaour tells his story from his deathbed, as does Adam Godley in John Banville's *The Infinities*. David Lodge's *Author, Author* has Henry James looking back from his deathbed at his life (in particular on his failure as a playwright). The same structure serves *The Death of Artemio Cruz* by Carlos Fuentes.

As devices go, the deathbed frame runs the risk of being cloying and melodramatic, but if handled well it can also be efficient and effective, since nothing frames a character's life more than his or her death.

Parts of this opening are very nicely handled. The narrator's voice has a sweet, callow freshness ("Her eyes gleamed like they did before they told me an old memory"), and her halting, insecure dialogue is effectively juxtaposed with Grandma's haughty resignation ("I am thankful, Holly, that the Lord chose to let me die peacefully."). There's the humor of opposites at work here: childhood vs. old age, naive vs. world-weary, life vs. death. And though a deathbed scene may not be the first place one looks for humor, it's as good a place as any to find it.

I wish that the oppositions here were even stronger, that the granddaughter was a little less syrupy-sweet, a little more profane. Sure, she loves her grandmother, but a child's fascination with old age is extremely limited; the young are far more interested in life than they are in death or growing old, things they can't begin to grasp, and therefore don't believe in. Here, the girl's veneration of her grandmother spills into sentimentality. While she points out Grandma's "once golden hair sprawled across the pillows" and her "gleaming" eyes, she doesn't smell the leaky catheter or any of the other unpleasant things that usually attend death at a ripe old age.

Yes, I know: the scene is meant to be tender. But to achieve tenderness it doesn't have to sacrifice authenticity or credibility. If the author wants to steer clear of catheters, that's fine, but something in that room should at least hint at the unpleasantness of death.

This opening is also marred by some other questionable choices, such as announcing the uniqueness of this event. To the extent that they depart from and shatter the routine or status quo of characters' lives, scenes are dramatic.

As presented here, however, there's no routine to depart from: before we get to the deathbed confession, we are told that Gramma has broken a long silence to speak to her granddaughter. This in itself is momentous, and the narrator responds with appropriate urgency ("I immediately dropped my book and ran downstairs"), stubbing her toe as she rushes to her grandmother's bedside, thereby undermining the genuine surprise of the deathbed scene. A more blasé approach ("I heard Gramma's bell again; she probably wanted me to massage her feet again.") would have set both character and reader up for an unanticipated, hence truly dramatic, scene.

Another problem: the author's use of modifiers, particularly adverbs. Note how many of the adverbs in this opening are implied or perfunctory. "I immediately dropped my book" (the immediacy is implied by the action of dropping). "Painfully stubbing my toe" (can a toe be stubbed with something other than pain?). "Finally slowing down a few feet from her bedroom door" (eliminate the adverb and what's lost?). Adverbs are to writing mainly what cornstarch is to cooking: they add nothing but bulk. Shakespeare shuns them (well, not always: "*Verily*, I swear, 'tis better to be *lowly* born"), favoring concrete nouns and active verbs, words that hit us where we live, in our senses.

Which isn't to say that adverbs can't be used effectively or that great artists haven't used them profusely. Joyce's *A Portrait of the Artist as a Young Man* is chockablock with adverbs:

> He feared *intensely* in spirit and in flesh but, raising his head *bravely*, he strode into the room *firmly*. A doorway, a room, the same room, same window. He told himself *calmly* that those words had *absolutely* no sense which had seemed to rise *murmurously* from the dark. He told himself that it was *simply* his room with the door open. [Italics mine.]

Similarly, in her novel *Asymmetry*, when Lisa Halliday writes

> Afterwards, Alice lay down to face the snow, which in the light of the balcony was falling more *calmly* now, *stealthily* and *evenly*, like an army of parachuting invaders

she adds gracenotes of wistfulness to an already melancholy moment. But while Joyce and Halliday use adverbs deliberately and even cunningly, beginning and published writers tend to use them thoughtlessly.

Why do writers overuse adverbs? Could it be because they're so easily abused? They come to us unbidden, automatically, sprouting like weeds in our prose, often clinging to other words like kudzu to a tree: "desperately lone-some," "devastatingly handsome," "firmly believed." Quietly, quickly, finally, carefully, cautiously, suddenly—these are some of the usual suspects. When we encounter them in our writing we should meet them with prejudice.

Strip away the useless adverbs, replace heavy-handed portentousness with a sense of business as usual ("There goes Grandma ringing her bell again."), thus setting the stage for genuine surprise, and this will be a most engaging opening.

Your Turn

Take a piece of writing, your own or someone else's, and eliminate all modifiers (adjectives and adverbs) from it. How has it changed? Now take the same or another piece of writing and squeeze as many modifiers into it as possible, making sure that each of the modifiers truly adds something that isn't implied or perfunctory, something precise and unanticipated.

64. The Sympathetic Medic

(Adjectives)

The relentless, screaming siren split the muggy Gulf coast night like bolt lightning rips a summer storm, hot and hard. A boxy fire-red ambulance zig-zagged through dark, foggy streets where other mothers stirred hamburger meat while their thirteen-year-old sons watched reruns of *The Simpsons* or whined for a new video game. Inside the ambulance a youngish woman in a marker-stained blue sweater dripped tears on her son's torn black tee shirt. A tired medic with a twenty-four-hour beard held up a fluid bag with one hand and checked pulse with his other. Cotton-candy fog from the bay moved in and circled scattered light posts in wisps outside the scratched windows. Bile tasting like guilt rose in her throat, and she felt she might add vomit to her tears.

The sympathetic medic tried to help. "Ma'am, he's probably gonna make it. His blood pressure and heart rate ain't real bad. Them pills just knocked him out a little with that beer. But don't think he got all that much from looking at his vitals. On an empty stomach, it'd hit him fast. Good thing that woman called 911 in time."

Crystal's racing pulse didn't slow. "Yes, thank God," she whispered. What woman? She forgot at whose house Will was supposed to be, and the woman who called her just said Will was being taken to the hospital. Thank God it was a little town, and she had been close by the kid's address. She swallowed the sour taste of panic in her throat. The medic's kind words didn't make guilt taste any sweeter.

Will is all I have left, she thought. I made a vow when Adam died to take up the slack, and once again I failed. I have to be stronger. Whatever it takes.

She should have monitored Will more closely. Was it true he was taking drugs? By thirteen Will should be planning high school courses, not following a pack of losers trying drugs and drinking beer. Her temples pounded like the Presbyterian gong in Shell Beach every Sunday. A familiar migraine was returning with its aura of dancing lights.

Up front the baby-faced ambulance driver complained, "This fog gets any worse, a putty knife would be more useful than them worn-out wipers."

Analysis

The relentless, screaming siren split the muggy Gulf coast night like bolt lightning rips a summer storm, hot and hard.

Modifiers—adjectives and adverbs—get a bad rap. English and creative writing teachers are known to despise them, and writers themselves haven't always embraced them with fierce devotion.

Voltaire: "The adjective is the enemy of the noun."

Twain: "When you catch an adjective, kill it."

Clifton Fadiman: "The adjective is the banana peel of the parts of speech."

Stephen King: "The road to hell is paved with adjectives."

Ben Yagoda: "Kicking things off with adjectives is a little like starting a kids' birthday party with the broccoli course."[15]

My feelings about adjectives are mixed. As those same English teachers will tell you, they tend to be lazy or perfunctory. That someone is "beautiful" tells us nothing about how they look; it merely casts an overarching judgment with respect to their physical appearance. Adjectives aren't descriptions; they're *opinions*.

With modifiers, you want to choose your battles. Just because every noun offers itself up for modification(s) doesn't mean you should modify it. By serving some nouns plain, you give more distinction to those you embellish. Think of adjectives as ketchup or hot sauce; put it on everything and it quickly wears out its welcome.

The opening paragraph of this first page, which finds us with a mother attending her son in the back of an ambulance, batters us with modifiers. *[R]elentless screaming, muggy Gulf coast, hot and hard, boxy fire-red* ... Taken individually, each of these modifiers may add something. Collectively they lose power and become monotonous.

Which doesn't mean adjectives can't be piled on to good effect. Do we really want to take a red pencil to Thomas Hobbes's description of life in the absence of society as "solitary, poor, nasty, brutish and short"? And what would Thomas Wolfe have done without his modifiers ("The nostalgic thrill of dew-wet mornings in Spring, the cherry scent, the cool clarion earth, the wet

---

15   Voltaire, cited in Mencken's *A New Dictionary of Quotation* (1946), but possibly apocryphal; Twain, from a March 1880 letter to student D.W. Bowser; Fadiman: quoted in Jon Winokur, *Advice to Writers*; Stephen King, *On Writing*; Ben Yagoda, *When You Catch an Adjective, Kill It: The Parts of Speech, For Better and/or Worse*.

loaminess of the garden, the pungent breakfast smells and the floating snow of blossoms....")?

Still, there are adjectives and adjectives. While "cool clarion" adds something essential to the "earth" that it modifies, what "screaming" adds to a siren is both perfunctory and predictable. As for "cotton candy," it adds nothing to the fog that helps us see the fog more clearly. In fact it fogs it up, adding connotations of innocent frivolity and sweetness where nothing of the sort pertains.

Lest my wariness of modifiers leads you to conclude that I think good writing should be boiled down to bleached bone, not so. The last thing good writing should be is bland, or, as the Germans say, *ohne Salz oder Fett*, "without salt or fat."

In the same way metaphors work best when forced on us by our need to make something clearer, the best adjectives are those imposed by necessity rather than those we indulge in or that arise automatically ("blind faith"; "abject poverty"; "raving beauty"). In *Catch-22*, in giving General Dreedle a "ruddy, monolithic" face, Joseph Heller adds something to that face that wouldn't be there otherwise. Likewise when in his story "The Circular Ruins" Jorge Luis Borges writes, "No one saw him disembark in the *unanimous* night," only a dunce of an editor would strike that adjective. When Ezra Pound said, "Go in fear of abstractions," he didn't mean don't use them. He meant use them boldly, bravely—and sparingly.

Our opening paragraph with modifiers applied more judiciously:

> The siren split the muggy Gulf coast night like lightning. Through dark, foggy streets where other mothers stirred hamburger meat and kids watched reruns of *The Simpsons*, the ambulance zigzagged. Inside it a woman dripped tears on her son's torn tee shirt. A medic with a twenty-four-hour beard held a bag of plasma with one hand and checked the boy's pulse with his other. Beyond the scratched rear window bay, fog circled light posts in wisps. Bile rose in the mother's throat.

What's sacrificed here by way of specificity of detail is more than made up for in rhythm and pacing, with some details left to the reader's imagination—which, given the chance and enough to go on, fills them in as well or better than the author in her version.

The rest of this sensational and potentially gripping opening is likewise overwritten, with the "sympathetic" medic's dialogue turning into a speech—as dialogue tends to do when in excess of two or three lines. Of the six lines spoken by the medic, any one would do to make his point. Given the circumstances, his prolixity seems especially out of place.

The next paragraph ("Crystal's racing pulse didn't slow ...") is confusing, with the mother who was "a woman" in the first paragraph referred to now by her first name, while a different "woman"—the one who phoned Woman 1 to inform her that her son was being taken to the hospital—is introduced. The author's failure to use the past perfect tense (it should be "She *had forgotten* at whose house Will *had been* ...") confuses us further.

The next paragraph dips us into the mother's stream of consciousness for some forced exposition ("I made a vow when Adam died ..."). Forced exposition is information forced into a character's dialogue. Though in this case the information is forced into *interior* rather than spoken dialogue, the result is as artificial. The second-to-last paragraph compounds this ("She should have monitored Will more closely") while stating things that, if not completely obvious, might be better learned elsewhere and not in the midst of such a dramatic scene.

The last paragraph of this page serves up its finest moment, with the ambulance driver's dialogue ("This fog gets any worse, a putty knife would be more useful than them worn-out wipers.") evoking his character while also describing the fog. If only it had come sooner. We might have eaten less broccoli.

Your Turn

Take a first page of your own or someone else's and void it of all modifiers (adjectives *and* adverbs). What's lost? Then add as many as possible. What's gained?

65. Home from Fairview

(Mental Illness / Abstract vs. Concrete / Similes and Metaphors)

Scoured clean as the sky after a storm or a tub after a good grouting, Ana Gates was home after nearly a month in Fairview Clinic. She should feel good about being back from that haven for sanity on the Sound, but it was hard to know what feeling good meant, though she was alive and that might eventually count for something.

Mornings were still rocky, the jittery sensation in her gut having less to do with anticipating the day and more to do with dreading it. Breakfast especially felt like a violation but she had to eat. She curled up by the front window, pulled her toast apart and washed part of it down with coffee. The warmth spread across her belly, the pain there less now, though she still sometimes felt the cramping from another miscarriage that made three a less than magical number.

She picked up the journal her psychiatrist Felix Beckman was having her keep and pulled the crocheted afghan around her. The cool of the house on Lake Waramaug made for the constant need of a covering even in spring. Only at the end of summer was it otherwise, as if the sun found it hard to reach them through the trees. She pulled the pen from the journal's spiral binding, the slender barrel solid between her fingers. A squadron of geese skidded onto the lake, flapped across its surface and took up positions, ever prepared for takeoff.

Emotions, Beckman had said, write about how she felt now, but her emotions were gripped and quelled by a mind that wouldn't let her rest. Maybe it would be easier to say what she should feel, what Peter and the rest expected, that she should be happy to be here, happy to be home, to be out. She should be a lot of things. She should be well, but people didn't always get to be what they should be.

Analysis

A woman comes home from a stay in a mental hospital. That's the subject of this first page. It could be the subject of the chapter as a whole, or of the entire novel to which it belongs. We don't know. We are only told that Ana Gates is "home after nearly a month in Fairview Clinic." The prose is strong; the handling of syntax, punctuation, and grammar unimpeachable. As written, this certainly works. Yet it could be less static and abstract. Let's examine it.

With its first sentence, the author dives into figurative language, serving up not one, but two similes in tandem ("like tractor trailers," I was tempted to add), with the heroine "scoured clean as the sky after a storm" and like "a tub after a good grouting." Though made of solid objects (storms, tubs, grout), since their meanings are figurative and not literal, similes and metaphors aren't all that stable or solid: they're symbols for things, not things themselves. Those similes put us—and this opening—firmly in abstract territory.

Each of the two similes also has its own problems, compounded by their union. What is "scoured clean"—the woman's body, or her mind? Presumably it's Ana's mind that has been scoured clean, or is this "scouring" a not-so-subtle reference to the three miscarriages alluded to at the end of the next paragraph? In their hunger for concrete experience, readers tend to take things literally, so reading these words one may picture a woman whose insides have been "scoured." If, on the other hand, it's Ana's mind that's been cleansed "like the sky after a storm," does it help to compare that mind to "a tub after a good grouting"? Does grouting a bathtub "scour" it?

Similes and metaphors are like those little stepping stools people keep to reach high shelves in their kitchens, to be used only when needed to help readers reach a solid impression or image. Here the grouted tub colluding with the storm-scoured sky isn't likely to help anyone.

The same sentence provides the first hint of action. "Ana Gates was home." As verbs go none is less active or concrete than the verb "to be." Look at the rest of the verbs in this opening paragraph: *should feel ... was ... feeling ... was ...* listless verbs tenuously attached to the protagonist's static state or condition of being or feeling. No other actions are implied or indicated.

The last lines of the opening paragraph give us the condition of Ana Gates's mind, with her unable to decide how she feels about being back home. We're told that she "should feel good about being back"; on the other hand, Fairview Clinic was a "haven for sanity." Then again, "it was hard [for her] to know what feeling good meant," notwithstanding that "she was alive and that might eventually count for something."

"Scoured clean as the sky after a storm" is one way to describe the mental state that's evoked by these thoughts. "Foggy headed" is another. One thing is for sure: Ana Gates is one confused heroine. But rather than be told as much, abstractly, would it not be better to let her confusion speak for itself through her solid actions and concrete perceptions?

Unlike the first paragraph, the second does give us a concrete and vivid picture of Ana in her present circumstances, bundled up in her afghan and looking out the window of her lakeside home while eating breakfast, pulling her toast apart. But even here the author resorts to bald abstractions ("Mornings were still rocky") instead of relying on the moment at hand to speak—not only for itself, but for the character's general state. If Ana feels jittery, her coffee cup might tremble as she brings it to her lips. If she dreads mornings, her dread might be evoked through a description of her breakfast from her point of view ("the bread crusts looked as appetizing as strips of cardboard."). Only when she swallows the toast and the "warmth spread[s] across her belly," do I feel myself in Ana's body, and, through her body, her psyche. But the effect is undermined by the paragraph's concluding clause, one that generalizes about Ana's cramping and her miscarriage from beyond her present state rather than from within it. The last clause of the last sentence expresses not Ana's viewpoint, but that of an intrusive author.

Here's what a more grounded version of this opening might look like:

> Ana Gates sat at the kitchen table of her summer cottage, pulling her toast apart and sipping black coffee while watching a squadron of Canada geese skid and flap across the surface of Lake Waramaug. The coffee cup trembled as she brought it to her lips. She braced herself, expecting a jolt of pain when the warmth reached her belly. But the moment passed. She sighed. Since her arrival home from Fairview three days before, the cramps had been coming less frequently.
>
> The crusts of toast on her plate tasted and looked like cardboard. She shoved the plate aside, took up the notebook that Dr. Felix Beckman had presented her with on her last day at the clinic, slid the slim fountain pen (also Felix's gift) from its spiral binding, and pressed its nib to the blank first page. "Write about what you feel now," Felix had suggested. So—what did she feel now? Emptiness. Cold. She drew the crocheted afghan more tightly around her shoulders. Even this late in May the winds off the lake turned the cottage into a refrigerator....

There's no rule against abstract openings. A famous novel begins, "It was the best of times, it was the worst of times," an opening that privileges grandiose abstraction over concrete events or particulars. Through a series of parallel constructions Dickens settles his readers into an epic whose events span generations and confront life's paradoxes across a comprehensive spectrum.

Opening *A Tale of Two Cities* with a specific dramatic event would have forced Dickens to narrow his panoramic view.

That said, we novelists of humbler ambition may wish to ponder whether an abstract, static opening is the best foot forward into our stories.

Your Turn

Render a character's emotional state by way of a scene in which they perform an everyday task or activity. For instance: a man mowing the grass who has very recently gotten some very bad news, a terminal diagnosis, or the rejection of a novel he has spent the last ten years writing. How does his recent bad experience color his—and our—experience of that routine chore? Use third person.

Do the same exercise again, with the same character doing the same chore, only now the recent news is good.

66. The Girls in the Band

(Modifiers / Statement vs. Implication / Less = More)

The bartender slid the keys across the bar toward Judy with such force they flipped over the edge and onto a barstool. The keys that had been aimed so mindlessly at her would open the doors to what were supposed to become the band's accommodations for the next two weeks. With a nod of the head pointing toward the rear of the building, the bartender informed us the rooms were located above the bar. Our eyes locked ... close friends don't need to talk some-times, you just know what each of us is thinking; and we both knew we were surrounded by bad juju, and this was just the beginning. Judy and I turned and walked outside to update the other four girls, who were still waiting in the van. Suspicions already raised, we voted on who would head up our little reconnaissance mission. As leader, we naturally drafted Judy. The first in line is always the first to be sacrificed, right?

Single file, we stayed close to each other for security. All six of us followed the fractured sidewalk that looked like it had lost a bet with a jackhammer to the back of the building. The paint covering the wooden entry door leading to the second floor was blistered and cracked, scars from its colorful life. The feelings of fight or flight were beginning to set in, intensifying our natural instinct to turn around and run away from the decrepit building; but obligation forced us to open the door.

In spite of the creaking groan of the rickety wooden stairs, and against my better judgment, I cautiously continued placing each foot on the next step. My eyes felt the need to scan the tunnel-like surroundings, in case I had to make an emergency escape, when the words fell from my mouth, "I don't like the looks of this, girls. Rooms above a bar—not a good sign." I said this with the air of confidence of a nineteen-year old; a confidence that existed only because I was not alone.

Analysis

This opening can be much improved without adding a single word. In fact, I'm going to subtract hundreds. First, though, let me say why.

NEVER STATE WHAT YOU CAN IMPLY. Years ago a dear writer friend gave me this useful bit of advice, which, whether he knew it or not, he got from French avant-garde poet, playwright, filmmaker (painter, photographer, chess player, etc.) Jean Cocteau. For a long time I clung to the injunction so fervently that I printed it out in BOLD CAPS, landscape format, and hung it on the wall over my computer next to that other sacred writers' commandment: NO POINT OF VIEW = NO STORY.

Since then, though I still cling tenaciously to the second injunction, I've loosened up a bit on the first. There are times, many in fact, when we writers need to state a thing outright, even when it has been or might be implied, in order to drive a point home or simply to draw more attention to it, or just to make sure certain implications don't slip under the reader's radar.

"Never state what you can imply" differs from "show, don't tell," that oldest of creative writing chestnuts, in that it allows for the fact that implication can't always be achieved through action or "showing." Sometimes—often in fact—we rely on the narrator's intervention to interpret or color characters' experiences and actions for us. There are also times when for pacing purposes an author wants to establish context more quickly than dramatization ("showing") permits. And while it's true that a story told purely through authorial summary ("telling") isn't likely to satisfy most readers, the same novel told purely through action and dialogue would in all likelihood be equally unsatisfactory. It would be like reading a movie, which is like drinking a steak.

I recall coming upon a "revised edition" of John Barth's *The End of the Road*, a black comedy I've invoked several times in these pages about a character named Jacob Horner (an ironic allusion to "Little Jack Horner") who suffers from nihilistic paralysis. I'd read the novel back in the seventies and much admired it. Curious as to what changes Barth had made, I did a page-by-page comparison with the original, only to find that the revision affected exactly one sentence. The sentence was "It hit me like a ton of bricks." For the new edition Barth cut the line. He did so, I'm sure, because it merely stated an emotion obvious to anyone reading the scene, without adding nuance or dimension to it. On the contrary, it flattened the sentiment into a cliché. Still, the sentence did add *something*: a beat to allow the moment to "sink in." If only Barth had not done it so tritely.

One of the best-known examples of the power of implication is Hemingway's famous short story "Hills Like White Elephants." Though the story is about a young woman facing an abortion, that word makes no appearance in it. Nor are we ever told directly how either of the story's two main characters—the woman and her male companion—feel about the prospect. Instead, all is implied through their terse, oblique, circuitous dialogue as they drink beer and absinth and await the train that will take the woman to wherever the abortion will be performed. The first overt reference to the procedure doesn't even appear until halfway through the very short story, where we read:

> "It's really an awfully simple operation, Jig," the man said. "It's not really an operation at all."
> The girl looked at the ground the table legs rested on.
> "I know you wouldn't mind it, Jig. It's really not anything. It's just to let the air in."
> The girl did not say anything.

Up to here, the characters have discussed 1) the shape of the hills in the distance, and 2) the taste of absinthe, nothing at all to do with the grim procedure awaiting the young woman. It can be argued that the true subject of "Hills Like White Elephants" is not abortion but avoidance. At any rate, nothing is stated; everything is implied. Our involvement in the story is heightened by the trust placed in us by the author, who dares to not describe or even label emotions for us, who would rather risk our misunderstanding than do so. That trust, that willingness to let us supply and interpret emotions, makes for a truly interactive reading experience. We become Hemingway's co-authors. We finish his story for him. As a result, it involves us more deeply.

Telling readers what to think or feel is the job of a propagandist. A story-teller's main purpose, on the other hand, is to create experiences for the reader, to involve us so deeply, so convincingly, so authentically in those experiences that we feel what characters feel.

In this first page of a memoir, at every turn the author feels compelled to both show *and* tell us what her characters are experiencing, so we're never allowed to draw our own conclusions. That the bartender shoves the keys "mindlessly" is implied by their flipping over the barstool. That the same bartender "inform[s] [the narrator and her friend that] the rooms [are] located above the bar" is likewise implied by his directional nod. That the two protagonists share the same thought (they're "surrounded by bad juju") is implied by their locking eyes with each other, as is the fact that their "suspicions [are] already raised."

The tendency to state what's implied persists through this opening, with us being told a) that Judy is the "natural" choice to lead her all-girl band in its reconnaissance mission to inspect their quarters, b) that the band members keep close together "for security," and c) as they make their way down the "fractured sidewalk that [looks] like it lost a bet with a jackhammer" and through a paint-blistered entryway "scar[red] from its colorful life," that "feelings of fight or flight were beginning to set in." In case we missed the point, we're furthermore informed that said feelings "[intensify their] natural instinct to turn around and run away." Got it.

The same opening with implications left to the reader:

> With a nod toward the building's rear, the bartender slid the keys across the bar so hard they flipped over it onto a stool. The keys were to the band's accommodations for the next two weeks. Judy and I locked eyes, then turned and went out to the van, where the other three members of *Ahead of Our Time* waited.
>
> Single file, we followed Judy down the fractured sidewalk to the back of the building. The blood-red paint covering the door leading to stairs was blistered and cracked. As we made our way up, to the sound of wood creaking under us I said, "I don't like the looks of this, girls."

The original runs 341 words; the revision 111. What, if anything, crucial is missed?

In Flannery O'Connor's most famous story, "A Good Man Is Hard to Find," wherein a southern matriarch watches—or rather listens—as one by one the members of her family are executed by two of a trio of escaped serial killers in the woods close behind her, never once are we told how frightened and horrified she feels. We aren't told how she feels at all. The horror implicit in the scene is left entirely to our imagination. Which makes it all the more horrific.

Your Turn

Take a scene from a story or novel that you or a colleague has written and try to cut it by more than half. Make as much use of implication as possible. Is the result better, or worse? Why? Discuss.

67. A Hole in the Heart

(Abstraction / Grounding in Scene / Metaphors / Subjectivity)

Sometimes you wake up with a hole in your heart and you're not sure why. It's a circle, carved by something you can't touch, something that opens up in your sleep and wakes you up, hungry. This morning, before I got on the plane, it was like that, like those lagoons left by old, erupted volcanoes. They pull things and people into them because the core of the earth, after it's shot out molten lava, is as hungry as I am.

Now, from 10,000 feet in the air, looking down at all these street grids, I still feel the hole in my heart. And the free-fall between me and the messy muck of being in the city again. I hate New York. Because when you're there, inside the grid, you can't see the whole picture, just what lies in front of you; you can get lost. Not like painting, where whether you're inspired to the point of bliss or you think you're losing control, the canvas is always there— whole in front of you like a map—and you're the one drawing lines of perspective. You can always find your way out.

Landing in LaGuardia all alone, it's cold. I forgot what this felt like, the sharp invisible burn through your clothes, going straight for the bone. I zip my jacket, wrap my scarf, and off I go onto the M60 into Manhattan. Straight through Queens. The houses with Christmas lights still on from six years ago, even in September; nothing's changed. Strolling through Harlem—an Old Navy now near the Apollo—and then there I am on 110th street, getting on the subway, on my way to Chelsea to see Lee. Lee, who told me to get my "painter ass" over here because it might change my life. And my life needs some change—in every sense of the word; in my pockets, definitely.

Analysis

The invention of airlines has fostered a grand tradition of novels and stories opening at cruising altitude, with characters bound toward (or departing from) the places where their stories have taken or are about to take place. One such novel, Erica Jong's scandalous *Fear of Flying*, honors that tradition through its brilliant opening line, "There were 117 psychoanalysts on the Pan Am flight to Vienna and I had been treated by at least six of them." Salman Rushdie's *The Satanic Verses* twists the convention by opening with its protagonists in mid-flight in more than one sense, having literally tumbled "without benefit of parachute or wings" out of their hijacked, blown-up jetliner:

> Gibreel, the tuneless soloist, had been cavorting in moonlight as he sang his impromptu gazal, swimming in air, butterfly-stroke, breast-stroke, bunching himself into a ball, spreadeagling himself against the almost-infinity of the almost-dawn, adopting heraldic postures, rampant, couchant, pitting levity against gravity. Now he rolled happily towards the sardonic voice. "Ohe, Salad baba, it's you, too good. What-ho, old Chumch." At which the other, a fastidious shadow falling headfirst in a grey suit with all the jacket buttons done up, arms by his sides, taking for granted the improbability of the bowler hat on his head, pulled a nickname-hater's face. "Hey, Spoono," Gibreel yelled, eliciting a second inverted wince, "Proper London, bhai! Here we come! Those bastards down there won't know what hit them!"

The opening in question, while offering no such sensational thrills and spills, plants us firmly in the tradition, with a painter poised to descend upon the New York City he/she left behind some unspecified amount of time ago, without regret, apparently, since she/he still hates the place.

If a successful opening is one that raises intriguing questions while providing enough information to ground the reader, this opening certainly succeeds. On the one hand, we know the protagonist is an artist (though of what sex and age we don't know; doesn't matter, we'll find out soon enough). We know that New York City has left a bad taste in her (let's assume she's a woman) mouth. We know, furthermore, that for some reason he/she has been compelled to return—possibly against her wishes. We know too that the protagonist is poor, or at any rate not flush. Else why travel into the city from the airport by bus—and by way of Harlem, to boot?

The author opens with a metaphor—a vague one about a hole in the protagonist's heart. Like all descriptions of feelings, though it tries through metaphor to obtain some concreteness, it remains abstract and subjective. However, no sooner does the author plunge us into subjective territory than she grounds us aboard a passenger jet at 10,000 feet.

A good thing, since readers like to be grounded. It gives those abstract first sentences something to congeal upon. But having done so, the author yanks us out of the airplane and into a spewing volcano, one that evokes the narrator's feelings but that doesn't feel organic; in fact it clashes with the image of New York City spreading out in its rigid grid below. In the next paragraph, where the grid of the city is compared to a canvas, the metaphor feels more appropriate to the narrator, a painter. It conveys not just the thought being illustrated, but the mind and personality of the character thinking it.

However appropriate they may be individually, taken all together there are too many metaphors here: perforated hearts, volcano craters, canvases, maps. At least one of them, I think, has to go. However seductive, metaphors and similes (a metaphor is an implied comparison, a simile an overt one) should be used as needed, and never forced. Their purpose is not to call attention to our prose—to adorn it with beads, baubles, and bottle caps, like a bowerbird adorning his nest; their purpose is to help readers see more clearly.

Like most good things in writing, the best metaphors come to us out of a sense of urgency, organically, through the need to be as clearly understood as possible. This is what so many young writers fail to appreciate: that a good style is—or should be—a means, not an end. Precision, clarity, authenticity—those are the ends. Make them your goals, and the windfall will be a winning style—and a unique one, since each of us is bound to be precise, clear, and authentic in our own special ways.

The rest of this opening gives us a tour through New York City, which, though well-written, feels more than a bit rushed, with the protagonist instantly transported "straight through Queens" to Harlem—a journey that anyone who's taken it will tell you is anything but instant. More can be accomplished here by way of exploiting the artist's gloomy mood through the description of this journey, tunneling through the city's Christmas-light festooned inferno, rumbling deeper and deeper into the past aboard that M60 bus.

Your Turn

Take a first page or scene of your own or someone else's and see if you can find opportunities for figurative language (metaphors or similes) in it. Remember that good metaphors are never gratuitous; they help us form a clearer image or idea. Bear in mind, too, that when you have a choice, metaphors tend to be more powerful than similes, since they *imply* rather than *state* a comparison, building more trust in our readers.

68. When I Met Lucia

(Abstract vs. Concrete / Opinions & Information vs. Evidence)

When Lucia and I met in the mid-1960s, we were thoughtful, idealistic young women. Knowing her really began after she realized what those around her always knew—that she was not crazy but a true individual, an independent thinker with an incredible imagination.

Her affinity for names began almost at birth when her parents were told before her Baptismal that the name they had chosen was not a saint's and would have to be changed. Her parents kept the name they originally selected and added two saints' names. Her identity was forged with two first names, two middle names and a surname. Her mother contributed the nickname, Boobie, which she kept—along with the many names she gave herself. She acquired the name Lucia as part of the Italian persona she assumed after several visits to Italy and a lifelong obsession with the Italian Renaissance.

Lucia understood from early childhood that she possessed characteristics that made her different from others—an only child, left-handed, born under the zodiac sign of Capricorn in the Chinese year of the Water Horse. Quite a combination of attributes and not easily understood. Few people are confronted with queries about what defines them and even fewer ask themselves. It becomes one of those mystery-of-life conundrums that when pondered reveal interesting truths—if answered honestly or at all. Lucia considered all aspects of her personality a means of gaining self-awareness. Left-handed people are visual thinkers, and Lucia epitomized this mindset.

"Nothing analytical, thank you very much."

"What about math?"

"No, I don't think so."

"Repetitive tasks?"

Again, not for Lucia, who was unlikely to engage in something that when considered, if she took the time to do so, was to her way of thinking so mind-numbingly dull. To delight her, one need only provide something to quicken the pulse and stir the heart, something to make her laugh and cry—simultaneously if possible. For her, Renaissance art, Barber's *Adagio for Strings* or watching Baryshnikov dance filled the bill.

Analysis

Nature abhors a vacuum. So does good writing. When writers fail to specify, when they leave the devil in the form of details to the reader, they have only themselves to blame when said reader fills in the blanks with less-than-authentic material.

In fiction what rushes in to fill the vacuum is cliché.

And cliché is the Number 1 enemy of good fiction. As Martin Amis has said, clichés don't just take the form of familiar phrases or figures of speech. There are also "clichés of the mind and clichés of the heart." Like a cancer, according to Amis, cliché "spreads inwards" from a book's language to its very soul.

But clichés don't thrive exclusively on pedestrian language; in fact they're known to flourish in the absence of words. I'm not (heaven forefend) talking about language for its own sake. I mean language that specifies, that lends authenticity through judiciously chosen details.

Hannah Tinti's "Home Sweet Home" tells the story of Pat and Clyde, who "were murdered on pot roast night." What raises Tinti's story high above the typical murder mystery is her emphasis on character, on providing each character in her tale with a set of ironclad specifics that render a generic experience impossible.

Take Pat, for instance, the adulterous housewife who falls victim to her lover's vengeful wife. On the eve of her murder she is

> ... thinking of James Dean. Pat had loved him desperately as a teenager,
> seen his movies dozens of times, written his name across her notebooks,
> carefully taped pictures of him to the inside of her locker so that she could
> have the pleasure of seeing his tortured, sullen face from *East of Eden* as
> she exchanged her French and English textbooks for science and math.

Another author might have written "as a teenager she had loved James Dean" and left it at that. But Tinti goes further—and further still ("When she graduated from high school, she took down the photos and pasted them to the inside cover of her yearbook")—to substantiate this particular specimen of a star-struck teenager. Similarly in *The Corrections* when Jonathan Franzen takes us on a tour of the flotsam in an aging couple's attic, he presents us not merely with a box of old recipes, but "recipes on brown paper calling for wilted lettuce." The level of specificity matters. It can make the difference between a good writer and a great one.

Over this nominally well-written first page the generic rules. Except for the temperature (which, though much is made of it, "hardly register[s]" with the protagonist), little is specified. A woman wanders through a generic library, scanning its generic stacks in search of a generic "list of book titles." She's looking for books about getting pregnant, but the author fails to share with us either the titles on Rebekkah's list or those she encounters on the shelves.

It's too bad, since it drains the scene of tone and texture, but also because it sacrifices humor, since those titles would surely occasion a chuckle. Even when Rebekkah pulls the first book on her list from a shelf, beyond its having been "recently published," we're left to imagine everything about it, from its cover illustration to its title. Another opportunity lost. A perfunctory scan of fertility book titles demonstrates that truth—if not stranger than fiction—is certainly as funny. Imagine Rebekkah's inner take on some of these:

The Rough Guide to Pregnancy and Birth
The Mother of all Pregnancy Books
Taking Charge of Your Fertility
The 5 Best Ways to Get Pregnant

Because the scene is rendered generically, there are no titles for Rebekkah to respond to, and so the chance to display her wit is likewise squandered.

Nothing wrong with engaging readers' imaginations and letting them do some of the lifting. But if readers are to do a good job—and not the hatchet job of cliché—we have to provide them with some tools. A few telling details go a long way, blossoming in the reader's mind into lush renderings.

Think of specific details as the ropes, nuts, cams, and hexes mountain climbers use, with the summit of vividly authentic description their devoutly wished-for goal.

Your Turn

Draft a scene in which a character in search of something (a book, a dress, a photograph, a record, a letter, or document of some kind) peruses the contents of a box, a file cabinet, a trunk, bookcase, wardrobe, or some other storage area or container. Render the object of the search, the character's ultimate purposes for seeking it, and the items encountered while searching for it all as specifically as possible so a sense of character emerges from the descriptions.

71. Five Years with Sam

(Poetry at the Expense of Meaning)

Prologue:
Not the wheel of dried figs kept in the drawer next to the sink, not the crema in the morning made on the old stove parked on a dirt floor in a kitchen the size of a walk-in closet, not the fresh figs sunset-garish and afternoon-warm on their thin branches, or the way my father's face went serene when he spoke of it, serene with a dash of the sad, not that I was the only child, a daughter and therefore a suspect heir to the little house connected to the vineyard, the farm where my father chased songbirds down with a slingshot, where what he brought down he learned to cook and what he cooked, they all ate, it was World War II, after all, and it was his home and I, his daughter and that land, and every step from the soles of my father's bare feet that the path between plants recalled, every sigh shot and sending up the soil from my grandmother's wearied and worried lungs, I was certain—bone-certain that they already belonged to me.

Chapter 1:
It had happened again. The bed up against the wall and the piles, five–six books deep that made a continual island of book indenting the mattress.

I had forgotten this.

Five and a half years with Sam had done that, undone that need to sleep with every book I was perusing at a given time. When they formed a perilous body, when they made it clear that no one occupied the second pillow on my bed, I began to gather them into the two crates the way I used to when I was in graduate school and a two-year dry spell had left me in a messy apartment and a bed meant only for reading, crying and the occasional hour or two of sleep.

I took the books to the scale and began weighing them, a stack at a time. Thirty-five plus ... as I suspected, there were one hundred and sixty-seven pounds of books in my bed. Enough to be a lover. The information made me sad.

Analysis

The first part of this opening of a novel confronts us with a host of negations bound by tortured syntax. Briefly, it tells us what the narrator—an only child—will (or won't: see below) inherit from her (Italian?) farmer father.

For all its twists and tangles, it's an alluring passage, attractively written, with biblically incantatory rhythms straight out of the Song of Solomon. Indeed, the set-piece passage, which serves more as an appetizer to the story at hand than as the main course, reads like a prose poem. "Not the wheel of dried figs kept in the drawer next to the sink, not the *crema* in the morning made on the old stove parked on a dirt floor in a kitchen the size of a walk-in closet, not the...." The temptation to keep quoting is strong; the words having the tug and energy of a strong tide. Like most good songs, they seduce by their rhythms even when their meanings are difficult or obscure. Poets can get away with that, I suppose.

Then again, as Ezra Pound once said, "Poetry to be good poetry should be at least as well written as good prose." (Pound, who was tried for treason during World War II and kept for twenty-five days in a cage, said many good and outrageous things.) Based on Pound's dictum, one may take issue with this opening passage, since—though it succeeds as prose poetry, fails at the level of prose. It fails for being at best unclear, at worst contradictory. Is the narrator inventorying those things that she feels "already belong" to her, or those that will not?

There's more than enough confusion to go around here, especially in the first paragraph's final clauses, which take us back to the same war that had Ezra spouting anti-Semitism across the airwaves, when the narrator's father "chased songbirds down with a slingshot," birds that "he learned to cook and what he cooked, they all ate"—"they" referring, presumably, to his family, and to the narrator ("it was his home and I, his daughter and that land").

Then again it strikes me that the narrator has yet to be born, that these are not her own memories, but communal ones of her father, passed down to her by others. Thus the steps "from the soles of [her] father's bare feet"—those of the boy with the slingshot—trod a path through the woods that in turn recalls ... the father's feet. This bit of poetic feedback gives way to one of a grandmother's "worried lungs" sending or shooting up their "soil" along with her sighs. By soil one may infer catarrh or something more sinister: chunks of ravished lung. It's not at all clear, and I for one can't be entirely sure that the confusion is mine and not the author's.

Of Wagner's music Mark Twain once quipped, "It's not as bad as it sounds." Of the first paragraph here I'd say it's not as *good* as it sounds, and it sounds very good. The opening's sweet music and sharp imagery are arrived at via sloppy syntax and slippery logic. Meaning has been sacrificed to music.

The second section of this opening is similarly compelling, and similarly challenged. Here the image is the singular one of a bed groaning under the weight of books that have displaced a romantic partner. The books are being gathered by the stack, and, for reasons unspecified, weighed. Apparently they have accumulated in the wake of a dissolved love affair or union. But here too a disregard for literal meaning in the name of poetry creates confusion and disorder where neither is warranted.

The scene opens with the bed groaning with books. The words "It had happened again," point to a sudden, unanticipated event (in fact the books have accumulated over time). The next one-line paragraph ("I had forgotten this.") suggests that the narrator has come upon this scene from a distance of time or space. From there we move to a mini-flashback of life with Sam, the narrator's partner, with whom the need to accumulate books was "undone." But the rest of the paragraph belies this topic sentence, telling how "when [the books] formed a perilous body" the narrator began to gather them ("... the way I used to when I was in graduate school"). So we have three beds full of books to lie with: the one before Sam, the one after, and one back in graduate school.

Which bed are we lying in here, now, in this scene?

This opening would be so much stronger were it less intent on poetry and more intent on clarity: if, for instance, it grounded us in a solid, particular moment with this narrator in one of her bedrooms full of books. Of course, that moment would need to attach itself to some specific, non-routine day or event, one that causes the narrator—and us with her—to look backwards or forwards at her life and tell a story.

Come to think of it, syntax and bedclothes have something in common. The author makes the bed that we, her readers, lie in.

Your Turn

Draft a musical opening, one that makes heavy use of rhythm and repetition or *parallelism*, as in the famous opening to *A Tale of Two Cities* ("It was the best of times, it was the worst of times ..."). See if you can do so with no sacrifice of precision and meaning. The subject needn't be grandiose; in fact the less grandiose, the better, possibly, since it will make for greater irony. Imagine an opening scene in which a parent struggles to get a recalcitrant six-year-old woken, dressed, fed breakfast, and ready to catch the school bus, written in the incantatory style of Dickens's famous opening.

72. Canary Wharf

(Overwriting / Sensationalism / Adverbs)

Madness belted out *Baggy Trousers* over screeching tyres and a roaring engine as a car sped through the back streets of Canary Wharf. Derelict warehouses lined the streets. Their windows boarded over in readiness. They were all due to be torn down to make way for the massive redevelopment, turning the dockside area into another financial hub.

Inside the car, with the windows down and the breeze rustling his short curly brown hair, Pete Carter sang along, at the top of his voice. A light tap of the brakes slowed the car and Pete swung the wheel over sharply.

Tyres squealed loudly in protest, struggling to maintain traction on the ancient potholed hardtop, and the rear of the car jolted violently, threatening to spin out of control. Deft work with the clutch and brake corrected the over-steer before he again trod heavily on the accelerator. With a roar from the engine, the car shot through the apex of the corner and raced away, down the deserted streets of the industrial estate.

Pete grinned broadly and a childlike giggle escaped his lips as the needle on the speedometer began to nudge 60 miles-per-hour.

He felt like a twelve-year-old on Christmas morning, rather than the supposedly responsible thirty-year-old adult, trying out his new toy. Except in this instance instead of a shiny new bike he was at the wheel of a top of the range Ford Sierra RS Cosworth. She was gorgeous bright red with gleaming alloy wheels. The price had been a steal—well, he'd paid a grand to a mate to pinch it out of a new car showroom. A bit of fancy work with the engine number and registration plate and the car was completely untraceable.

Susie, his missus, had gone ape shit at him when he arrived home with it. When their two girls were safely strapped into their new car seats, pushchair in the boot, and plenty of room left for a load of shopping, she'd see the sense in it. It had better be soon; she'd made him sleep on his lumpy old couch that really wasn't very comfortable.

Analysis

Two things good writers can't do without: a love of language and a love of truth. Not the factual truth, necessarily (though even in works of fiction getting the facts straight doesn't hurt). I mean emotional or aesthetic truth, the kind of truth an author brings to bear (for instance) in choosing a character's name, deciding it should be Alice and not Esther.

No one else may care about such things. Good writers do. They are determined to get even the smallest, least significant details just right. So they work and keep working, fine-turning their words to within a tolerance that would make a Swiss watchmaker proud.

Here, in this opening, truth and language are at odds with each other, with the author more intent on showy syntax than on clear, precise communication.

The story opens with a man—Pete Carter—driving at breakneck speeds down the blighted streets of Canary Wharf, now a high-rent financial and shopping neighborhood in East London, but still derelict at the time when the story takes place. My first assumption is that this is going to be a high-impact thriller, with Pete a fugitive on the lam. In fact, Pete is a gooney thirty-year old, and the car he's putting the hammer down on is a brand new Ford Sierra pinched from a dealer showroom on Pete's behalf by a contract thief.

It's all a bit over the top. Still, given fewer infelicities of language and detail, I might be willing to go along for the ride.

The third paragraph offers some examples. It begins: "Tyres [British spelling] squealed loudly in protest, struggling to maintain traction on the ancient potholed hardtop, and the rear of the car jolted violently, threatening to spin out of control." For all its kinetic energy, the sentence feels passive, with the car doing the struggling and the protagonist nowhere to be seen. And do we really need to know that the tires (or tyres) squeal "in protest," and furthermore that they do so in "struggling to maintain traction," i.e., grip? A less showy description might read, "As Pete struggled to keep it on the road, the car's tires squealed. Its rear end jolted over potholes."

Next sentence: "Deft work with the clutch and brake corrected the over-steer before he again trod heavily on the accelerator." A bit more overwrought than necessary: "He corrected for the over-steer, then hit the accelerator again."

Last sentence: "With a roar from the engine, the car shot through the apex of the corner and raced away, down the deserted streets of the industrial estate." Since apex usually refers to the top of something, its relation to a corner may be a factor of British usage. Likewise, in British English "shot through" may mean something other than what it sounds like—namely, that Peter has driven off the road, in which case how does he end up back "on the deserted streets of the industrial estate"? The image I'm left with is of a car shooting through a high guardrail and vaulting through space toward a perfect two-point landing on another street—the sort of thing you see in movie chase scenes all the time, but which, on paper, at least for me, is more absurd than exciting.

In the next paragraph, proud Pete (as he has every right to be, having executed that last Hollywood stunt) grins "broadly" and "a childlike giggle escape[s] his lips." I want to know, first of all, why the giggle has to "escape," since nothing else about Pete is inhibited. A paragraph later, when we're told that Pete's a "supposedly responsible thirty-year-old," I can't help wondering who does the supposing, and whether he (or she), too, should be locked up before being loosed on the back streets of London? As is so often the case with adverbs, these fail to earn their keep.

We read further to learn that rendering the stolen vehicle "untraceable" took nothing more than "a bit of fancy work with the engine number and registration plate." And what about those "gleaming alloy wheels" and that "gorgeous bright red" paint? As targets of theft go, Pete's dream car is as discreet as a wailing fire engine. Within an hour he'd be in jail—or "gaol," as the English spell it.

As for Pete's having done all this to please Susie, his wife and the mother of their two children, wouldn't she have been happier with a minivan or an SUV? Apparently so, since when Pete gets home (in the last paragraph) Susie goes "ape shit"—an abrupt diction drop, by the way, and hard to reconcile with phrases like "he again trod heavily on the accelerator."

Half of this opening's problems stem from an overeager author's urge to flash his writing credentials, to be linguistically clever rather than clear and precise, from having put the style cart ahead of the substance horse.

Were it mine to edit, I'd solve the other half of this opening's problems by entering the action as Pete pulls into his driveway, and let readers discover what he's done through the dialogue with his wife, who, knowing him, smells something fishy. I'd even consider narrating the scene from Susie's point of view so the reader doesn't have to smell all that burned rubber.

And leave the car chase to the movies. They do them so well.

Your Turn

Take a page that you've written—preferably one involving a dramatic event—and overwrite it. Make it as lavishly and sensationally over the top as possible. Toss in perfunctory modifiers and gratuitous metaphors/similes. Have fun. Then do the opposite, strip it down to bleached bones and understatement, just the dry facts.

73. Kidnapped

(First Sentence / Grounding Scene / Flashback / Revision / Past Perfect)

Our father kidnapped us on a January afternoon, the day before Faye's eighth birthday. I was twelve and should've known better. A few days earlier at the grocery store Mom had bought yellow cake mix, chocolate frosting, candles, and icing. She'd asked me to please bake the cake when I got home from school, as I'd done a few months earlier for my own birthday. Birthdays weren't a big deal in our new three-person family—money was tight and Mom worked a lot of nights tending bar at Roughboys back then—but there was always a little something: if not quite a celebration, then at least an acknowledgment. A cake. A simple gift or two after a macaroni and cheese dinner, or hot dogs, or take-out. But for some reason I hadn't connected those dots, that it didn't make sense for him to take us on this unannounced trip while those cake ingredients sat untouched on Mom's kitchen counter.

He was sitting in his '67 El Camino outside our school in Emeryville, smoking a Kool, one booted foot up on the glossy dashboard heavily greased with Armor-All, "Southern Nights" by Glen Campbell crackling from one working speaker. It still seems like yesterday. A second cigarette was tucked behind his ear, the one with the ragged earlobe. A couple years earlier, at a backyard barbeque, he'd been toying with his new fishing rod, showing one of his friends how to cast properly. My mother had told him not to do that with so many people around, and, the way I remember it, about two seconds later, on his backswing, he'd hooked his own ear, tearing the lobe clean away.

The junior high was across the street from the elementary school Faye attended. My job after school was to meet her so we could walk home together. I hadn't minded this the year or two before, but by junior high I'd started to feel self-conscious: my friends getting rides from their older siblings in high school, while I moped down the sidewalk alongside my little sister with her pink boots and pink hair ribbons and pink Shaun Cassidy lunchbox.

Analysis

Sometimes a little editing is all we need. Let me walk you through my revision of this good opening, which begins:

> "Our father kidnapped us on a January afternoon, the day before Faye's eighth birthday."

Not a bad opener, but not as good as it could be. In killing two birds with one stone, it does, or tries to do, too much. Better one bird, one stone:

> "Our father kidnapped us on a January afternoon."

Or:

> "Our father kidnapped us the day before Faye's eighth birthday."

The problem with the second version—and it's a problem in the given draft as well—is that, since we don't know who Faye is, instead of raising the pertinent question, "Why did the narrator's father kidnap him?" we are left asking, "Who is Faye?" That bit of *false suspense* spoils the opening, diffuses its energy. We have to read on until the end of the final paragraph to learn that Faye is the narrator's "little sister."

Likewise, though the first part of the second sentence ("I was twelve") provides useful context, the second part ("and should've known better") teases us with its vague self-searching. Should have known better than what, or who? *Why* should the narrator have known better? It asks and answers questions not yet raised in the reader's mind. Before we drift into existential queries, let's have more of the experience, please.

The event pointed to by the tantalizing opening sentence has barely been engaged—in fact it hasn't been engaged at all—when the third sentence ("A few days earlier at the grocery store ...") yanks us out of it and into a flashback. Rule 1 for flashbacks: until and unless you've invested us in a scene, don't flash back (or away) from it! The point of a flashback is to illuminate the scene from which it digresses, to add dimension and tension to it. The depth of our investment in the primary scene, the amount of suspense generated by it, determines how long a flashback it can support. In this case, since the primary scene hasn't yet left the station, it can hold a flashback of exactly zero words.

After the narrator and his sister have gotten into the car with their mysterious father—that's where the flashback belongs, and where, having shortened it, I relocated it. In my revision, the "had" in the flashback's first sentence ("A few days earlier at the grocery store, Mom had bought yellow cake mix, chocolate frosting ...") has been deleted. It's not necessary, since "Days earlier" makes it clear that the scene takes place in the past before the past that we're in, or the past perfect. My rule about "had": use it when necessary. For instance, the next use of the past perfect "had" ("*She'd* asked me to please bake the cake") is warranted, since it takes us to a moment *before* the narrator went to the grocery store with her or his mother: a past (cake request) before the past (grocery store) before the past (father/car scene). Other "hads" have been cut.

Much of the rest of that long first paragraph ("Birthdays weren't a big deal in our new three-person family ...") is implied or anyway not crucial enough to warrant weighing down this dramatic opening with less-than-crucial material. The respective ages of the narrator and her or his sister are—or will soon be—made clear by the fact that she or he is in junior high while she or he is in elementary school. Whatever else isn't crucial can be discovered later. We need to get to the "kidnapping" promised by the first sentence, to the father waiting in his car, to that event.

Once we get to it, we want to be kept in the moment(s), with digressions (in the form of flashbacks and exposition) occurring at points of high, or at least sufficient, tension, and cunningly distributed between actions ("'Get in,' said my father" / "My sister and I got in my father's car"), such that, though our engagement in the main scene is interrupted, the brief interruptions *add* dramatic tension. They enhance more than they annoy.

The cunning distribution of exposition and action throughout a scene is called *pacing*.

The same opening page revised:

Our father kidnapped us on a January afternoon.

He was sitting in his '67 El Camino outside our school in Emeryville, smoking a Kool, one booted foot up on the glossy dashboard heavily greased with Armor-All, "Southern Nights" by Glen Campbell crackling from the one working speaker. A second cigarette was tucked behind his ear, the one with the ragged earlobe.

"Get in," said my father.

Farley Junior High was across the street from the elementary school my sister Faye attended. Normally after school I would meet her and we'd walk home together. While my friends got rides from older siblings, I moped down the sidewalk alongside Faye with her matching pink boots, hair ribbons, and Shaun Cassidy lunchbox.

My sister and I got in my father's car. "Where are we going?" I asked.

"Vacation," he said.

I should have known better. It was the day before Faye's eighth birthday. Days earlier Mom asked me to bake a cake, as I'd done a few months earlier for my own birthday. It didn't make any sense for our father to take us on a "vacation" while the ingredients for Faye's birthday cake sat untouched on the kitchen counter.

Your Turn

Revise a first page—your own or someone else's—in which no scene/action is engaged until well down the page such that the first line launches us directly or as quickly as possible into a scene.

74. A Twice-Drowned Narrator

("Titanic Lit" / Dead Narrators / Details / Baroque vs. Austere / Devices)

THE END: FINN—APRIL 10, 2012

I drowned three times. First, in the relentless rain of Ireland, second, in the deep gloom of mourning that settled over my mother, and third, in the freezing waters of the North Atlantic.

Even when the sun blazed down fierce as the devil there was the bleakness that settled in our bones like a great damp. Once in a blue moon Mam would pull me into her lap, rocking and singing and hanging on to me for dear life, calling me Michael, her wee angel, and ask me where we were going because sweet Jesus she was lost at sea.

It's sad, how in moments of despair when all a body wants is hope, a still small voice will tell you the truth you don't want to hear. Because, you see, I'm NOT Michael! I'm Finn, and it's sad how precious few blue moons there are.

Yes, those are definitely my shoes, there in the museum case. Now who would have thought the likes of me would be famous for my shoes. And such a sad pair as that. I wore them the day I stepped onto the *Titanic* and the day I floated free of it, April 15, 1912.

I'm not sure if I was five or almost six when it happened, but after my death I discovered that time is an inexact measurement. Time raced ahead of me, pulling me backwards and spun me around so I met myself arriving. Even now, as the centenary of Titanic's maiden voyage approaches, it continues to fling me forward, years speeding past me until I come to a full stop without my growing an inch or aging a single day. I've never felt more like a child but I've never been wiser. I've never been more me. And now, I'm almost free. I have five days to keep a promise. Five days to break a spell.

Visitors come to marvel at the miracle of my shoes, awed that a pair of innocent shoes survived the terrifying chaos when hundreds of people perished. The little shrine of the shoes celebrates a moment in time. But not what they imagine. I know their secret. You'd think a dead child's shoes would make them grief-stricken, entirely. But then I've known miracle shoes before and I know how they can capture a soul with magic. I've seen them cast a spell. I've seen them break a mother's heart. I can't go back to Mam shoeless. Sure, she'd skin me alive. Losing my shoes is a sin and I lost TWO pairs in the one day.

Analysis

Though more than a hundred years have passed since she struck an iceberg and sank, the *Titanic* maintains its grip on the imagination. It is our modern Fall of Man myth, the Industrial Age's answer to the expulsion from the Garden of Eden. But whereas Adam and Eve's sin was eating of the fruit of the tree of knowledge, modern man's transgression took the form of *hubris*: specifically the audaciousness attendant to building the world's largest floating object, calling it "unsinkable," and naming it after a race of mythological giants who, overthrown by Zeus, were consigned to the depths of a watery underworld. And though today it may seem as if the myth was born on that cold April night in 1912, the fact is it took forty years—until Walter Lord published *A Night to Remember* in 1955—for the *Titanic* to resurface in memory. Nothing like two world wars to make one forget.

Since *A Night to Remember* was published (speaking of first pages, Lord's masterpiece has one of the most captivating prologues ever written, guaranteed to send shivers up your spine), countless works of fiction have—I was going to say "exploited"—have availed themselves of the *Titanic* legend. The heroine of Danielle Steele's *No Greater Love* survives the sinking. In Richard Peck's YA novel *Ghosts I Have Been*, Blossom Culp can see into the future: too bad, since she's on the *Titanic*.

A more recent example of "Titanic lit," *The Girl Who Came Home* by Hazel Gaynor, concerns a group of Irish immigrants. Beryl Bainbridge's *Every Man for Himself* was shortlisted for the Booker Prize. The oddest of all fictional treatments of the *Titanic* legend must be Donald Newlove's yet-to-be-published *The Welles Requiem*. It takes place aboard a passenger train on which a fictional Orson Welles directs a movie that in turn is set aboard the doomed liner. (N.B. the set occupies a series of flatcars.)

The most interesting fictional treatment of the *Titanic* disaster was one written fourteen years *before* she sank. Penned by a struggling science-fiction author Morgan Robertson, *Futility* tells the story of the world's biggest ocean liner and how, on its maiden voyage, on a freezing April night, it strikes an iceberg and sinks, carrying its cargo of fabulously wealthy passengers to the bottom of the Atlantic. The name of Robertson's fictional doomed passenger ship? The *Titan*.

In the Titanic opener under consideration here, a narrator who is either Michael or Finn greets us with news that he has "drowned three times." According to my dictionary, to *drown* is to "die through submersion in and inhalation of water," meaning our narrator is categorically dead and therefore speaks to us from the Great Beyond.

Since I've already delivered my spiel about ghost narrators, I won't go into it again here. Suffice it to say that, as narrative sleights of hand go the "dead narrator gambit" strikes me as a little too easy, a bit too glib. It also requires suspension of all four laws of thermodynamics.

The next two paragraphs of this beguiling (and beguilingly written, in a lilting brogue) opening evade the double drowning flourished by the first paragraph, and read like non sequiturs. Only with the fourth paragraph do we come to realize that our ghost narrator is visiting a museum wherein artifacts from the *Titanic* are on display—including the shoes he was wearing when the ship went down with him on board.

As for the narrator's presence in that museum, it's treated *informationally* ("Visitors come to marvel") rather than as a particular *experience* ("Museumgoers crowd around me, jostling each other for a better view"). The "little shrine" holding that pair of shoes is labeled, not described. Readers might wonder: is the display case set into a wall, or on a table? What do the shoes look like? How badly worn are they? We're left to imagine such things with no help from our ghostly narrator, who doesn't see for us through his eyes. Nor do we know where this museum is located, or the context of the exhibit. Do those things matter? When it comes to details, how many are too many, and how few are too few? When should authors specify, and to what extent?

In *How Fiction Works*, his eloquent inquiry into technique in the modern novel, novelist and critic James Wood has this to say:

> I confess to an ambivalence about detail in fiction. I relish it, consume it, ponder it. Hardly a day goes by in which I don't remind myself of [Saul] Bellow's description of Mr. Rappaport's cigar: "the white ghost of the leaf with all its veins and its fainter pungency." But I choke on too much detail, and find that a distinctively post-Flaubertian tradition fetishizes it: the overaesthetic appreciation of detail seems to raise, in a slightly different form, [the] tension between author and character....

In defense of detail, however, Wood alludes to a moment in George Orwell's essay "The Hanging" in which Orwell describes the prisoner stepping around a puddle to avoid wetting his shoes while being led to the gallows.

In a similar moment in *War and Peace,* as he is about to be executed by firing squad, the condemned man adjusts his too-tight blindfold. "The avoidance of the puddle, the fiddling with the blindfold," writes Wood

> are what might be called irrelevant or superfluous details. They are not explicable; in fiction, they exist to denote precisely the inexplicable. This is one of the 'effects' of realism, of 'realistic' style.

That these details are superfluous, that they are "irrelevant," is what makes them potent. Reading them, we ask ourselves, "Who would make up such a thing?" No sooner is that question raised in our minds than we *believe*. I call them "authenticating details." They may be imaginary or real, and apply to both fiction and nonfiction.

The question of detail points toward a much bigger stylistic choice we make as writers, namely: to be minimalists or maximalists? Lush or lean? Ornate or pared to the bone? Baroque or Puritan? Carlyle or Hemingway? Much depends, of course, on the subject that we are treating. Written in a lush style, a stark tale like Hemingway's "The Killers" would be an odd duck indeed. That said, we need look no further than Cormac McCarthy's *Blood Meridian* to find stark matter treated with baroque splendor:

> Spectre horsemen, pale with dust, anonymous in the crenellated heat. Above all else they appeared wholly at venture, primal, provisional, devoid of order. Like beings provoked out of the absolute rock and set nameless and at no remove from their own loomings to wander ravenous and doomed and mute as gorgons shambling the brutal wastes of Gondwanaland in a time before nomenclature was and each was all.

As writers, we may choose correctly from either end of the baroque–puritan continuum, or find our sweet spot somewhere in the middle. But as James Wood also points out, "There is a way in which even complex prose is quite simple." Wood goes on to cite Marilynne Robinson's novel *Gilead* by way of illustration, asking of the following passage "Is [it] ... an example of simple or complicated prose?"

> This morning a splendid dawn passed over our house on its way to Kansas. This morning Kansas rolled out of its sleep into a sunlight grandly announced, proclaimed throughout heaven—one more of the very finite number of days that this old prairie has been called Kansas, or Iowa.

But it has all been one day, that first day. Light is constant, we just turn over in it. So every day is in fact the selfsame evening and morning. My grandfather's grave turned into the light, and the dew on his weedy little mortality patch was glorious.

Back to our ghost narrator looking at those shoes salvaged from the *Titanic*. We learn that he "has five days to keep a promise," and furthermore that the dead child's shoes on display have secret magical qualities, that they have "cast spells" and broken "a mother's heart." How much of this is to be taken literally and how much is metaphorical remains to be seen.

A dead narrator (whose name is both Finn and Michael and who has drowned thrice, lastly aboard the *Titanic*); a pair of magical shoes dredged up from the depths of the North Atlantic; a spell to be broken; a promise to be kept. It's a lot to digest in a page that, while providing quite a lot of information, also raises many questions, chief among them: beyond that its narrator met his fate aboard the *Titanic*, what will this story be about? This fabulous opening places an enormous burden on whatever follows it, since whatever else is revealed about Finn-Michael, his life must turn out to have been more interesting than his death—a hard act to follow, or rather to precede. Can all the promises held out by this opening possibly be kept?

Speaking of floating vessels, for my money the museum scene could do with some ballast in the form of grounding in concrete details. Were this opening mine, I'd establish the action with the first sentence: our narrator looking at a pair of shoes in a museum display case. I'd make the museum particular, not general. It may be crowded or empty, but it should be a *gritty* museum, rather than as spectral as our narrator.

To sum up: a compelling if convoluted opening. I suspect there's a great story to go with it, albeit one with a surfeit of imaginative devices.

Your Turn

This prompt has to do with details. Write a scene in which a character or characters discover an object inside a box or some other container that in turn has been hidden somewhere. The scene should be written such that, the closer we get to the object in question, the greater the level of descriptive detail. To wit: if the description of the room or field or construction site in which the box or container is hidden is six sentences long, the description of the box should be ten or more sentences, while the description of the object inside the box should run half a page or longer. The idea is to slow the action while building suspense toward and drawing interest to the focal object.

75. Meatloaf Night

(Child's or Child-like Perspective / Dialogue / Constraint = Style)

Tonight was meatloaf. It was quiet and just our forks.

Then Mom said, "I think I'll give her a call later."

Dad didn't answer.

Mom said, "What?"

Dad said, "These challenges ... well, don't you think they're par for the course to adulthood? Maybe she needs a little space to find her way."

That was about Steffi. I looked at her chair. It is an empty place and just three people now.

Mom said, "I hardly think I'm being overbearing."

Dad said, "I know, hon. I didn't say you were."

Mom said, "It's not like I'm demanding to know what color her socks are, or, or, what she had for lunch."

Dad said, "Okay, Celie."

Mom put down her glass and did a sigh.

I said, "Is Steffi an adult?" I used to be the one in the higher grade, before my extra years.

Mom picked up her fork. She said, "In my opinion, eighteen years old is still very much a part of adolescence."

Dad said, "Some would argue adolescence is an art fact."

I didn't know "art fact."

Dad looked at me. He said, "An art fact is anything made by humans. Like tools, or—"

Mom made her voice loud and said, "Until Stephanie graduates from college and gets a job, she is not an adult."

Some people don't believe I'm older. After we moved here a girl came in our yard. Holly. Me and Steffi were digging to India because Steffi said it is better than China.

Holly said, "Hi."

Steffi and me both said, "Hi."

Holly said, "The people who lived here before only had boys."

Steffi said, "Gross," and they laughed.

I said, "Yeah, gross."

Analysis

First-person narratives come with severe limitations, and none more than those in which the narrator is—or, in the case of this first page, has the mentality of—a child. Not only are diction and syntax restricted, so are the narrator's perceptions. Can a child or child-like narrator be competent, let alone stylish?

To render child-like perceptions in a first-person narrative without being childish: that's the challenge confronted—and largely met—by this opening passage in the voice of a character who, though physically older than his eighteen-year-old sister, is emotionally and mentally much younger.

Literature offers many examples of child or child-like narrators whose voices are equally convincing and compelling. "Benjy" Compson, who narrates the first part of Faulkner's *The Sound and the Fury*, comes to mind ("Through the fence, between the curling flower spaces, I could see them hitting."), as does Holden Caufield, who narrates J.D. Salinger's *A Catcher in the Rye*. Through his masterful control of idiom and syntax, Salinger simultaneously conveys both Holden's irreverence ("... and all that David Copperfield kind of crap") and his suffering soul. As one early reviewer noted, he manages to "understand an adolescent mind without displaying one."

In his charming first novel, *In the Cherry Tree*, author Dan Pope does something similar for a group of adolescents coming of age in suburban Connecticut in the early 1970s. In Pope's novel, though the sensibilities and behaviors of his young characters are decidedly those of children, there's nothing the least bit juvenile about Pope's writing or his novel. On the contrary, in its seeming innocence it is extremely sophisticated, a perfectly clear window through which the reader enters Pope's world to re-experience his own adolescence.

"Timmy was playing with his peter. I saw him, I saw him, I saw him."

"He was doing what?"

"Shaking his peter."

"I won't hear another word of this kind of talk."

"But he was playing with it."

"I was not. I was scratching."

"Leave your brother alone, Daphne."

The author of the first page under review here does something very similar, and almost as well. One problem is strictly technical and easily fixed: the wobbly handling of tense starting with the opening sentence, where "tonight" belongs to a present-tense narrative, while the rest of the sentence ("was meatloaf") is in the past tense. Several lines later the narrator looks at Steffi's chair in the past, only to see it in the present ("It is an empty place"). Since nothing organic or intrinsic warrants or is accomplished by these discrepancies, they sound an off-note.

Otherwise, stylistically this opening's eccentricities, along with the severe *constraints* imposed on it, make it strong. Notice the simplified vocabulary and short sentences, and how the attributions are positioned at the start of each line of dialogue (Mom said, "What?") rather than where they would usually come, at the end, ("What?" Mom said.). This intentionally clunky, repetitive approach makes sense, given the narrator's age. It is sophisticated in its lack of sophistication, while still entirely readable.

So much of a good style comes down to *constraints*, to the limitations that we impose on ourselves, to what we choose *not* to do. Antithetically, a poor style often comes down to a lack of selectivity and restraint, using every tool and technique in our kit bags. Result: a catch-as-catch-can, hodge-podge style. Which is no style at all.

The dialogue itself has many merits; we get a strong sense of a family sitting down to dinner, of their overlapping, disjointed, sparring voices. Within half a page I feel that I know these people, that they are real. The narrator's diction seals the effect, with Mom not sighing, but "[doing] a sigh," and the narrator casting a positive light on the years she has stayed back in school by calling them her "extra years." A nice touch.

My only concern about the scene is that it succeeds only in conveying routine without hinting at any event or conflict, and without presenting readers with so much as the shadow of what might be in store by way of a plot. Maybe that's coming in a page or two. I hope so, since otherwise I will probably feel disappointed.

Your Turn

Take an opening—your own or someone else's—and revise it by applying severe constraints to the style. For instance, allow yourself no words of more than two syllables, or sentences of more than eight words. Use no adjectives or adverbs. Have each sentence begin with the next letter of the alphabet. Write in rhymed couplets. Use no articles. Come up with your own unique, severe constraints. Is the result stylistically weaker or stronger?

IV.

Some Exemplary Openings

BELOW ARE SOME EXEMPLARY FIRST PARAGRAPHS AND PAGES FROM published works. Note what information they supply and what questions they raise, and how the status quo or routine in the characters' lives is established or broken. At what point (if any) and to what extent do these openings promise some unique event or series of events? What is the ratio of background to foreground? How quickly do these openings engage your interest?

> We had been preparing for months, slowly ridding ourselves of the possessions we had once thought essential. By the time we left, everything that was ours fit into three brown vinyl suitcases. My parents told me this would be enough, but, like so much they said, these words of comfort were not particularly plausible. Still, there was consolation. On our last day in Russia, as the fall of 1979 slid into winter, my brother Viktor lost his piano.

The opening of Aharon Levy's short story "The Piano" drops us into the middle of events (*in medias res*) on the day when the narrator and his family are leaving their home under less than ideal circumstances and with only the barest possessions. While generous with information, the opening raises pointed questions. What has happened to force this family into this situation? Most provocative of all is the paragraph's ultimate sentence, by which we learn that, as far as the narrator is concerned, his brother Viktor's loss of his piano is a "consoling" factor. Clearly, there is sibling rivalry at work here, and possible humor set against a backdrop of dire circumstances.

> One August afternoon, when Ajay was ten years old, his elder brother, Aman, dove into a pool and struck his head on the cement bottom.
> —"Surrounded by Sleep," Akhil Sharma

317

You may remember this sentence from another short story about brothers referenced in the "Opening Strategies" chapter. That the events of the story are to be experienced from ten-year-old Ajay's perspective is made clear from the first sentence, which presents us with the story's inciting incident in the form of a sensationally dramatic event. We are held in suspense as to the consequences of Aman's accident. Did he survive? If so, did he suffer serious and permanent damage? More importantly, what was the relationship of these two brothers? How does Aman's accident change that relationship?

> When I was seventeen and in full obedience to my heart's most urgent commands, I stepped far from the pathway of normal life and in a moment's time ruined everything I loved—I loved so deeply, and when the love was interrupted, when the incorporeal body of love shrank back in terror and my own body was locked away, it was hard for others to believe that a life so new could suffer so irrevocably. But now, years have passed and that night of August 12, 1967, still divides my life.

The aforementioned opening to Scott Spencer's novel *Endless Love* makes explicit the fact that the author has chosen the story's *inciting incident*—a fire that the narrator protagonist sets to the home of the girl with whom he is infatuated—as his jumping-off place. Though at the time of that event (which had unplanned and tragic consequences) the narrator was clearly not in his right mind, the perspective here is that of a considerably older and wiser person looking back at events with objective clarity, bringing the understanding he's gained in the intervening years to bear on his youthful indiscretions. The main question raised: why did this narrator, who speaks to us in such a rational voice now, commit such an irrational act?

> Spring had come to my hometown. When I got off the bus at the entrance to the contamination zone, Oles was standing at the guard station in a lightweight uniform instead of his padded military jacket, his gun swung loosely over his back. The thaw seemed to have improved his unusually sullen mood; he nodded his appreciation of the flowered fabric I'd brought for his wife and let me pass through the gate without even looking at my documents.

This opening of Katherine Shonk's "My Mother's Garden" (also quoted earlier) likewise begins *in medias res*. Note how the author avoids mentioning Chernobyl or "nuclear reactor" or "meltdown" in her first paragraph. Instead we read the words "contamination zone" and wonder: what sort of "contamination"? Is this an example of *false suspense*, of an author capriciously withholding information from us to arouse curiosity? Perhaps, but the facts become clear soon enough. Meanwhile we know it's Spring, and the homely image of the "flowered fabric" along with that season associated with freshness and renewal plays curiously against the notion of contamination and the image of a uniformed, gun-wielding guard. There is clearly trouble in this Paradise.

> My clothes have failed me. I remember the green coat that I wore in fifth and sixth grade when you either danced like a champ or pressed yourself against a greasy wall, bitter as a penny toward the happy couples.

Not only does this opening to Gary Soto's nonfiction story "The Jacket" make clear both its theme (the significance of clothes) and its subject ("the green coat that I wore in fifth and sixth grade"), the narrator's attitude ("bitter as a penny") comes through loud and clear. This is a tale to be told not with mature, objective calmness, but with resentment and regret. Such a sour approach might turn us off were the theme one of greater intrinsic import (death, illness, war). Instead, we have bitterness directed toward an article of clothing—an object of little consequence in the grand scheme of things. Which is the point—and intrinsically funny, as is the essay itself.

> Two things to get straight from the beginning: I hate doctors and have never joined a support group in my life. At seventy-three, I'm not about to change. The mental-health establishment can go screw itself on a barren hilltop in the rain before I touch their snake oil or listen to the visionless chatter of men half my age. I have shot Germans in the fields of Normandy, filed twenty-six patents, married three women, survived them all, and am currently the subject of an investigation by the IRS, which has about as much chance of collecting from me as Shylock did of getting his pound of flesh. Bureaucracies have trouble thinking clearly. I, on the other hand, am perfectly lucid.

This in-your-face opening to Adam Haslett's story "Notes to My Biographer" is a perfect fit for its subject/narrator, a borderline case megalomaniac who may (or may not) have done the things he claims, and whose over-the-top personality is the subject of the narrative that it drives. Reading it is like watching a train wreck. Though you feel as if you should, you can't take your eyes off this overbearing narrator. Nor can you quite disbelieve anything he says.

It was one of those midsummer Sundays when everyone sits around saying: "I drank too much last night." You might have heard it whispered by the parishioners leaving church, heard it from the lips of the priest himself, struggling with his cassock in the vestiarium, heard it from the golf links and the tennis courts, heard it from the wildlife preserve where the leader of the Audubon group was suffering from a terrible hangover. "I drank too much," said Donald Westerhazy. "We all drank too much," said Lucinda Merrill. "It must have been the wine," said Helen Westerhazy. "I drank too much of that claret."

The next paragraph of "The Swimmer," John Cheever's most famous short story, begins, "This was at the edge of the Westerhazys' pool." In fact, Cheever's story has as much to do with swimming pools as with drinking. One even can argue that its protagonist, Neddy Merrill, who on the day on which the story is set has gotten it into his head one morning to swim across the county via a series of swimming pools, is equally lubricated by alcohol and chlorinated water.

The premise is, of course, absurd: no matter how many pools are in it, one can't possibly *swim* across any county. What Neddy actually swims across is his entire existence, but to know that you need to read the story. What this opening accomplishes—and what Cheever does splendidly throughout his story—is a subtle melding of surreal symbolism and gritty reality. For instance, the name Westerhazy, which manages somehow to be simultaneously symbolic, authentic, and absurd. Like the story that carries it, it strains credulity without breaking it.

You come in out of the oppressive bright sunlight through one of the double swinging doors that flap behind you, announcing your presence. It is afternoon-empty, a few people on stools or scattered around the tables in back who nod in your general direction. You order a shot of tequila and take your usual spot where the bar slopes around toward the bags of chips and pretzels, near the bartender leaning against the rows of bottles.

Though momentarily stylish, writing in the second person, as Susan Buttenweiser does in her story "This Bar," is always a gamble. You're betting that the reader will willingly accept the role of your story's protagonist. Here, out of that "bright sunlight" we—or rather "you"—enter this bar like a B-Western gunslinger, Hopalong Cassidy on the Sagebrush Trail. Apart from the "chips and pretzels," everything—including the scattered barflies "who nod in your general direction"—fits that bill. Will a brawl ensue? Will guns be drawn? That's the cliché expectation aroused by this opening, one that, to (your) relief, won't be met.

> I spent the early '90s shopping for tattoos and letting strangers finger me in public parks. Not complete strangers: I'd met them at a dance club, or a cafe, or my job telemarketing. San Francisco was in recession then and the rents were cheap, the weather too warm and the sound of steel drums filled the parks. It was the year my divorce was final. I cried every day.

This opening of Chris Lombardi's memoir-essay "San Francisco in the 1990s" does exactly what its title promises: gives us that city then from the author's unique and deeply personal perspective. The first line informs us in no uncertain terms that the author will hold nothing back, that this is an uncensored, unexpurgated offering. The "sound of steel drums" filling the parks functions as an authenticating detail, something so specific on reading it we surrender at once to the author's authority: she was *there*. And though set a decade after its outbreak, it's hard to read this opening without being reminded of the AIDS epidemic that decimated San Francisco.

> I first heard Personville called Poisonville by a red-haired mucker named Hickey Dewey in the Big Ship in Butte. He also called his shirt a shoit. I didn't think anything of what he had done to the city's name. Later I heard men who could manage their r's give it the same pronunciation. I still didn't see anything in it but the meaningless sort of humor that used to make richardsnary the thieves' word for dictionary. A few years later I went to Personville and learned better.

This opening of *Red Harvest*, crime/noir author Dashiell Hammett's first novel, comes loaded with *voice*, or rather voices—that of the jaded, slangy detective narrator, and that of the "red-haired mucker named Hickey Dewey" who calls a "shirt a shoit." Thanks to those pungently articulated voices, we get two character evocations in one brief paragraph. The narrator's weary worldliness reaches us through that third sentence, with its suggestion that he's been around the block more than once and met all kinds of men there (including some who could "manage their r's"). And though we can't see this narrator, we can imagine the dark half-moons under his eyes and him wearing his tie somewhat askew, and that the cuffs of his shirt aren't what they used to be.

Jesus came into my room and I tried to keep reading, but it was hard with him standing there all caked in the blood of our sins, arms hanging at his sides, like he'd just stand there forever until I looked up. I laid down my magazine, open to the article about diet programs that deliver. "Christ," I said. "I was planning on having a me night."

With respect to getting the reader's attention, one can do worse than have Jesus Christ himself walk into the opening of a story, as Kristin Kearns does in "Sleeping with Jesus," a title that, the story goes on to demonstrate, is meant to be taken literally. As with John Cheever's "The Swimmer," what gives this opening its authority is a balancing of the sensational (Jesus) and the banal (a magazine article "about diet programs that deliver"). The latter makes the formal more "real" by dragging Christ, if you will, down to earth. Under the circumstances, the spoken line "Christ" has an ironic double meaning that's both funny and unsettling. Who could resist reading on?

I get a phone call from the past saying, "It's time your son met his father." There's not a whole lot I can do because she's flown him halfway round the world for the purpose. I remember some letter a couple months back, and with me busy it getting misplaced and forgetting about it and, knowing me, surely she can't expect anything else. From experience I've found that most worries disappear when you stop worrying about them.

This opening of Ezra Kyrill Erker's "Weekend with the Boy" promises all kinds of discomfort not only for its narrator, but for the boy and the father in question. Though unprepared for, the confrontation has been set in motion and is inevitable. The paragraph's last line ("most worries disappear when you stop worrying about them"), by which the narrator wishes to assure us and himself, does nothing of the sort. It does the opposite, in fact: it assures us that there is much to worry about. Ergo—since misery loves company—we keep reading.

I write this sitting in the kitchen sink. That is, my feet are in it; the rest of me is on the draining-board, which I have padded with our dog's blanket and a tea-cosy.

Inexperienced authors often fail to ground their readers in the concrete actions, settings, and other experiences of their characters. This happens especially with narrators, third- or first-person, who tell their stories from no clear or particular vantage point or perspective. No such issue with this opening to Dodie Smith's romance *Capture the Castle*, in which the narrator is firmly (if only partially) ensconced in her kitchen sink. An opening that gets its feet wet.

> I am living at the Villa Borghese. There is not a crumb of dirt anywhere, nor a chair misplaced. We are all alone here and we are dead.

In 1934, when this opening to Henry Miller's *Tropic of Cancer* first appeared in print (in Paris; an official American edition wouldn't appear until twenty-seven years later, when the ban was lifted), it was considered as impudent and revolutionary as the pages that followed it. In fact the book didn't even call itself a "novel," though no other term applied. As Miller himself tells us a page later:

> This then? This is not a book. This is libel, slander, defamation of character. This is not a book, in the ordinary sense of the word. No, this is a prolonged insult, a gob of spit in the face of Art, a kick in the pants to God, Man, Destiny, Time, Love, Beauty ... what you will.

Miller meant to shock—and did, back then, though compared to much that's been written since his books seem mild and even dull, while Miller himself comes off today as a misogynistic noble savage of American letters. Still, though his work hasn't dated all that well, one must grant these opening lines their iconoclastic due. "We are all alone here and we are dead" is still one heckuva way to begin a novel. Imagine how it must have struck people in 1934. Whether one admires Henry Miller's convictions or not, he had the courage of them.

In the end—with respect to beginning—perhaps that's all or most of what we need: the courage of our convictions, the willingness to plunge headlong into the worlds of our stories, and—along with that willingness—the authority to compel our readers to take the plunge with us.

v.

Some Exemplary First Sentences

THE FIRST SENTENCES BELOW ARE OFFERED WITHOUT COMMEN-
tary. Come to your own conclusions as to whether they work for you, and why.
What do they tell you? And what do they make you want to know? What
moods, attitudes, perspectives, and other qualities do they convey? Do they
evoke character? If so, how?

Collect your own favorite first sentences to add to this list. Why do you
like them? How are they perfectly suited to initiate the novels, stories, essays,
or memoirs that go with them? Can you come up with alternative first sentences
that might be as good or better?

If you are interested in stories with happy endings, you would be better
off reading some other book.
—*The Bad Beginning*, Lemony Snicket

I lost an arm on my last trip home.
—*Kindred*, Octavia Butler

I had just come to accept that my life would be ordinary when extraordinary things began to happen.
—*Miss Peregrine's Home for Peculiar Children*, Ransom Riggs

This is my favorite book in all the world, though I have never read it.
—*The Princess Bride*, William Goldman

You better not tell nobody but God.
—*The Color Purple*, Alice Walker

Coraline discovered the door a little while after they moved into the house.
—*Coraline*, Neil Gaiman

I was born twice: first, as a baby girl, on a remarkably smogless Detroit day of January 1960; and then again, as a teenage boy, in an emergency room near Petoskey, Michigan, in August of 1974.
—*Middlesex*, Jeffrey Eugenides

The snow in the mountains was melting and Bunny had been dead for several weeks before we understood the gravity of our situation.
—*The Secret History*, Donna Tartt

It began in the usual way, in the bathroom of the Lassimo Hotel.
—*A Visit from the Goon Squad*, Jennifer Egan

We slept in what had once been the gymnasium.
—*The Handmaid's Tale*, Margaret Atwood

By our second day at Camp Crescendo, the girls in my Brownie troop had decided to kick the asses of each and every girl in Brownie Troop 909.
—"Brownies," Z.Z. Packer

Of course, I had not always been a drunkard.
—*The Drinker*, Hans Fallada

The food ladies from the church went home hours ago.
—"Milk," Lisa Allen

My father has asked me to be the fourth corner of the Joy Luck Club.
—*The Joy Luck Club*, Amy Tan

Jane's husband, Martin, works for the fire department.
—"The Fireman's Wife," Richard Bausch

First Lieutenant Jimmy Cross carried letters from a girl named Martha, a junior at Mt. Sebastian college in New Jersey.
—"The Things They Carried," Tim O'Brien

Uncas Metcalfe's Raleigh had been stolen.
—*The Natural History of Uncas Metcalfe*, Betsey Osborne

It was a pleasure to burn.
—*Fahrenheit 451*, Ray Bradbury

Not for the first time, an argument had broken out over breakfast at number four, Privet Drive.
—*Harry Potter and The Chamber of Secrets*, J.K. Rowling

Joost had two problems: the moon and his mustache.
—*Six of Crows*, Leigh Bardugo

If commercial success is your goal, this book won't have been in your didn't stories aren't. Good writing doesn't equal a commercial book. If artistic success is your goal, possibly this book has helped you even more—either way, I hope it has helped and wish you good luck.

Afterword:
Artistic vs. Commercial Success

SAY YOU'VE EXTRACTED EVERY LAST OUNCE OF WISDOM FROM THE preceding pages. You've tended to every injunction and made every possible improvement to your opening: you've avoided default omniscience and false suspense, you've grounded your openings in time and place, you've started with (or as close as possible to) an inciting incident, you've either avoided a framing device, or used one shrewdly; you've made sure whenever possible and practical to provide your readers not with inert or abstract information and conclusions but with the concrete experiences from which those things might be drawn. You have avoided autobiography and sentimentality. You've done everything "right," which is to say you've done everything right *your own* way, in a way that's authentic and true and particular to you, and not just a hodgepodge of good advice earnestly obeyed.

You've written a fine first page that sets the tone and serves as a template for all those that follow, meaning all the pages that follow are equally fine. Meaning you've written a fine book or memoir or story.

Will it be published?

Maybe. For here is the truth: that good writing, however good it may be, is not all that determines whether something gets commercially published or not. It may be among the last things, lagging behind such considerations as the author's platform, her "web profile," and previous sales figures, the timeliness of her subject, and conditions of the market in whatever category or genre she has chosen to write in.

The great graphic designer Milton Glaser summed it up well: "The model for personal development is antithetical to the model for professional success." Artistic and commercial success are often two entirely different if not antithetical things. It's up to you to decide which kind of success means more to you and aim for it.

If commercial success is your goal, this book won't have hurt your ambitions toward it. Good writing never hurt a commercial book. If artistic success is your goal, possibly this book has helped you even more.

Either way, I hope it has helped and wish you good luck.

Subject Index

Works and Authors Cited Index

From the Publisher

A name never says it all, but the word "Broadview" expresses a good deal of the philosophy behind our company. We are open to a broad range of academic approaches and political viewpoints. We pay attention to the broad impact book publishing and book printing has in the wider world; for some years now we have used 100% recycled paper for most titles. Our publishing program is internationally oriented and broad-ranging. Our individual titles often appeal to a broad readership too; many are of interest as much to general readers as to academics and students.

Founded in 1985, Broadview remains a fully independent company owned by its shareholders—not an imprint or subsidiary of a larger multinational.

For the most accurate information on our books (including information on pricing, editions, and formats) please visit our website at www.broadviewpress.com. Our print books and ebooks are also available for sale on our site.

broadview press

www.broadviewpress.com